A BUCKET OF
SUNSHINE

A DEDICATION

Flight Lieutenant Geoff Trott, RAF

This book is dedicated to the memory of my directional and positional consultant, good friend and close companion from the Cold War days, described in this book. Geoff Trott was a talented, accomplished and professional navigator. His calmness, ready wit and dry sense of humour were a constant support and delight to me during good times and not so good. Geoff was not a career officer and was all the more good company for that. Indeed he was a member of the 'Supplementary List' club, whose badge was a ladder with all but the bottom rung broken! Geoff enjoyed his rugby, sailing and beer and loved his family above all other things.

In 1996 Geoff died far too young, of cancer, at the age of fifty-three. He had just retired from the RAF after a career that had seen him rise to the top of the Search and Rescue specialisation. He is pictured above during his first SAR tour flying Westland Whirlwinds from RAF Brawdy in his home nation of Wales. Note the prominence of the crossed keys of his No.16 Squadron badge! Geoff was married to Sonia for thirty-one years and they had two lovely girls, Nicola and Joanna. Sonia also died too young, again of cancer, ten years after Geoff. I am grateful to Nicky and Jan for their permission to make this dedication and for the photograph that they allowed me to use.

A BUCKET OF SUNSHINE

LIFE ON A COLD WAR CANBERRA SQUADRON

MIKE BROOKE

A group of us at RAF Idris after a morning's flying. Geoff Trott is extreme left, with the author on the right. The folically challenged officer in uniform is Squadron Leader Suren. (Gp Capt Tom Eeles RAF (Ret.))

First published 2012

The History Press
The Mill, Brimscombe Port
Stroud, Gloucestershire, GL5 2QG
www.thehistorypress.co.uk

British Library Cataloguing in Publication Data.
A catalogue record for this book is available from the British Library.

ISBN 978 0 7524 7021 4

Typesetting and origination by The History Press
Printed in Great Britain

CONTENTS

Acknowledgements

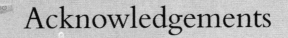

First, I would like to acknowledge the part my youngest brother, Richard, played in the conception of this book. Although he was not able to follow me and join the RAF as aircrew, due to colour blindness, he has maintained a lifelong interest in and love of aviation. It was he who, over lunch one day, suggested that I write down all the stories I used to regale him with. It was also Richard who told me that there were precious few books about the RAF's role in the Cold War, let alone an insider's view of life on a front-line strike/attack squadron based in Germany.

I would also like to thank my wife Linda, who has stoically put up with my long disappearances into the study and my mental retreats to the 1960s. Not only that but she was my constant proof-reader and critic. Her knowledge and practice as a teacher of the English language and her experience as an avid reader have had more than a significant impact on the readability of this book.

My mother, who is a nonagenarian and living with us, was also but perhaps less critically, another sounding board for my tale. I also want to acknowledge her, and my late father's, support and guidance during my childhood and those early years when I left home to fulfil my desire to fly.

I want to thank my commissioning editors, Jay Slater and Amy Rigg, also Emily Locke and all the team at The History Press for their help, guidance and support in my first venture into the publishing world. I hope that you agree with me that they have done a fine job in the production of this book.

In addition, I would like to thank Mach One Publications for allowing me to reproduce a section of the *Pilot's Notes Canberra B(I) Mk8* as an appendix in this book.

Unless otherwise credited, all pictures are from my own collection. The Canberra on the front cover came to me via Patrick Camp and Bob McLeod.

Mike Brooke
Normandy, 2011

Introduction

Wing Commander Michael C. BROOKE, AFC RAF(Ret)

Mike Brooke was born in Bradford, West Yorkshire on 22 April 1944. After a grammar school education he joined the RAF as a trainee pilot in January 1962. Subsequent to passing through all-jet flying training he was posted to No.16 Squadron in RAF Germany, where he flew the Canberra B(I)8 in the low-level, night interdictor, strike and attack roles.

On completion of this tour he was selected for the RAF Central Flying School course where he was trained as a qualified flying instructor. Three flying instructional tours followed, then, in 1975, Mike attended the Empire Test Pilot's School (ETPS) and graduated as a fixed wing test pilot. After graduation he spent five years as an experimental test pilot at the Royal Aerospace establishments at Farnborough and Bedford, at the latter commanding the Radar Research Squadron. At the beginning of 1981 Mike returned to ETPS as a tutor, where he spent three years teaching pilots from all over the world to be test pilots. In 1984 Mike was awarded the Air Force Cross (AFC) for his work within the flight test community; HM Queen Elizabeth II presented the medal to him at Buckingham Palace in November that year.

After attending the RAF Staff College's Advanced Staff Course he spent six months at HQ Strike Command, where he was a member of the Command Briefing Team. In 1985 Mike was promoted to Wing Commander and given command of Flying Wing at RAE Farnborough. A wide variety of aircraft came his way, including helicopters such as the Gazelle, Wessex and Sea King. After three years at Farnborough, he returned once more to Boscombe Down, this time as Wing Commander Flying, in charge of all flying support activities and deputy to the chief test pilot.

The end of Mike's RAF career came in 1994, when he decided, at the age of fifty, to take voluntary redundancy. He then spent five years in part-time aviation consultancy, working as a test pilot instructor with the International Test Pilots' School and Cranfield University, and as a developmental test pilot for the Slingsby Aircraft Company.

In 1998, Mike moved to Texas to fly for a company called Grace Aire, who aimed to give flight test training in their ex-RAF Hunter jet trainers, gain US Department of Defense flight test contracts and display the Hunter at Air Shows. Sadly, the company went into liquidation after two years so Mike returned to Europe, choosing to live in northern France.

In January 2002, he returned to RAF service as a full-time reservist pilot, commanding one of the RAF's eleven Air Experience Flights, which give flying experience to members of the UK's Air Cadet organisation. He finally retired from the RAF in April 2004, on his sixtieth birthday. Mike has flown over 7,500 hours (mostly one at a time) on over 130 aircraft types, was a member of the Royal Aeronautical Society, a Liveryman and a Master Pilot of the Guild of Air Pilots and Air Navigators, is a Freeman of the City of London and is a Fellow of the Society of Experimental Test Pilots. He also flew many historic and vintage aircraft with the Shuttleworth Collection, the Harvard Team and Jet Heritage.

This book is a sometimes irreverent and mostly humorous insight into life on an RAF squadron on the front-line of the Cold War in the mid-1960s. It describes in detail the aircraft, the Canberra B(I)8, and its nuclear and conventional roles and weapons and the flying that went with them. Mike tells his story, warts and all, with amusing overtones in what was an extremely serious business, when the world was standing on the brink of nuclear conflict with its potentially catastrophic outcome for the whole world.

Mike is married to Linda; they have four children and seven grandchildren. They live in France where they have restored a 230-year-old Normandy farmhouse and created a garden from a field. Mike is a licensed lay minister in the local Anglican church, which he and Linda helped to found in 2003. Linda is following in his footsteps and training for the lay ministry in the same church.

Prologue

It is the summer of 1960. I am sixteen years old and I am fishing, sitting on the banks of the River Ouse in Yorkshire, not far from the RAF flying training base at Linton-on-Ouse. I can hear the distinctive whistling of the de Havilland Vampires as they fly their training missions. I know Linton quite well because on many weekends I hitchhike or take a bus there as a Staff Cadet at the RAF Volunteer Reserve Gliding School.

I have flown solo in a glider on several occasions and am about to be sent to Somerset to do an advanced gliding course, where I will learn to soar; that's stay up a bit longer than the 5 minutes that's usually the case in the Vale of York.

Suddenly, there is a noise off to my right; it is an ascending, rushing noise. I look in that direction. Round the bend of the river, at what seems only tree-top height, banking sharply, is a Hawker Hunter – the RAF's premier single-seat day-fighter. No sooner have I taken this in than a second one appears, in a loose trail position, echoing exactly the movements of the first as they rapidly reverse the bank angle to follow the course of the River Ouse. They pass me almost seemingly within touching distance; I can see clearly the silver-helmeted pilots in their cockpits.

As quick as the adrenalin has hit the pit of my stomach and the hairs risen on the back of my neck, they are gone. Only the sound of the air folding itself back into place remains. I am left breathless, though I haven't moved a muscle, and I feel an overwhelming conviction, perhaps for the first time in my life, that one day I must do that myself. I resolve there and then that whatever else I try to do with my life, the first thing to attempt is to fly.

It is the summer of 2000. I am fifty-six years old and I am sitting on the banks of another river, fishing. I am content, the fullness of nature surrounds

A four-ship formation in transit. (Sqn Ldr S. Foote, OC 16(R) Sqn)

me, the fish are biting and the air is warm. I am thinking about nothing in particular.

Suddenly, there is a noise off to my right; it is an ascending, rushing noise. I look in that direction. Round the bend of the river, at what seems only tree-top height, banking sharply, is a Jaguar: the RAF's premier single-seat day-fighter. No sooner have I taken this in than a second one appears, in a loose trail position, echoing exactly the movements of the first as they rapidly reverse the bank angle to follow the course of the river.

I watch and the same rush of adrenalin occurs, the hairs on the back of my neck tingle and, as the Jaguars disappear and the air folds back into place. I muse that I am so thankful that I did, after all, get to do that myself, in several different aircraft types including the Hunter and the Jaguar. I realise that I miss it now and, with a regret that has no name, I'll never do it again.

A pair of 16 Squadron B(I)8s take off for a bombing and gunnery sortie. (Gp Capt Tom Eeles RAF (Ret.))

B(I)8 XM 272 just airborne; the QRA shed is in the background. (Sqn Ldr S. Foote, OC 16(R) Sqn)

1

Baptism of Air

'Daddy, when I grow up I want to be a pilot.' Some might say that you can't do both, but I said these words immediately after being set down from my first flight in an aeroplane. I was six years old and I'd just spent 10 minutes sitting on a large cushion in the front seat of an Auster, probably ex-Second World War, with a handlebar-moustachioed pilot who was definitely ex-Second World War (well, at least his moustache was). We had just flown from Southport Sands on a 10-minute 'Round the Marina and Back in Time for Tea' trip. I've no idea how much it cost my parents from their modest income, but it was worth every penny!

From then on I had an abiding interest in anything that flew: birds, butterflies, moths, but most of all aeroplanes. That interest was nurtured and encouraged by my father, who had always wanted to fly, but had been prohibited from doing so by his overbearing mother. When he finally, and clandestinely, went along to volunteer as aircrew in 1939 it turned out that two other things mitigated against his desire: an eyesight defect and the fact that, as an engineering draughtsman, he was in what was known as a 'reserved occupation'. He spent his war as a member of the Home Guard, literally, for me anyway, Dad's Army.

Throughout my childhood we visited every air show in reach. There was an annual one at nearby RAF Yeadon (now Leeds-Bradford International Airport) and I well remember walking back after the show, on a fine summer's evening, lost in thoughts of being able to learn to fly.

As soon as I was old enough, I joined the Air Scouts and then the local Air Training Corps squadron. Along with fishing and rock-climbing, the ATC soon became one of the most important things in my life. The whole environment was immersed in a sense of being up close and familiar with military aviation and, for me, was a dream come true. We learned Morse code, went shooting, practised foot drill, we had our very own functioning Link Trainer, but most excitingly we actually went flying, at least once a year!

The 'Link' was the world's first effective flight simulator. It had electrically and vacuum-operated instruments and moving parts. It could mimic the pitch, roll and yaw of an aircraft in flight, as well as simulate the progress of a flight from one place to another. The cockpit was a generic one, with most of the current instruments, knobs and levers. What's more, it was all connected electrically to a wheeled device, known as the Crab, which drew an ink trail on a map resting on a nearby glass-topped table. It was a real boys' toy!

As I advanced through the rank structure to sergeant, I was given increasing responsibilities for operating and supervising other cadets in the Link Trainer. Of course this meant that I had to become more proficient than them, so I did tend to 'hog' it! Whatever my level of expertise, which I don't recall as being particularly good, it did increase my desire to do that sort of thing for a living. As did our annual summer camps at RAF stations, which always included at least one air experience flight. In my time with the ATC I flew in a Scottish Aviation Single Pioneer, several times in a Chipmunk, a Beverley, a Hastings and, most excitingly, in a de Havilland Vampire trainer. Little did I realise that a couple of years later I would learn to fly it.

As I approached my sixteenth birthday, I discovered that I could apply for a sixth-form scholarship with the RAF. This would, if I were successful, give my parents an additional small income while I stayed on at grammar school taking my A-levels. I would also have a reserved place at the RAF College at Cranwell, subject to achieving acceptable results in the exams. I filled out the plethora of forms and waited impatiently.

After what seemed an interminable time to an impatient teenager, I was sent a rail warrant to travel from Leeds to London and on to the RAF Aircrew Selection Centre at Hornchurch in Essex, where the initial round of interviews and tests were to be inflicted. This in itself was an adventure. Up to then I had rarely been out of t'North, let alone Yorkshire. Our next-door neighbour, Arthur Spoor, was a travel agent and so, in the view of my parents, a well-travelled man of the world. Accordingly, I was sent round to get a briefing on how not to get lost on the London Underground.

Suitably briefed I left my parents standing on the platform as the train left Leeds City station for London King's Cross. I don't recall being at all worried by the prospect of travelling all that way on my own and looked on it as a great adventure. Having arrived at King's Cross, I tracked down the Underground station and successfully found the right line, the green one, and an hour or so later, alighted at the correct station. A street map of Hornchurch had been despatched with the rail warrant, so I successfully navigated my way from the station to the main gate of RAF Hornchurch. This was an edifying result, as my stated first choice of aircrew category was navigator. This, in turn, stemmed from my love of geography and maps!

As I made my way to the Candidates' Barrack Block, I realised that I was treading the same ground as some of those Battle of Britain fighter pilots I had spent most of my formative years reading about. The two days of medical tests, interviews, aptitude tests and just sitting around waiting for the next event went by in a blur. The intervening evening was a real eye-opener as I fell in with some more experienced southerners and was taken on a tour of Soho, where we sampled some of the female anatomical education that was on offer.

On the second day there was a filtering out of the candidates, for all sorts of reasons; the main one seemed to be colour blindness. By late afternoon less than half the original number of us were left in the running. We were then told that we would be going by coach to the RAF College at Cranwell, in Lincolnshire, to complete the rest of the scholarship selection procedures. The next morning, duly fed with a good RAF full-fry, we boarded our springless RAF coach for the 150-mile journey north. I don't know how long it took, but it felt like several lifetimes.

Eventually, we arrived at Cranwell and were accommodated in an aged building that was probably built personally by Lord Trenchard when he started the college in 1920; it had the grand name of Daedalus House[1]; I was hoping that I wouldn't emulate Icarus!

Then followed a series of team and individual verbal and physical exercises, all designed to test our organisational and leadership skills, as well as seeing how we expressed ourselves. The only part I really remember is the question, 'Who would you most like to bring back from history to see the world today?'; my answer was, 'The Wright Brothers.' There were yet more discussion and Q&A sessions, as well as more interviews. When would it all end? Well, after two days, we were sent on our way, with not the slightest hint as to where we stood.

After a couple of weeks back in the real world of school, ATC, coffee bars and Friday nights at the Mecca[2] or the cinema ('t'pictures' in West Yorkshire parlance!), a brown manila envelope turned up in the post. It turned out to be a case of 'good news and bad news'. The bad news first: I had not won a RAF sixth-form scholarship, so no money for Mater and Pater. The good news? I had passed all the tests and medicals sufficiently well to be offered a place in training as a navigator in Her Majesty's Royal Air Force. The letter went on to offer me one of two choices. Either a reserved place at the RAF College, subject to me gaining two A-level passes, one of which had to be a science subject, or a direct entry place in training, once I had reached the minimum age of seventeen and a half years of age.

It didn't take me long to decide; the direct entry meant that I could leave school and start flying in just over six months time! I told my parents that was what I wanted to do and they were very supportive; it became obvious that they had resolved not to repeat my paternal grandmother's obstruction to my Dad's dream. I returned the appropriate form to the RAF. The next half-year was going to be very long.

To help the time go by more quickly, I threw myself even further into ATC activities and was selected for an advanced gliding course, which I completed successfully in the summer of 1961. I had become the proud owner of a 250cc BSA C15 motorcycle and had passed my test at the first attempt. I had also picked up, on the back of the BSA, a new girlfriend! Life and the future looked immensely rosy – roll on the New Year!

Notes

1 I believe that it still graces the environs of Cranwell and houses the Headquarters of the Air Cadet Organisation, which in terms of personnel numbers is now larger than the RAF! The continued use of this old building enhances the view that I once overheard a US Air Force Colonel express when he saw the one-eyed navigator and peg-leg pilot dismount from their Canberra: 'You Limeys! You never throw anything away!'

2 The name of a chain of dance halls.

2

Apprenticeship

The Officer Training course for which I had been selected started on 16 January 1962; I was seventeen years and eight months old. At that time the world was turning, not just into a new year, but more and more into a planet split between two superpowers – the United States of America and the Union of Soviet Socialist Republics. The bombs had been getting bigger for some years now; the atom bomb was old hat – the hydrogen bomb was the new terror over the horizon. The Cold War was hotting up.

After the disaster for the USA of the shooting down of Gary Power's U2 reconnaissance mission over Russia, and Premier Kruschev's belligerent response, there was a new, younger man in the White House. Here was a man who seemed to be willing to take on the USSR more directly. His name was John Fitzgerald Kennedy; like his native country, he would be henceforth known by his initials.

In the skies above us a new race was on – the Space Race. At the time I joined the RAF, Russia had a definite lead down the back straight, but things were moving in the west. The Soviets had successfully launched and recovered a dog from space and the Americans were trying hard to catch up, using a chimpanzee called Ham. Both sides had men waiting in the wings. With the cancellation of the Blue Steel project, the Brits had backed out of the race. To rub salt in that particular wound, the Italians launched their first rocket into space on 12 January 1962. Three days later I, and about fifty other likely lads, arrived at No.1 Initial Training School, RAF South Cerney, Gloucestershire, to start our Officer Training.

South Cerney was a grass airfield with a tarmac perimeter track and had last been active as a relief landing ground for the Central Flying School at RAF Little Rissington, about 15 miles away. In 1962, however, the only aircraft that came near the place were USAF B-47 bombers flying into nearby Fairford. The sole activity on the airfield now was the regular strings of hot, panting bodies running round the perimeter-track with varying loads on their backs.

There were four months to be endured – four months of foot drill, rifle drill, sword drill, mathematics, public speaking, RAF Law, physical exercise of all kinds and even lessons in Officers' Mess etiquette. Aerodynamics and meteorology were about the only things we were taught that seemed to have anything to do with aviation. However, the main result was the forging of friendships in adversity.

We started by inhabiting cold, stark barrack blocks, with about twelve to a room, then, after a month, we moved to what was called No.2 Officers' Mess, with its wooden huts and individual hutches, but a 'proper' officers' dining room. At around this time, during one classroom session a staff officer had come in to ask whether any of the Cadet Navigators would like to become Cadet Pilots. He explained that there was a shortfall in the number of trainee pilots on our course. He then sugared the pill by explaining that anyone who didn't make it through training as a pilot would be automatically re-streamed to navigator training.

The staff officer said that he didn't want answers right away, but should any of us wish to take up the offer then we should report to his office by the end of the day. During the mid-morning break, I pondered this possibility. Since going through selection, almost a year ago, I had completed an advanced gliding course and was feeling much more confident about my ability to pilot an aeroplane. I had also learned that I had passed all the aptitude tests required for selection as a pilot. My gliding instructors had been surprised when I told them I was aiming to be a navigator. By the end of that day I had duly reported back with a positive answer and so, by that evening, I was a Cadet Pilot.

As a lad of fairly short stature, curly blond hair and a tendency to chubbiness, I was, and hopefully still am, one of those lucky souls who look young for their age. However, when I was going on eighteen it was occasionally a drawback. For instance, one day we had to report for some sort of physical fitness session and I had acquired a new, red tracksuit; most of the other guys were in the RAF issue kit. When we were lined up the Sergeant Physical Training Instructor stood in front of me and, due to his massive build, towered over me.

'What are you doin' 'ere?' he growled.

'I've come for the PT, Sergeant,' I replied nervously.

'Well, kids from the married quarters don't join in with the courses. Go home!' he ordered.

'But I'm not from the married quarters, Sergeant, I'm on the course.'

He looked surprised, muttered something about his sadness at getting older and walked away. This happy problem would bug me many times in the future. For instance, for some years to come I frequently had to show my RAF Identity Card to pub landlords!

After three months at South Cerney, we were sent on a six-day field exercise in the Brecon Beacons, where it was hoped that boys would be turned into men. A reasonable hope I suppose, but it was more like a grown-up Scout camp; lots of hard exercise up and down mountains; semi-arctic weather for some of the time; and lots of messing about with ropes, pulleys and bits of wood. The best bit was getting a turn in the cookhouse with what appeared to be a disaster waiting to happen in the shape of a pot-bellied, gas-fired heater called a Hydraburner.

The thing that I remember best about those few days was when one of our erstwhile staff, Flight Lieutenant Dave Goodwin, beat the hell out of the campsite in a single-seat Hawker Hunter on the penultimate day. Cheered mightily by that, and after a long, sore-footed march to Abergavenny, we piled on to another suspensionless RAF coach and, despite the discomfort, slept all the way back to Gloucestershire.

Our reward was to be graduation to No.1 Officers' Mess for our final month. This was it. We now felt like proper *Officer* Cadets. We were, at last, inhabiting rooms in a building that had been built expressly for the purpose of housing officers. After the weeding out of more of our comrades, who were persuaded to seek employment elsewhere, we had come to the final hurdle. En route to this point we had gelled into a fairly cohesive band of brothers, special friendships had been forged in the fires of duress and we were all eager to escape into the world of the 'real' Royal Air Force, wherever that might take us.

Our passing out parade was held in early May on the parade square, which was surrounded by flowering cherry trees. The day was fine, warm and there was a light south-westerly breeze nudging small, fluffy cumulus clouds across the sky. The reviewing officer was Air Marshal 'Bing' Cross; the then boss of Bomber Command. During the rehearsals I had slipped and fallen while carrying my rifle. This carelessness had broken a finger on my left hand so I was now unable to carry rifle or sword. I was thus accorded the privilege of being a 'spare part' at the back of our flight.

After much rehearsing under our, by now, much beloved senior drill instructor, Flight Sergeant Jim Maunder, we had reached a level of skill and presentation which he deemed just acceptable. We thought we were fit for parading outside Buckingham Palace! We marched on to the parade ground, watched by the staff and many families and friends, and then waited. Eventually the hour arrived and, as the Air Marshal took his place on the dais, our parade commander brought the parade to the 'Present Arms', the band struck up and a huge, white Victor bomber appeared from behind the barrack blocks and swept majestically over the parade ground. It was almost impossible not to turn and follow it with my eyes; in fact, being at the back and of short stature, I did sneak a longer look than I should have and very nearly lost my hat in the process. Nobody seemed to notice.

After much marching back and forth, many fine but forgettable words and the prize-giving, we finally left to the strains of the RAF March Past, all wearing our ever-so-thin Acting Pilot Officers' rank tapes with great pride. Now, finally, was the time to retire to the mess and partake of tea with visitors and staff, make phone calls or send telegrams to parents who, like mine, were too far away to be there and then just let go for the evening. What was next we wondered?

3

Learning the Basics

For me it was back to my native Yorkshire, to RAF Leeming in the Vale of York. During my time at South Cerney I had teamed up with a few like-minded individuals and had made some new, close friends. I was now learning that a feature of RAF life would be that those new, close friends will be posted elsewhere and that you will have to go through it all again at the next place.

An impish young man called Colin Woods and I had struck up an alliance against authority very early on. Together we had paid the princely sum of £50 to buy a 1934 Lagonda saloon car from one of the staff at South Cerney. This thing was a monster with a bonnet that seemed about 9ft long, under which was a 3½-litre straight-six 'marine' engine. I didn't have a car driver's licence so, fortunately, I didn't drive it on the public road. However, I knew how to drive a car because I had driven the Air Training Corps Gliding School Land Rovers all over RAF Linton-on-Ouse and Colin had given me more lessons on the narrow twisting roads of RAF South Cerney. The greatest difficulty with the Lagonda was that the pedals didn't come in the right order and it was extremely easy to accelerate when you should be braking, and vice-versa! When we had left South Cerney, Colin had bravely taken the Lagonda the 250 miles north, to his home in West Hartlepool, where he thought he might have a buyer. We even hoped for a bit of a profit. Sadly, it was not to be, the machine broke down and when Colin finally got it back, extensive woodworm was found in the coachwork and she had to be laid to rest. I think I got a tenner back!

In mid-May 1962, Colin, some others from South Cerney and I turned up at No.3 Flying Training School, RAF Leeming, to learn to fly. We had, as usual, received lots of paperwork to be completed during the short leave period between courses. The reporting details stated that we should arrive before 4 p.m. and go to the Ground School for an address by the senior staff. There would then be a written exam and in the evening we would retire to the Officers' Mess Bar, where we would meet our flying instructors.

After we had taken our seats a stream of senior officers gave us the repeated message that we were there to work and not play. The Station Commander seemed very young to me; I concluded that he must be one of the 'high fliers' I'd heard about. Perhaps there was hope for rapid career progression in this business? Then the exam papers were handed out. We were given half an hour to complete the twenty or so questions.

Some of them were a bit strange, like: 'Who is responsible for controlling the height of trees on the airfield?' Multiple-choice options:

A The Senior Air Traffic Control Officer (SATCO)
B The Station Commander
C God

I'd no real idea but I gave it my best effort.

After that we returned to the Officers' Mess, where we were told to change into PE kit and were given a series of demanding physical exercises, including some rather strange jumps and hops, at the back of the mess, in full view of those eating dinner. After showering and eating we were told that we were to report to the bar, where we would meet our flying instructors – and that they would expect us to buy the drinks. It seemed that we had hit the ground running! Nevertheless, a pleasant, if expensive, evening was passed in the company of our would-be instructors, much beer was consumed and respectful banter exchanged. And so to bed.

The next morning, after breakfast, we were told to make our way back to the Ground School again. There we were addressed by a series of officers all claiming to be the men who had addressed us the previous afternoon. Rats began to be smelled. At least these chaps appeared to be the right ages for their ranks. Then we started the serious work of receiving books, publications, filling in endless arrival proformae – just how many times do you have to write your full name, rank and service number for the station to keep track of you?

When we returned to the mess for lunch, the first person I bumped into was my flying instructor. I greeted him and asked him if he had slept well; it seemed sensible to be polite. Then I noticed that he was chatting to the Chief Flying Instructor and the Station Commander – neither of whom was wearing the correct badges of rank. When the question mark so obviously appeared above my head they could no longer keep their faces straight, in fact they became extremely bent.

They were all from the senior course in residence and they had obviously arranged the previous afternoon's and evening's events; no doubt with the collusion of the aforesaid senior officers, who had probably thought that it was a 'wizard wheeze'! Apparently the whole introductory 'exam' was dreamt up in collusion with the staff. The answers to most of the questions was actually 'none of the above'! They had got away with it because most of them were graduates and ex-University Air Squadron members, so their average age was well above ours. We were just about all school leavers and not many of us were over twenty. The joke was on us, but in the evening they said they would help us entertain our real flying instructors.

Then there was lots of 'admin' to do; the most exciting part of which was to be issued with our flying kit, including two light blue flying suits, the silver 'bone-dome' and its inner helmet and oxygen mask. The least exciting part was to be issued with a whole armful of documents and APs (Air Publications), including our Pilots' Notes and the AP 1234. The latter was a weighty tome, in two parts, that told one all one needed to know, and lots of things one didn't need to know, about aviation and all its related sciences. Along with all these books there were the plethora of ALs (Amendment Lists), which had to be incorporated in the said volumes. I sat on the floor of my bedroom that evening, surrounded by pages extracted and pages to be incorporated, trying desperately not to mix them up. Then after all those had been done there were the 'Handwritten Amendments'. My spirits finally rose when I came across the following instruction: 'AP1234, Part 4, Chap 6, Page 3, Line 7: For "heliocoptre" insert "hicopleter".' Even to this day you can tell someone who joined the RAF as a pilot in the early 1960s through the fact that they will refer to those whirling dervishes of aviation as hicopleters!

By now, we Acting Pilot Officers had met up with the other half of our course, the Sergeant Pilots. These were all ex-airmen who had been selected as potential NCO pilots.[1] They increased the average age of the course to something more fitting and, as we were to discover, brought us some very useful corporate experience of service life.

After a few weeks in the classroom we were finally allowed near the aircraft, which was the Hunting Percival Jet Provost Mark 3 – known universally as the JP 3, or more often as the 'constant thrust, variable noise machine'. This sobriquet was an allusion to the miniscule thrust of the Rolls-Royce Viper engine; a power unit originally designed for a short life in the Jindivik radio-controlled pilotless target drone. In Ground School we had spent many hours in what was called the Procedures Trainer, a real JP 3 cockpit section furnished with all the correct dials, knobs and switches. This training aid was there to help us learn all the checklist items required throughout a flight, from before starting the engine to shutting it down again and getting out and leaving the aircraft in a safe and tidy condition. We were constantly reminded that we should know all the checks and emergency procedures by heart before we would be allowed to fly on our own. In fact, if we didn't it would not go down well with our flying instructors, known as QFIs[2] and who were to be invariably addressed as 'sir'.

So it was that the day finally dawned when I was to make my first flight with my instructor, Flight Lieutenant Wally Norton. It was a nerve-wracking, exciting, scary and exhilarating experience. The actual handling of the aircraft was not too much of a mystery to me. With the exception of the fact that we were not constantly descending, it wasn't so different to flying a glider. There was, of course, the additional throttle lever, which fell easily into my left hand, to control the output of the Viper jet engine only a few feet behind me, and the fact that we were zooming round the sky at about 200mph!

With Wally's gentlemanly and patient help I gradually picked up the various motor skills, got better at remembering my checks and learned to speak correctly on the radio. After a couple of weeks, during my twelfth flight, he suddenly announced that I was to land and take him back to the dispersal area where he would get out and I was to go and fly a circuit all on my own. On the way he asked me what my callsign was, I told him 'Romeo 56, sir,' and he said, 'Practise it and don't go using mine!'

We were marshalled back onto our spot on the dispersal line and Wally dismounted. A rather crude wooden triangular device was then put on his seat and the groundcrew fastened all the straps round it. This contraption was called a 'dummy' so I hoped that there was still only one dummy in the cockpit. I then restarted the engine and called ATC for permission to taxi. But I was wrong, there were two dummies in the cockpit!

Out of the habit of the last twelve flights I used my instructor's callsign! The controller must have been used to this and Wally was up there beside him. He replied with my own callsign and let me loose on the aviation world.

Everyone had said that your first solo would be something you would never forget and it's true. The excitement, tempered with an overwhelming desire not to screw up, led to a tightening in the throat and butterflies in the stomach. These feelings soon gave way to elation as I lifted-off and committed the act of solo aviation in a powered aircraft for the first time in my life. The elation was rapidly replaced by concentration on getting everything right. After all, this first solo flight was only going to last a few minutes, just the time it would take to make a single circuit of the airfield and land. I concentrated on achieving the right height and speed, making my turns level and accurate, and flying exactly parallel to the runway.

I made my pre-landing call on the radio, remembering to use my own callsign, and took a very quick look at the empty seat to my right, probably just to reassure myself that Wally hadn't sneaked back in while I wasn't looking. I also realised that while I was alone in the aircraft I wasn't alone in the air and soon took my eyes outside to look for the other aircraft in the circuit with me. Soon, all too soon, I was on the final approach, full flap and undercarriage down and locked, with three green lights, speed coming back through 100kts, height steadily reducing. It looked reassuringly the same as on the previous three circuits, which had satisfied Wally, so I pulled the throttle smoothly back to the stop, eased the stick back to reduce the rate of descent and about 200 yards into the runway the wheels contacted terra firma in a satisfyingly soft way. The landing was much better than the minimum standard of being one I could walk away from. I taxied back to dispersal sporting a very large grin. Wally met me with one of his own.

This was the memorable beginning of a year in which I eventually amassed all of 166 hours, learned many aviation skills, such as formation flying, aerobatics, recovery from spins and stalls, how to get your jet safely home without the engine and low-level and high-level navigation. Flying on instruments provided a big challenge and flying at night was one of the most enjoyable things I did.

From my gliding days I had experienced the thrilling beauty of flight. I soon learned, despite the hard work and occasional moments of terror, that it never goes away. We could fly as high as 30,000ft in the JP but, because the cockpit was not pressurised, only for a limited time. Up there the sky was bluer than ever I'd seen it and the ground seemed all of its 6 miles away. There was wonder in seeing the clouds from above and turning around to fly through your own condensation trail. One day, as I was descending from high altitude, a day on which there were lots of very large cumulus clouds around, I spotted Leeming airfield under one of these clouds. It looked so small, such a long way down. It's an image that has stayed with me to this day.

Then there was low-level flight. We flew our low-level navigation exercises at about 200mph and 250ft above the ground. Things seemed to rush by so quickly at first, higher up the sense of speed diminishes rapidly. Navigation became much more difficult because you couldn't see so much; the plan view of the world had disappeared. But we were taught the right way to find our way about and stay alert so that we didn't fly into the ground or obstacles, like power lines. Once I got the hang of it I found that low flying was my favourite exercise.

Another joy was night flying. Before becoming a QFI, Wally had been a night-fighter pilot, flying the Javelin, so he was an aficionado of flying around in the dark. He soon passed his enthusiasm and skill at this special slice of the aviation cake on to me. Flying around in the dark was so entirely different to doing it in daylight. Generally speaking the horizon was hard to perceive and on a cloudless and moonless night the only difference between down and up were the size and distribution of the lights.

Nevertheless, over northern England it was a wonderland of patches and ribbons of light, occasionally eclipsed by clouds passing below. When there was a full moon it was a little more like day flying, but the cockpit was dark, except for the very selective lighting of the instruments. Before going off in the dark we had to spend time in the cockpit trainer feeling for various knobs and levers with our eyes shut so that we could locate them without looking. We had to do this until it was second nature. In flight, the flying technique we had to learn was to blend instrument and visual flying. We had to start any manoeuvre with a good look in the direction we were going to go and then initiate the manoeuvre watching only the flight instruments. Once we were happy that the aircraft was doing what we wanted, then another look outside for other aircrafts' lights (not easy to see against urban backgrounds) and then constantly cross-refer with the instruments.

After about five months, as summer melted away into autumn, we started the formation flying phase. Wally was a member of the station's four-ship formation team, so I was very much looking forward to this and set off on my first trip with eager confidence. It turned out to be over confidence! Formation flying is a completely different skill.

The correct position in space near another aircraft is defined by lining up with three points on the leader. In the JP we used a diagonal line fixed by putting the navigation light on the end of the tip-tank of the other aircraft in line with its pilot's head and then staying abeam the tailplane by looking straight down the elevator hinge line. That alignment gave an echelon position at the correct distance away – about half a wingspan gap.

Line astern was a bit easier: keep in line with the leader's fuselage and hold vertical position by splitting the wing in half with its trailing edge. Somehow fore and aft distance wasn't too hard, although all you had to go on was the apparent position of the leader's tailplane in your windscreen. To maintain any formation position requires constant small adjustments with the flying controls and throttle to keep all the alignments right.

I just couldn't get the hang of it and became far too worried about hitting this other aeroplane only a few feet away. After a couple more trips it wasn't getting much better. The next event was a shock – I found that I was flying a fourth (and potentially final) sortie with 'The Boss', Squadron Leader Paddy Glover. He was a cheerful, puckish chap and had not appeared to be anyone to be frightened of. However, I then remembered that if you didn't pass a sortie with The Boss, then you were 'chopped', you failed the course. It didn't matter how nice he was, you were still on your way back down the A1 to Nav School.

Wally was kind enough to give me an encouraging grin as The Boss and I left the Operations Room and I tried hard to quell my nerves. At first I was doing quite well, but that was just in straight flight and gentle turns. We then did several changes of formation, from echelon port to line astern and then into echelon starboard. Paddy was occasionally teaching, occasionally admonishing and then I felt a prod in my side. He told me that he had his dinghy knife[3] out and was going to push it against me until I got closer to the leader.

I didn't have the spare capacity to check whether he was bluffing or not, but it worked! It was just like the time when my Dad had been pushing me up and down on my first bicycle and, just when I thought, 'I'll never get the hang of this,' off I went and suddenly realised that Dad was standing still and getting smaller behind me.

'That's it,' said Paddy quietly, 'You've got it now.' And just to prove the point he called the leader and asked him to 'Wind it up a bit.' The turns got steeper with more G, the climbs and descents also got steeper with much more speed variation. Now I was really beginning to enjoy myself. After an exhilarating tailchase and recovery for the formation break we landed with Paddy barely saying another word.

'Don't worry,' he told Wally, 'You've got him for a bit longer.'

The winter of 1962/3, which was memorable for a two-month period of snow, gales and freezing north-easterly winds, brought other challenges and adventures in its train. It started on Boxing Day 1962. That day I had said my goodbyes to my parents and girlfriend in West Yorkshire and set off to return to RAF Leeming on my motorbike. As I travelled north it started to snow. By the time I had reached the Officers' Mess I resembled the abominable snowman, at least from the front I did. I slowly unfolded my frozen limbs and escaped into the centrally heated balm of my room to thaw out. In those days the RAF did not shut down between Christmas and New Year so we were there to resume our flying training on 27 December. However, the weather had other ideas. During the next two months we were able to fly spasmodically between periods of snow, frozen runways and howling northerly gales.

On one occasion Chris Blake and I were sent on a formation sortie, led by an instructor called Joe Hickmott. While we were away from base a huge cumulonimbus cloud passed over Leeming and dumped an inordinate amount of its frozen cargo all over the airfield. Once the shower had passed we were recalled, so Joe called us into close formation to fly home and land. We actually flew through the aforementioned snowstorm as we approached Leeming from the south to land into the teeth of the biting wind on runway 36. Once we were in clear air Joe brought us into echelon starboard so I was on the outside formating on Chris, who, in turn, was formating on Joe. Joe told us to extend the usual 5-second period between following each other on the left-hand break to 20 seconds to give us extra space on landing (SOP). Because Chris and I had been concentrating hard at keeping tight formation we both wondered why he had decided this change to SOPs. As soon as we had turned through 180° to fly downwind and looked at the airfield, the penny dropped. The runway was no longer visible under a new blanket of snow; you could only see where it was by the lights sticking up through the snow on either side.

Joe landed well ahead of Chris and by the time I was touching down Chris was a good distance ahead of me. However, he seemed to be pointing the wrong way. It must be very slippy I thought. I tried a touch on the brakes and soon confirmed my diagnosis. This would be interesting. By now Chris had got his jet pointing the right way and was about to clear the runway onto the almost invisible taxiway. As he skidded out of the way I came to a slithering halt in his place. Phew! A very slow and gingerly return to the dispersal area then followed. But Jack Frost still had something up his sleeve. Joe, being the good guy he was, came to see if we were OK. Chris had dismounted but I was still in my cockpit when he got to me. Having ascertained that I was getting over the experience, he said a few encouraging words and jumped down from the back of the wing. Whereupon he slipped on the ice and broke his arm!

During that terrible winter many of us had another flying experience. Leeming became the centre for a few days for the airdrop by helicopter of supplies and feed for the hill farmers of the North York Moors and the Dales. When we were not flying we were pressed into service as air-delivery operators in the back of the SAR Whirlwind helicopters pushing out bales of hay to sheep cut off by the drifts while hovering over snow-covered fields. It was a cold job but qualified us for a tot of rum when we got back!

Of course there were the other potentially bad things that happened. Like a 500mph head-on meeting with the JP of fellow student George Millington, as we both flew around a towering cumulus cloud, at the same height, but in opposite directions. Thankfully we didn't both break into each other – but it was close! Then there was the time when I had been doing solo circuits at another airfield, RAF Topcliffe, and hadn't, until it was too late, noticed some really bad weather coming in from the north, the direction of Leeming and 'home'. Having set off to fly back to base, clear of the cloud because I wasn't yet allowed to fly in clouds on my own, I had to fly lower and lower to stay clear of the descending gloom. To find my way to Leeming I followed the main east coast railway line north and then turned left at Northallerton station to follow the main road west to Leeming Bar, from where I should be able to see the airfield. The trouble was that by the time I got to Northallerton the cloud was much lower than we were supposed to fly over built-up areas and I vividly remember flying down the High Street trying to be as quiet as possible! I did get back safely but had to fill out a report for unauthorised low flying.

By May 1963 there was exactly half the original course left: seven officers and seven NCOs. Over in the USA the *Mercury Seven* astronauts were the aviation heroes of the day; I secretly liked to think that I was now one of the 'Leeming Seven'. We fourteen were the very first of a new training regime in which the coveted RAF wings, signifying that you really were a pilot, would be bestowed upon students at the end of their one-year basic course. But we were told that we were only actually 'probationary' pilots and that our bright new, shiny badges were to be sown on with thin thread until we had passed our advanced training.

Nevertheless, after a couple of days of rehearsals, the Wings Graduation Parade took place on a May morning, almost a year to the day since I had graduated from Officer Training at South Cerney. I was just nineteen years old. Again there were lots of mums and dads, friends and siblings there to watch, along with our flying instructors. This time my parents were there along with my brothers.

The day went by in a bit of a haze: parade with a formation flypast, church dedication, lunch in the Officers' Mess, farewell to families and bags packed ready to go on leave. The commissioned 'Leeming Seven' had been earmarked to go to RAF Valley for Advanced Flying Training on the brand-new, minuscule, swept-winged trainer the Folland Gnat. I was really excited and all my worldly goods and chattels had already been despatched to Valley in a large wooden box a couple of days previously.

But it was during the afternoon of the big day itself that Paddy Glover had sought us out and taken us aside to give us some bad news. He told us that the introduction of the Gnat was behind schedule, so the powers that be had decided that the first course would not start, as previously planned, in June, but would be delayed until September and would consist of only that summer's graduates from the RAF College at Cranwell.

We would now be going to No.8 FTS at RAF Swinderby in Lincolnshire to fly the elderly and very nearly obsolete DH Vampire. Disappointment was an understatement; I was devastated. No modern, swept-wing, brand new, nearly supersonic jet for me. Flat, boring Lincolnshire instead of the seaside beauty of Anglesey! What's more, the wooden crate with all my bits and pieces was probably right then rumbling up the A5 on the back of an RAF 3-tonner! I returned home to Pudsey on my 250cc BSA in a blue funk; two weeks' leave was OK, but now I wasn't much looking forward to the next phase of training. I wanted modern swept wings not twin-boomed antiquity!

Notes

1 NCO pilots were very common in the RAF of the Second World War but their numbers were reducing. After the advent of the Military Salary in the early 1970s all pilots were commissioned officers.
2 Qualified Flying Instructors, a formal qualification gained by passing the QFI Course at the Central Flying School (CFS).
3 The dinghy knife was worn in a sheath sown onto the upper, outer leg of the flying suit and was there so that, should the single-seat dinghy in the ejection seat suddenly inflate, you could use the knife to puncture it. The knife would also function as a survival tool.

4

Climbing Higher

RAF Swinderby lay alongside the A46, about halfway between Newark and Lincoln. There the A46 follows the course of a Roman military road – the Fosse Way. During the Second World War RAF Swinderby was one of the numerous bomber stations in Lincolnshire and, before its role change to jet pilot training in the 1950s, it had been a training base for future transport and bomber aircrews, using the venerable Vickers Wellington.

It wasn't long after our arrival that we were back in Ground School being taught about this rather strange-looking aircraft, the Vampire, with its bulbous nose, stubby fuselage and twin booms holding the empennage in place. We had to learn about its engine, its electrical, pneumatic and hydraulic systems and its safety equipment. Our course was one of three in training at Swinderby at any one time and our numbers had been increased by those who had passed out successfully from other Basic Flying Training Schools; most of these fellow students were friends or acquaintances from South Cerney days.

After grinding through seemingly interminable lessons we learnt that the Vampire's wooden nose section was held together by glue (it was a direct descendant of the 'Wooden Wonder' – the DH Mosquito). We learned that the centrifugal jet engine (a direct descendant of Whittle's original) was so much more robust than the more 'modern' axial flow jets, like the Viper, and that the ejection seat was an older model than the one in the JP. Of course there were also the inevitable lectures on meteorology, aerodynamics and 'officer development'; these mostly seemed to repeat what we'd already suffered at Basic FTS. After all, it was only the aircraft that had changed and that, it seemed to us, not for the better!

It was like holding lessons in a museum. This impression was greatly enhanced when we discovered that we were going to be the penultimate Vampire course in the RAF and that as individual aircraft became too difficult to mend, they would be scrapped rather than repaired. We just had to hope that enough of them would survive old age long enough to see out our course and the next! Later we would see a diminutive figure in a long brown coat, carrying a hide-faced hammer, who would tap various parts of an aircraft, a wing-tapper rather than a wheel-tapper. This curious behaviour usually led to the aircraft on which he had played his odd timpani disappearing over the horizon, never to be seen again.

When we did get finally airborne it turned out to be a challenge to learn to handle this old lady and, especially, her engine correctly. However, with much more thrust available than in the JP and not that much more weight, she did slip through the air quite well. Climbing speed was 250kts[1] (about 100kts more than the JP) and aerobatics could be flown at between 200 and 450kts.

Despite her age the Vampire was pressurised, whereas the JP was not, so we could fly higher and stay up there for longer without any bad effects, such as the bends. It took about 20 minutes to get to 40,000ft. The flying training syllabus was more of the same: circuits, stalling, spinning, practise forced landings, aerobatics, instrument flying, night flying, formation flying and, of course, low-level and high-level navigation. My instructor, Flight Lieutenant Pete Young, also threw in a few extra-curricular, low-level ground-attack lessons for free. These really excited me and it became my aim to go to a Hunter squadron at the end of the course.

We were due to graduate by the end of October 1963 and the syllabus was designed to give us about 75 flying hours each, so the pressure was on. Still, it was summer and I have happy memories of us moving chairs out of our crewroom onto the grass behind the aircraft line and sitting there, like so many Battle of Britain pilots. That summer was, for me, idyllic. I had bought an Italian Racing Red 1934 MG PA Midget for the princely sum of £120, there was a reasonable selection of nightlife in Lincoln or in the Officers' Mess, and I was getting to grips with the flying and enjoying every minute of it.

Of course, there were those times when things either got hilariously silly or downright scary or, sometimes, both: like the time when I was the third aircraft in a formation being led by one of our instructors. We had just got to the best bit of the trip, called the tailchase, which was a game of 'follow-my-leader' through a series of increasingly demanding aerobatic manoeuvres. That day there was lots of what the weather folk call 'fair-weather cumulus' and our gallant leader started climbing up the side of one, inverting his aircraft to pull over its top and then diving down the other side, before rolling away from it and pulling up to climb the next one. He'd done this about three times and the clouds had got progressively bigger.

So coming down the side of the third one, with our cockpit canopies still facing the cloud, he called for us to extend our airbrakes to help control the speed. What I then saw in front of me was the number two aircraft's undercarriage start to extend and then it suddenly disappear into the cloud.

By now the leader had rolled his aircraft through 180° and was starting to pull up for the next manoeuvre. I thought I ought to let him know that our number 2 had taken his leave of us when I heard a faint and slightly high-pitched voice on the radio, saying that he was OK and that he had '3 greens', signifying that his undercarriage was safely locked down. This, of course, was a complete mystery to our leader. I rejoined formation with him and we went home; we didn't see number 2 again until we got back on the ground. He had landed safely, shaken and not a little stirred.

What had happened was not that uncommon in the Vampire. The three levers that operated the hydraulically actuated stuff, like flaps, undercarriage and airbrakes, were clustered together below the throttle, on the left lower side of the pilot. You had to learn to find them by feel as there was usually, and especially during formation flying, no time to look for them. Unfortunately my fellow course member had knocked the undercarriage lever to the down position instead of selecting the airbrakes out. It probably slowed him down even more quickly, as at the time he was actually about 100kts above the undercarriage lowering speed limit. The Vampire suffered quite a strong nose-up trim change when the landing gear was lowered, even at normal speeds, so the trim change at 350kts must have been both a big surprise and difficult to stop; hence his rapid disappearance into the cloud.

Another episode I remember all too well occurred on my solo night, high-level navigation sortie. I was to fly a triangular route from Swinderby to Bristol, then to overhead Heathrow and return to Swinderby, all at about 40,000ft. It was a beautiful late summer night with not a cloud in the sky and what the older instructors used to call a 'bomber's moon'. Everything went to plan and the views were outstanding; I could see from coast to coast and was feeling happy and very self-satisfied. Later in my career I would always watch out when I started feeling like that!

But on this night I was king of the world. As I flew north from London I could see the towns passing below me and I started to count them off, ignoring my radio navigation altogether. Well it was such a beautifully clear night, who needed it? I had identified Newark and Lincoln well ahead of me and asked permission of the radar controller for a visual descent directly to Swinderby. He readily gave it and soon handed me over to the Swinderby Approach controller. As I had no need of any further radar service I asked him if I could go directly to the airfield and he handed me over to the local controller. I could now see the airfield clearly and asked permission to join the circuit. He told me that I could and that I would be the only one in the circuit. I had the place to myself.

As I turned to go downwind, parallel with the runway, I thought I saw another set of navigation lights to my right. But when I made my radio call the controller replied, 'Roger, you are number one,' confirming that I was alone in the landing pattern. I did my pre-landing checks and, as I turned onto the final approach, I saw another set of lights to my right and yet another ahead of me. I made my final call to 'roll', that is to make a 'touch-and-go' landing, and I was cleared to do so.

When I touched down and then applied the power to take-off again I could have sworn that there was another aircraft just above me, but I didn't have the time to look properly. As I turned downwind again, this time to make my final approach and landing for the night, the controller asked me if I had my navigation lights on. I looked down to check the switch and when I looked up again there was a Jet Provost in front of me and I was overtaking it rapidly. I turned right to avoid it and, just as I was about to complain to the controller, I noticed that the airfield identification beacon had been moved quite a distance while I'd been away and that the A46 had disappeared altogether.

A huge shot of adrenalin accompanied my realisation that I wasn't at Swinderby at all! But where was I? What was going on? How had I got it so wrong? I called the controller, as nonchalantly as I could manage, to tell him that I was leaving the circuit for about 5 minutes and that I would call him when I wanted to come back to land. All I had to do now was climb to 2,000ft, find out where I was and then sneak back to Swinderby.

I was pretty sure that I hadn't flown north beyond Swinderby so I set off heading north-west, flying as slowly as I dare. It didn't take me long to realise what I'd done. I'd misidentified Grantham as Newark and Sleaford as Lincoln and the airfield in between the two towns was RAF Barkston Heath, which was the relief landing ground for the RAF College at Cranwell. As soon as I had established that, I set off for Swinderby as fast as I could, rejoined the circuit and landed. Nothing was said when I got back to the squadron operations room, no severe words from the duty instructor. Silence. I'd got away with it.

Well, I had until the next day when I was summoned to the Flight Commander's office. He told me that he had received a call that morning from our Chief Flying Instructor, a frighteningly large Wing Commander, whose opposite number at Cranwell had complained about a rogue Vampire upsetting some of his students and instructors in the circuit at Barkston Heath the previous evening. While I'd had the morning off, the wheels of investigation had turned and identified me as the guilty party. There was no point in denying it. I had to write a 'formal official' letter of apology and spend seven consecutive days as the Station Orderly Officer. No more socialising for a week!

The course soon passed by. Before we knew it the last week was upon us. I had only one solo flight left before the final assessments: aerobatic competition, final navigation test and the final handling test – all of which would be flown with the more senior instructors – all called 'Sir' with a capital S.

When my turn to fly that last solo trip came up, one of my classmates was also due to fly the same sortie at the same time. So we agreed that 30 minutes after take-off we would meet up over Gamston airfield at 12,000ft and have a bit of a dogfight. So, half an hour after departing Swinderby, I headed for our rendezvous and it wasn't long before I spotted a Vampire, not quite over Gamston but close enough. As I closed in at about 300kts, I noticed that he had the flaps and undercarriage down; he was practicing a stall – what a swot! So I kept up my overtaking speed and dived behind him to pull up in a barrel roll in front of his nose. Having done that, I wheeled back round and found that he had recovered from his stall and was accelerating slowly. So, with the airbrakes out, I closed up on his starboard side to come into fairly close echelon formation. As I did so I noticed two things: there was someone occupying the right-hand seat, which would not be the case with a solo student; and the very large fleet number on the side of the nose was the wrong one! So - airbrakes in, full power, rapid roll to the right and disappear downwards as fast as possible! Did he see my number? Who was it?

When I got back and signed in, I casually inquired as to who was flying fleet number 14.

'Oh, that's the Chief Instructor, Wing Commander Carson, doing a final handling test on one of the students on your course, sir,' came the reply. Thankfully the supplementary question as to why I should wish to know didn't come. When I got to the squadron operations room, I signed in very quietly and made a quick getaway to the crewroom. Thankfully, bearing in mind my previous misdemeanour, I never heard any more about it. Except for a bit of insulting banter from my oppo about my lack of navigation skills in not being at the rendezvous!

Actually I did quite well on my final navigation test, especially at the low-level phase and the final handling test result was a solid pass. Sadly, my aerobatics were not quite good enough to win me the trophy; but I thoroughly enjoyed the flight.

So that was it. We had passed the course and all we needed now were our postings. A couple of days later most of us found that what we had asked for was nothing like what we'd got. I'd asked for Lightnings or Hunters and I learned, with not a little disappointment, that I was going to a two-man strike/attack Canberra squadron in RAF Germany; which one they didn't yet know. I would get that news when (and if) I passed the next phase of training – operational conversion. But before I left Swinderby the RAF had one more surprise for me.

Because of the design of the Canberra's cockpit there was a maximum thigh length allowed, otherwise ejection could lead to loss of the kneecaps. As I was barely 5ft 7in tall I didn't think that I would have a problem, nevertheless I had to report to Station Sickquarters and get measured.

I duly turned up and sat on what I later learnt was an anthropometric measuring chair that was in the corner of the room with various measuring scales painted on the wall alongside it. The medical orderly came in and looked at the scale measuring horizontally from my buttocks, pressed up against the wall behind me, to my left kneecap.

'Plenty of room for you,' he said cheerily. I could have told you that, I thought as I stood up to leave and pursue a more worthwhile activity, like having lunch in Lincoln. Just as I was doing so he asked me to sit down and sit up; I wondered what he was up to now?

'Are you sitting as upright as you can, sir?' he asked, as he put a ruler horizontally on the top of my head. I stretched up as far as I could and said, 'Yes. Is there a height limit as well?' Then he did that thing that all medical folk do when something is wrong: he left the room without saying a word and came back with the Medical Officer. He then repeated the ruler on the top of my head procedure while they both totally ignored me. Tutting noises and sucking of teeth was all I got in the way of any information as to what was going on.

Records were then retrieved from the office and more sucking of teeth ensued. Eventually I could stand it no longer.

'What's the problem?' I asked (I had been tempted to mimic Bugs Bunny with a, 'Nahhrr, what's up Doc?' but thought better of it). The ruler was then reapplied and I was asked to slide out from under it.

'Look at this, young man,' said the Doc. I looked at the far end of the aforementioned ruler, which was an inch or so below a red line.

'See that red line?' the MO asked.

'Yes,' I replied, wondering whether this was some new form of colour blindness test.

'Well, that represents the minimum back length for our aircrew to be pilots.'

I pointed at the by now, well-worn RAF Pilots' Wings on my uniform jacket and said, 'Well, how have I got these then, sir?'

'A very good question,' he responded, 'We'll have to look into this. You're not leaving the station yet are you?'

'No,' I said, with a strong conviction that the alternative would not have been acceptable!

'I'll let the Chief Instructor know about this and leave him to decide what to do,' was the ominous closing medical bulletin.

Needless to say I didn't sleep too well that night. Had I gone through all this to still end up at Navigation School, but two years late? I was listlessly hanging about the mess the next morning when I got the message to go and see the Chief Instructor, the rather imposing Wing Commander 'Kit' Carson. I hesitantly knocked on his door and was immediately given a booming invitation to enter. I gave him my smartest salute and stood to attention in front of his desk.

'Relax, Brooke,' he said, so I removed my hat and stood at ease.

'I've had a look at all this fuss that the quacks are making about your back length,' he said. 'It's all nonsense. You've done well throughout your training and we've spent far too much on you thus far to make you start all over again. You don't want to be a navigator now, do you?'

'No, sir.'

'I see that you did at first, and that's where this problem stems from. When you went through aircrew selection at Hornchurch, you passed all the aptitude tests for pilot with flying colours. So when you applied to change streams from Cadet Navigator to Cadet Pilot that was all they looked at. If they'd have looked at your detailed medical papers and your anthropometric measurements you'd never have been accepted and you might now just be passing out of Navigation School. So consider yourself lucky and go off to fly the Canberra. I did a tour on the Canberra with No.16 Squadron at RAF Laarbruch in Germany. If you get there you'll have a ball. Best of luck!'

Little did he know how things would turn out. But one thing was clear in my mind: I now knew why I'd had so much trouble seeing out of the Vampire, even with the seat in its fully up position. I wondered whether the Canberra would be the same. Well, I'd find out soon enough.

Notes

1 For the non-aviators or landlubbers a knot is equal to one nautical mile per hour, which equals 1.15mph. A nautical mile is a distance equal to 1 minute arc of latitude and that is taken as 6,080ft.

5

The Canberra

I must now introduce a major player in my tale: the English Electric Canberra. Before they built the Canberra the only aircraft the English Electric Company had designed and developed were the Kingston flying boat and the ultra-light Wren, both machines having flown in the years well before the Second World War. The Preston-based firm had produced a long line of successful industrial electrical products, such as generators and heavy motors for locomotives and trams. During the Second World War the government tasked English Electric to build several types of aircraft on behalf of other aircraft manufacturers, which were then flown away from the airfield the company had built at Samlesbury, near Preston. One of the most numerous of these was the Handley Page Hampden. By 1945 English Electric had gained a lot of expertise in the manufacture of all-metal, twin-engined, medium bombers. After the war multiple mergers brought English Electric into the world of computers and retail electrical goods, such as washing machines and fridges; indeed my parents had both of these EE products in the early 1950s.

The Canberra had its origins in a 1944 Air Ministry requirement for a successor to the de Havilland Mosquito. The Air Staff wanted a high-altitude, high-speed bomber with no defensive armament that could outclimb and outrun the fighters of the day. Several aircraft manufacturers submitted proposals and English Electric were shortlisted to proceed with development studies. Their new design team was headed by the former Westland Aircraft chief designer, Mr W. Petter. In May 1945 English Electric was awarded the contract to produce and develop a protoype, jet-engined, medium bomber capable of flight at high altitudes and speeds.

However, postwar military reductions slowed the process and the prototype did not fly until May 1949; oddly enough on the afternoon of Friday the thirteenth! The aircraft was a simple and very smooth aerodynamic design, looking a bit like a scaled-up Gloster Meteor, with a shoulder wing. The fuselage was circular in cross section, tapered at both ends and, cockpit canopy aside, entirely without protrusions; the line of the large, low-aspect ratio wings was broken only by the tubular engine nacelles.

The original development was also delayed by the provision of suitable powerplants. Armstrong Siddeley had offered an engine, curiously called the Beryl, with about 4,000lb of thrust, but this was insufficient power to give the projected bomber the required performance. Rolls-Royce were developing a similar axial-flow turbojet, but a considerable time passed before it was ready for installation. This engine, the first in a long line called Avon, would develop 6,500lb of thrust and so was selected and installed in the wings.

After a two-year test and development programme, the production model, styled the Canberra B2, first flew on 21 April 1950 and entered RAF service with No.101 Squadron in May 1951, just two years after the flight of the first prototype. In a testament to the aircraft's benign handling characteristics, the pilots' conversion course consisted of 20 hours in the Meteor and 3 hours under supervison in the B2; at this stage there was no dual-controlled version.

With a maximum speed of 470kts (871km/h), a standard service ceiling of 48,000ft (14,600m) and the ability to carry a 3.6-tonne payload, the Canberra was an instant success. It was flown by a crew of three: pilot, navigator and bomb aimer. All were equipped with ejection seats, with the pilot sitting under the low bubble canopy ahead of the other two crew, who occupied a rather claustrophobic cabin at the rear end of the pressure cabin. The bomb bay ran the whole length of the cylindrical section of the fuselage behind the cabin and could carry up to six 1,000lb bombs in tandem on triple carriers. The bomb aimer had to get out of his seat and go past the pilot, whose seat was offset to the left, to lie on a couch and aim the bombs, looking down through the transparent nose cone, using a contemporary visual bombsight.

There were three fuel tanks above the bomb bay, containing around 11,000lb of fuel. The forward and rear tanks (nos 1 & 3) carried the most fuel and the 2,400lb of fuel in the centre tank (no.2) was usually held until last. Auxiliary tanks could be fitted to the wingtips, bringing the maximum fuel load up to about 15,000lb; the tip tanks were jettisonable. A full fuel load gave the B2 a maximum endurance of about 4 hours and a range of about 1,600 nautical miles (nm). A special overload tank could be fitted in the bomb bay, but I never came across this fitment in any of my 2,500 hours flying many marks of Canberra. However, the overload tank was certainly used on 21 February 1951, when RAF Canberra WD 932, piloted by Squadron Leader A. Callard, flew non-stop from Aldergove, Northern Ireland, to Newfoundland. The flight covered almost 1,800 nautical miles (3,300km) in 4 hours 37 minutes. The Canberra was being flown to the US to act as a pattern aircraft for the Martin B-57, which would be built under licence.

Fuel management was entirely manual, using the two pumps in each tank. If fitted, the tip tank fuel was fed by air pressure to the engines via the no.3 tank. Once that fuel was consumed the best course of action was try to keep the forward and aft tanks in balance and leave the centre tank till last. When that tank got down to 1,250lb it was definitely time to land!

The Canberra had a hydraulic system, pressurised to 2,700psi by pumps on each engine. This operated the undercarriage, wheelbrakes, single-stage flaps, airbrakes and bomb bay doors. The aircraft showed its ancestry from a long line of industrial electrical machinery in that the electrical system had a multitude of spring-loaded, electro-mechanical solenoids to connect its various parts. When the Battery Master Switch was switched on there was an audible *thunk* from the bowels of the machine as various connections were completed!

The crew all entered the aircraft by a door on the starboard side of the nose. This swung up and was retained there by a metal strut; the door was quite heavy and it hurt like hell if it fell down when you were mounting the machine! The door was lockable, but all Canberras seemed to have the same key; replacements could be bought from any Ford agent as the key fitted the doors of the Ford Anglia! The pilot's cockpit was immediately inside the door, with the bomb-aimer's couch, bombsight and instruments off to the right at floor level. The rear cabin was off to the left, with its two ejection seats, desks and navigation equipment, directly behind the pilot. The navigators also had control of the electrical generation system.

The Canberra B2 reeked of immediate postwar design (if you can use such a technical term for the rather haphazard layout of some of the equipment and instruments). It also had a very special and unique smell. Years later when I flew the Canberra again that smell took me straight back to my very first flight in the aircraft. However, there was a modicum of organisation to the pilot's instrument panel, with the main flight instruments grouped together in a sensible way. The three fuel guages and their associated pump switches, arranged vertically, were to the right as were the engine-related dials. Much like in the Vampire, the panels were all painted black and there were little lights on stalks sticking out all over the place.

Flying at high altitudes required that the cabin and cockpit were pressurised, using filtered air from the engine compressors. Temperature could be controlled via a single, spring-loaded switch and there was a small circular window in the bubble cockpit canopy that was electrically heated to keep it frost free. This rather curious feature was known as the Direct Vision or DV window. In the B2 the cockpit heating was notoriously poor for prolonged flight at or above 40,000ft, where the outside air temperature (OAT) could be as low as -56°C. One modification was that the rear cabin occupants were provided with electrically heated socks; Heath Robinson was alive and well! In 1963 VHF radios were fitted and there was, of course, an internal intercommunication system (intercom); in the mid-1960s the main radios became UHF. The B2s and T4s of the early '60s were fitted with radio navigation and landing aids, such as Gee, Radio Compass and ILS (Instrument Landing System).

One feature of the Canberra which was novel to me was the engine starting system. Unlike the Jet Provost and Vampire, which used electric motors to wind-up the engine until there was sufficient airflow to allow the fuel to be ignited, the Canberra used large, black-powder cartridges that looked like brass shell cases. When these were electrically ignited they produced a large amount of gas at high pressure that was channelled into the starter turbine. This was like a little jet engine that very rapidly whirred up to the amazing rotational speed of 64,000rpm. Through a geared drive it rotated the engine itself up to about 1,200rpm. At that point fuel was introduced and ignited by spark plugs in a couple of the combustion chambers. The cartridge starter unit was in the bullet-shaped housing that stuck out of the front of the engine. The early marks of Canberra had a single breech system with room for just one cartridge. The later marks, except the PR9[1], had a triple breech so that three cartridges were loaded for starting. The cartridge starter system gave the aircraft real independence when away from base. There was no need for external power units and a spare set of six cartridges were housed in the spacious tailcone of the aircraft, which was easily accessed via a hatch underneath the rear fuselage. Starting the Canberra was always an impressive sight and sound, with the exhausted black gas coming out of three vents around the forward engine cowling accompanied by an impressive bang and loud whoosh.

Eventually the English Electric Canberra was built in twenty-seven versions, which equipped 35 RAF squadrons and the air forces of fourteen countries worldwide. The T4 trainer version came along a couple of years later, along with a two-man photographic reconnaissance version, the PR3.

Notes

1 The PR9's 207 Avon was started by AVPIN, an isopropyl nitrate liquid operating a similar turbo-starter unit. Each engine had an AVPIN tank, which had to be replenished when required.

6

Operational Conversion

Because I had finished Advanced Flying Training in early October and my Canberra conversion course was not due to start until mid-December, I spent several weeks being sent on what the RAF calls 'Temporary Detachments'; that was really a means of occupying young men who can't be sent on leave! So, I ended up hanging around various RAF stations, mostly in Lincolnshire, which isn't the most engaging of counties in late autumn. I spent some time at RAF Binbrook making coffee for the folk installing the new Lightning simulator and a very enjoyable week being a checklist reader and amateur co-pilot for RAF pilots on what was known as a 'Refresher Course' at RAF Manby. The latter was great fun and I flew sorties in the twin piston-engined Vickers Varsity, the multi-engine trainer of the times; it was also used as a flying classroom for the Basic Navigation School students. I committed aviation in this clattering flying machine several times with a Flight Lieutenant Lincoln, inevitably known as 'Abe', who had just spent two years flying for the British Antarctic Survey. He seemed to me then to be positively ancient and had a wonderful repertoire of flying stories. The Varsity was a splendid old beast and I was told that its ancestor the Wellington was much in evidence in the cockpit. Funnily enough, I would get to know the Varsity much better about twelve years later when I flew it as a test pilot at RAE Farnborough!

Autumn soon turned to winter and I was allowed a couple of weeks leave at home in Yorkshire. But the day soon came when I packed my cases and loaded them into my precious little MG and set off for RAF Bassingbourn, the home of No.231 Operational Conversion Unit. That was where all future RAF and overseas Canberra aircrew were taught the vagaries of the venerable English Electric Canberra. There were three marks of Canberra based at Bassingbourn: B2s, PR3s and T4s. The T4s were used commonly by both the Bomber and PR training units, who had their own hangars and aircraft dispersal areas.

I arrived at RAF Bassingbourn, north of Royston, after a long and cold journey from Yorkshire in my draughty little 1934 sports car. On my arrival I found out that I was on a small course of six, made up of three two-man crews, all of us destined to join Canberra B(I)8 squadrons in RAF Germany. Inevitably the first get-together was in the Officers' Mess bar on the night before the course started, which was just one week before we all went away again on Christmas leave! The RAF often moves in very mysterious ways!

When I met the other five, I discovered that I already knew one of the navigators, a tall Welshman called Geoff Trott. We had been on the same Officer Training and Basic Flying Training courses. However, Geoff had failed the pilots' course by not going solo before the allotted flying hour limit, so he'd left RAF Leeming after only a couple of months. But the RAF was as good as its word and he then went through navigator training, so here we were together again almost two years later. We thought that this was a good enough foundation to form a working partnership as a bomber crew.

The other guys on the course were happy with this and we all had a good evening getting to know each other; Ken Lilley and Ron Ledwidge were the other two pilots. Cranwell graduate Ken had come from that first Gnat course that I had so narrowly missed and Ron had been flying the mighty Avro Shackleton with Coastal Command. They had already teamed up with the other two navs, Alec Wedderburn and Martin Fortune, so all was complete. Of course, we all knew what was coming first – Ground School – it always does; so no flying before Christmas!

Along with us we had three Southern Rhodesian Air Force pilots doing a short conversion course. Two were straight out of training and one, a redoubtable, grizzled character called Wally, was an ex-DC3 driver. Wally introduced me to a hangover cure called the Reineck: lager and tomato juice mixed with ice! But it worked and I used it for many years afterwards. The Rhodesians were a gregarious, if a bit loud, bunch and had a wealth of stories about their wonderful country. Looking back on what we learnt about it then makes today's self-inflicted woes of Zimbabwe all the more sad. Indeed, I found that I was learning a lot about the wider world and aviation from mixing with other folk who were not as young and inexperienced as I was. For instance, Martin Fortune had worked for the Forestry Commission and Ron had a good repertoire of tales about his time flying the Shackleton. Just one of my favourites went as follows.

Ron's crew was on a 12-hour Atlantic patrol. It was the early hours of the morning and they were flying at 500ft, well out to sea on a steady track back to their base at Kinloss, in northern Scotland. All was very quiet and dark on the flight deck when a microphone clicked on; it was the navigator.

'Skipper, turn right through 60°.'

'Roger.'

About 2 minutes later, 'Good, now turn left 90°.'

'Roger.'

Then another 2 minutes later, 'OK, turn right again through 60°, back onto our original track.'

After a short pause the captain switched his microphone back on, 'What was that all about?'

The nav replied, 'I'd dropped some stew on my chart and I didn't want us to fly through it!'

We spent the first three weeks of 1964 either in the classroom, 'flying' the Link Trainer (ah, memories of the Air Training Corps!) or waiting for the grey winter weather to clear sufficiently for us to carry out our first training sorties. It was during the classroom phase that I acquired a nickname that would stay with me throughout my operational tour and, with some folk, well beyond. It was 'Noddy'. This was due to being accused of 'nodding off' during lessons and the coincidence of a new dance called 'The Nod', at which I became a bit of an exponent. I suppose my youthful looks, diminutive stature and the fact that I could still get away with not shaving for up to three days also helped!

At one party with the instructors, one of them, the leprechaun-like Paddy McCormack, came over to me with a photograph. It was a picture of him and his eleven-strong Liberator crew during 'Ops' in the Second World War. He told me not to worry about being nineteen; he said, in his engaging Irish brogue, 'Dis is what oi was doin' when oi was nointeen.'

My instructor was Flight Lieutenant Bob Brinkhurst, a tall, rather pale-faced and grey-haired Canadian on an exchange tour. Back home he had flown and instructed on the RCAF Avro CF100 Canuk, a large, twin-jet, all-weather fighter. It soon came to light that Bob had experienced a hair-raising incident during his conversion to the Canberra. During a flying exercise in which the aircraft is flown on a steady heading, at gradually reducing airspeed with one engine at full power and the other idling, Bob's ejection seat had fired of its own accord and he suddenly found himself outside! He had to act very quickly as they were flying at only 3,000ft above the ground. He managed to get away from the seat and open his parachute just in time. His instructor, Flight Lieutenant Jim Cox, also did a wonderful job of recovering the aircraft from its ensuing unusual attitude and bringing it home in 'convertible' mode, with the wind whistling over and round the cockpit. Perhaps that was why Bob was pale and grey-haired!

We first flew together on 28 January 1964 and, to my mind, the course was finally underway. The Canberra was very different to the compact jet trainers that I had flown so far. For one thing it was so big. Its length, at 65½ft, was not far short of that of an Avro Lancaster bomber and the Canberra's wingspan was almost twice that of the Vampire. The other very different aspect was that, for the first time, I could actually see the front of an engine – it wasn't buried inside the fuselage. Indeed, we were taught during our external inspection to reach up and give the compressor a push to make sure that it rotated freely. And I could walk, albeit with a bit of a crouch, underneath the wing – no more getting down on hands and knees to check the undercarriage – plus I could easily enter and inspect the interior of the cavernous bomb bay. From there I could see the electrical fuel pumps at the bottom of the fuel tanks above my head.

Getting aboard was also very different – no climbing up and over into the cockpit, but a rather somewhat undignified crawl up via the entrance door on the starboard side of the nose. The seating arrangement in the T4 was extremely unusual in that the right-hand (instructor's) seat was pivoted from a beam at its top end. It was swung forward to let the navigators into the cabin and then back to let the student pilot clamber across into his seat. The instructor then strapped in with the seat in its rearmost position and when both front-seat crew were happy with the myriad connections they had to make, the instructor's seat was swung to its central position. Then the ground crew removed the small access stepladder and shut the door.

Those first few sorties in the T4 were quite hard work and included operating the Canberra through its whole flight envelope, climbing above 40,000ft and out to its maximum speeds of 450kts and 0.84 Mach no. It took me a little while to adjust to flying with a yoke instead of a stick and to handling two throttles. We stalled aircraft and with that big fat wing the T4 didn't fully stall until the speed got down to around 70kts.

But the most important and most difficult new thing to learn was how to cope with an engine failure, especially at the most critical times, such as just after take-off and just before landing. The minimum speed at which a trained pilot was deemed to be able to fly the aircraft safely away after an engine failure on take-off (EFATO) was 140kts. And that was the speed at which our instructors would start chopping back a throttle just after lift-off. For safety's sake they had to tell us it was going to happen, but until they did it you didn't know which foot you were going to have to push with. Absolute full rudder was required and that took a force of about 180lb! There was also a need to apply quite a bit of lateral control, as well as making a radio call and carrying out the emergency drills. By the time that the aircraft reached 1,000ft the appropriate leg was shaking and it all felt as if things were teetering on the edge of disaster. Of course, practise makes perfect, but the EFATO was always a trial. Especially when the speed at which it was initiated was reduced as you got better at it!

We also had to learn how to make a successful landing with one engine not working and, even more challenging, to make a missed approach without losing control. The normal landing speed of the Canberra T4 and B2 was around 90kts so the approach speeds were very similar to the Vampire. The last and equally important new thing to learn was how to handle the aircraft and the old Avon engines in icing conditions. The T4 and B2 had no anti-icing system, like a hot air feed, to melt any ice that formed on the front of the engine. And if the ice accretion got too much there was a real risk that the engine would choke and flame-out. In the trainers I'd flown, icing wasn't really a problem because the engines were buried deep in the fuselage. But the Canberra's design meant that the front faces of the engines were just a few inches inside the intake. This made them very vulnerable to ice formation, which happened readily in the sub-zero, stratocumulus clouds that hung over East Anglia in the winter.

The trick was to set the engines at a particular rpm; this was for technical reasons that are too tedious to explain. Then the problem was that during the approach the thrust from the engines was sometimes too high at other times it wasn't enough. So we had to learn how to manage the aircraft's drag – not something that the Canberra was over-endowed with – by modified selection of the undercarriage and the flaps. It was a trick that we needed to know and to practise, although during our course we also had to do it for real on several occasions!

After about 10 hours' dual instruction I was judged fit to go 'solo' so I was let loose, with Geoff in the back, for a half-hour flight. Then it was time to move on to the B2. Although the B2 and the T4 don't differ that much, we pilots had to spend about an hour sitting on a small, fold-down seat alongside our instructors who occupied the only pilot's seat while we watched him fly the aircraft. Differences in cockpit layout were pointed out but it seemed to me that it wasn't going to be much different from the T4. In the back Geoff was being shown similar differences by a navigator instructor. After the hour was up the two brave staff men got out and left us to fly together for about another hour.

The course then progressed steadily with navigation exercises, instrument and night flying and we learned how to drop bombs. This was done from medium level, about 10,000ft, onto targets in the Wash. Geoff had actually done this before in the Varsity, but it was my first time to experience what I'd seen in countless war films of my youth.

'Left, left . . . steady, right, steady . . . BOMB GONE!'

However, the bombs weren't the huge Tallboys and Grand Slams of the war, not even the 1,000 pounders. No they were tiny 25lb versions of those, incongruously painted an attractive duck-egg blue.

These practise bombs contained a small explosive charge designed to give a bright flash and white smoke, so that the range personnel could triangulate on the impact point and calculate where the bombs had fallen. Bombing brought the teamwork between pilot and nav into sharp focus. It was important for the pilot to make his corrections accurately and quickly and to keep the aircraft flying absolutely straight, with no sideslip. As for the nav, he had to use the sight correctly, assessing the drift imposed by the wind and anticipate the drop point correctly before he pressed the bomb-release button. To do all this he had to unstrap from his ejection seat, having replaced the safety pins, and then clamber down onto the couch in the nose, so that he could see the target out of the Perspex nosecone.

The other time that he had to do this was for the low-level navigation exercises, which were flown on special routes around the UK at 500ft above ground level (AGL). This was an important exercise for us as we were going to be practising our operational roles at low level in Germany, at 250ft AGL. Another thing that I had to be given experience and practise in was a manoeuvre called LABS. This acronym stood for the Low Altitude Bombing System and was a method of delivering a nuclear weapon from low level. The manoeuvre consisted of arriving at 430kts at a pre-calculated pull-up-point and then, not surprisingly, pulling vertically upwards at a load of 3.4G (just over three times the force of gravity) until half a loop had been achieved. During this pull-up, depending on the delivery mode, the bomb would be released and fly to the target in a graceful parabola.

Once the nose had passed through the horizon on the way down, full aileron and a modicum of rudder was applied to roll the aircraft so that the wings were again level and the ground was back where it belonged, beneath you. By then the aircraft was in a dive of about 30° nose down. The final bit of the manoeuvre was to level off at the original entry height and speed, but going in the opposite direction.

When I was briefed on the LABS manoeuvre I thought that after all the aerobatics that I'd so enjoyed in training it would be easy. How wrong I was! Everything had to be done on the instruments – looking outside was going to be strictly *verboten!* After all, we were told, we would have to do these manoeuvres in cloud and/or at night for real and we would therefore be practising them in cloud and/or at night on the squadron. Needless to say, it took a lot of practise (my logbook shows twenty-nine manoeuvres flown) before we started to feel that it was second nature. Geoff had to help by calling out airspeeds, timing to the bomb release angle (usually about 60° nose up) and the roll-out point; stuck in his virtually windowless cabin that must have been even more disorienting for him than me!

We only had two notable incidents during our course. One was on St Valentine's Day when the three crews on our course were all launched on navigation exercises. The weather wasn't great – overcast and cold – but the forecast was for it not to get any worse. That was important because none of us had yet gained our instrument ratings, which meant that we shouldn't fly if the cloud base at Bassingbourn was going to be below 1,000ft. It wasn't, so off we went. Up at 40,000ft it was, as ever, clear and blue. In fact the cloud tops were not high at all. After an hour and a half, thanks to the consummate skill of my navigator, we were back over Bassingbourn descending to join the Ground Controlled Approach (GCA) pattern to land. But when I levelled off at 2,000ft I couldn't see the ground at all. There was a layer of cloud below me. I crosschecked my altimeter with Geoff's and he confirmed that we were indeed at 2,000ft. Air Traffic Control (ATC) hadn't mentioned this when I started to descend, so I asked them what the cloud base was; '2,000ft' was the reply. So I apprised the controller of what I was seeing. There was a stunned silence, followed by, 'Standby, we'll check.' At this point I was told to change radio frequencies to contact the final controller. I called but got no reply. I went back to the previous frequency with the same result. I decided to call the local controller in the tower and found that I was actually talking to the GCA man! Not only had the weather gone bad, but also the VHF radios were playing up!

The first GCA didn't go at all well and when I got to 1 mile and 300ft (well below the height I was supposed to come down to) I still couldn't see the runway, so I opted to go around and try again. The problem now was that we were getting short of fuel. Both the front and rear tanks were virtually empty and the centre tank was falling rapidly. By now everyone on the ground was trying to overcome the radio problems and get not only me but also the other two unrated pilots down. I heard Ron ahead of me land successfully, so that boosted my confidence, then I remembered that he had 1,000 more flying hours than I did!

As we climbed away from the airfield at 2,000ft, still above that layer of cloud, I told Geoff that if we didn't get in this time we would climb out to the east, towards the North Sea and eject when the fuel ran out.

'OK, boyo,' was the cool reply. I really concentrated hard for this second and last attempt; I think that the controller did too. Suffice it to say that this time at about 300ft I saw the runway lights and a white Verey cartridge fired by the runway controller from his caravan alongside the touchdown area. We were going to make it! I throttled back and we touched down in just the right place. You could hear the sighs of relief everywhere! Ken Lilley landed just after I'd cleared the runway. There was a bit of an inquest afterwards but we students didn't hear much about it.

Our second disturbing incident took place a couple of months later. During a long, high-level night navigation exercise, one of the engine-driven electrical generators failed – the red warning light showing up on my instrument panel. As Geoff had control of the generators he followed the checklist and switched off the appropriate switch. Immediately the other generator failed. We were now running on the batteries.

We had been told in Ground School that there was a particular type of fault with the voltage regulator that could drive the good generator off-line, so Geoff switched the originally 'failed' generator back on. Nothing changed. This was where the checklist ran out of advice, so I told him to turn that one back off and turn the other one back on. Nothing changed. We were still some distance from base, so we decided to put out an emergency call and turn towards Bassingbourn as, in a direct line, it was closer than our diversion airfield of RAF Marham in Norfolk.

The batteries in that old B2 must have been aging as well, because it wasn't long before the voltage started to fall. So I called Bassingbourn to tell them that the good weather would allow us to make a visual approach and that I would be turning off the main radios. I also said that I would turn one back on and call them when we were going to land. We made our way back with virtually no electrical equipment running, navigating visually and descending gently, avoiding all the various civilian air traffic zones in our way.

It took a bit longer than we had first estimated, but we were eventually in sight of our airfield and I positioned us for a straight-in approach. As promised I switched one of the main radios back on and transmitted my position and intention to land. By now the battery voltage was very low and few of the cockpit lights were working. Geoff was calling out speeds and heights from his instruments, illuminated by his torch, and I was concentrating on the approach angle. We heard nothing from ATC, but I just assumed landing clearance and touched down. Then just as we were about to turn off the runway onto the taxiway, all the airfield lights went out! It was suddenly very dark and I tried to taxi very slowly, but in the end I got Geoff to dismount and walk in front with a torch. We found an empty apron and parked the aircraft. Geoff found some wheel chocks and we shut down and walked to the dispersal huts where the groundcrew worked from and all the aircraft documents were kept.

When we walked in we were greeted with astonishment. The few people left there were just packing up for the night, it was gone midnight by now, and they thought they'd put the last B2 to bed!

'We were told that you'd diverted to Marham,' said the Chief. 'No one heard you land!' I told him that he wasn't alone – ATC had turned out all the lights with us still turning off the runway!

We found out that the generator problem was genuine, but that our recovery actions had been hampered because the switches were wired in reverse, to the wrong generators. This hadn't previously been discovered because the generator switches stayed on all the time and that it was only when there was a fault that were they operated. ATC hadn't heard our final transmission and had assumed that, following our electrical failure, we were diverting to Marham, despite the fact that it was about 20 minutes flying time further away. In fact, all of the controllers had left the control tower before I'd made my last transmission and it was one of the ATC assistants who was left to tidy up and turn out the lights. He just hadn't heard us and our navigation lights by then were so dim that there was nothing to see!

We finished the course two days after my twentith birthday and Geoff and I, and Ken and Alec were posted to No.16 Squadron at RAF Laarbruch, within the command of RAF Germany (RAFG) and NATO's Second Allied Tactical Air Force (2ATAF). A couple of our instructors were very pleased for us, as they had served on 16, so we were extensively briefed on the squadron history and customs over several pints at the end of course party! Ron Ledwidge and his navigator, Martin Fortune, were to go to No.3. Squadron at RAF Geilenkirchen. It was now time for a spot of well-earned leave.

7

To Germany

After a week at home I had received my travel orders to proceed to RAF Laarbruch via a trooping flight, from Gatwick Airport to RAF Wildenrath, and then by RAF coach to Laarbruch. I studied the maps I had at home but couldn't find anywhere in northern Germany with the name Laarbruch! Well, I'd find out soon enough.

But why was the RAF in Germany anyway? There were six RAF airbases in all and lots of ancillary units; and that was a fairly small contingent compared with the Army presence at the time. The British Army of the Rhine, or BAOR, had many more bases, firing ranges and exercise areas. They were all part of NATO forces, based all over Western Germany, retained and reinforced there since the end of the Second World War. NATO's presence in Germany was to form part of the overall deterrent to any further expansionist ambitions of the USSR.

How had it all come about? It had all started when three elderly men met at a Crimean seaside resort on the Black Sea called Yalta on 12 February 1945. The war was all but over when Winston Churchill, Franklin Delano Roosevelt and Joseph Stalin sharpened their knives ready to carve up what was left of a shattered and broken Europe. At the age of seventy-one, Churchill was exhausted by the effort of leading a coalition government in its task of vanquishing the Nazis. Although only sixty-three, but because of his lifelong polio Roosevelt was not a well man and died only two months later of a cerebral haemorrhage. Also sixty-three, Joe Stalin was the most robust and focussed member of the group. Churchill may have been distracted by a General Election, due to take place in July, and Roosevelt was definitely distracted by the need to concentrate on the war against

Japan. Whatever the reasons, the European joint was carved up in such a way as to give the largest portion to the Russians.

In early July, only a few days before the British General Election result would see Churchill ungratefully dismissed by the public, he again went to meet Stalin and the new US President, Harry H. Truman, in the German city of Potsdam. However, there was strong disagreement over the fate of Poland and where the new German borders should be drawn. The meeting was curtailed with only one agreement: to meet again on 31 July. And when that happened one wonders whether Churchill or Stalin was the most surprised to find the rather bank manager-like Clement Attlee sitting in the UK seat. Stalin now knew he was on to a winner and brushed aside all attempts at compromise on borders and calls for free elections in the new Eastern European Bloc.

This freeze in previous Allied relationships was the first act of a new war: the Cold War. During a trip to the USA the following March, Churchill (who else?) coined a term that would become a well-used phrase in the political lexicon of the next forty years. In a speech in the Mid-West town of Fulton, Missouri, he said, 'From Stettin in the Baltic to Trieste on the Adriatic an Iron Curtain has descended across the continent.' Over the coming years that line on the map would indeed become a curtain of steel mesh, barbed wire and land mines.

The only concession that had been wrung out of the various conferences was that Berlin, the erstwhile capital of Germany, would be subdivided into four portions, each governed by one of the four main allies: Britain, the USA, France and the USSR. A joint Control Commission was set up in June 1945 to oversee and adjudicate. With the USSR occupying over half of Germany, West Berlin had become an isolated island some 200 miles inside the new Eastern Germany.

So the new geopolitical reality was that Germany was cut in half, the eastern portion along with Poland was to be occupied by the USSR, while the western half was to be shared by British, French and American occupying forces. Reparation agreements were established and a new West German government, centred at Bonn, would be brought into being and nurtured into a democracy. An uneasy standoff then took place for the next four years. Russian intransigence was on show at most, if not all, international diplomatic encounters. Stalin still held the country and its politics in his iron grip; the party unfaithful would spend their remaining days freezing in the Gulag. As during the Siberian winter, their days were usually bleak and short.

In the rest of the world, communism started to impose its influence on a wider scale. The West saw this as a sign of possible Russian-inspired 'colonialism' and so began to work on ways that it might defend itself cooperatively. At the end of February 1948, the centre-right government of Czechoslovakia, under President Benes, was overthrown by the Communist Party. Barely a month later, on the first day of April, the Russians, with no warning, imposed rigid checks on all road traffic into Berlin from the west. This action was the opening shot in a fire-fight that would bring about the Berlin Airlift, a monumental application of air power to an apparently insoluble problem. In March 1949, eight Western countries reached agreement on forming a new alliance; it would be called the North Atlantic Treaty Organisation – NATO, another acronym for the Cold War lexicon.

In May of that year the Russian blockade of Berlin was lifted, but very rigid lines were now drawn in the European soil. Everyone knew where they stood and the main protagonists had nuclear weapons, with intercontinental ballistic missiles and massive bomber forces to carry them. By the time I arrived on German soil, in May 1964, the Korean War and the Cuban Missile Crisis had come and gone and another East v West conflict in the Far East was just warming up. The UK had also repressed communist-inspired conflicts in Malaya and Kenya. The Space Race was well under way, its noble aims underwritten by the development on both sides of ever bigger and more capable rocket systems. The jet engine had come into all forms of aviation giving more speed and carrying capacity.

West Germany was the frontier with the forces of the Warsaw Pact. NATO forces stood there at constant readiness to respond, should the opposition decide to strike. But one of the problems was that of perception. Since 1940, in what they called the Great Patriotic War, the Russians had lost over 20 million of their population; more people than all the other nations put together. They were now paranoid that it might happen again. They saw NATO as a threat massed on all their European borders.

It was a stalemate to end all stalemates. It was called deterrence and given the appropriate acronym MAD: Mutually Assured Destruction! So, into this potentially white hot, Cold War arena came one small, very-young-looking-for-his-age, still-under-twenty-one-and-unable-to-vote, Flying Officer with all of 330 flying hours in his logbook. What could he do?

As I left Leeds station on the evening's last train to London I wondered what I was in for. I arrived at King's Cross at some ungodly hour and made my way by taxi to Victoria station. There I spent several hours in the 24-hour News Cinema, where there were some newsreels, many cartoons and the film *High Noon*. When I stepped out again it was daylight and I caught the stopping train to Gatwick (no Express in those days). Nevertheless, I arrived in good time, found the trooping check-in desk and waited some more. I was actually quite excited because, strange though it may seem for someone who had been flying since the age of sixteen, I had never been on a commercial aircraft before. It wasn't long before I was. However, my response to the question, 'Would you like a window seat, sir?' with, 'Yes, please, the one with the window in front of me,' didn't go down at all well! Within an hour, we had crossed the sea and were landing at Wildenrath. Another hour later I was being driven through the gates of RAF Laarbruch and my new home.

Laarbruch was a new NATO airbase, built in 1957 right on the Dutch border, west of a German town called Kevelaer. The airfield had a 7,500ft-long, east–west runway, equipped with ILS and Precision Approach Radar (PAR). There were four squadron dispersal areas in each quadrant, each with its own hangar. South of the main runway were the technical, administrative and domestic sites. The base had its own primary school, cinema, bowling alley, NAAFI supermarket, two churches and an American Base Exchange (BX). There were contingents of the USAF and the Royal Signals Regiments sharing the station with the personnel from a Canberra PR7 photographic reconnaissance squadron (No.31), an RAF Maintenance Unit and, last but by no means least, No.16 Squadron, equipped with the Canberra B(I)8.

I was dropped off at the Officers' Mess, booked in and then lugged my bags three blocks east to find my small, but perfectly formed, room on the first floor with a view over the tennis courts. I was here – what next?

8

The Squadron

When I had finished unpacking, showered and changed I wandered down to the Officers' Mess for a bite to eat. It was lunchtime and I soon bumped into Geoff; it turned out that he'd been at Laarbruch for a couple of days and was settling into his room in the same block as me. It was a fine Saturday so, after lunch, we sat out in the warm sunshine at the back of the bar and enjoyed a couple of drinks together. Geoff said that one of the couples on the squadron was holding a party that evening and that I would be very welcome to go along and meet some of the squadron guys and gals. As I hadn't really slept much for a couple of days I took my leave of him and went back to my room to catch up.

We met again that evening, which was still warm and sunny, in the back garden of the Officers' Married Quarter of one of the squadron pilots, Jim Seeger. All I really remember was meeting lots of folk, whose names I would have forgotten by the morning, drinking too much Amstel beer, not eating enough food and being helped back to my room by my kind and much more sober navigator! Sunday was totally forgettable. Then came Monday and, for the first time in several weeks, work.

No.16 Squadron was housed in an area in the north-eastern quadrant of the airfield. This area comprised a large hangar, a dozen dispersed aircraft parking areas, known as pans, and a wire-enclosed, gated area for two nuclear-armed aircraft on Quick Reaction Alert (QRA). Aircraft access to and from the aircraft dispersal pans to the eastern end of the east–west runway was by two connecting taxiways that also ran past the hangar. Vehicle access was via a road from the technical and domestic site to the south. This road passed through the approach path, about 500m from the beginning of the runway, round to the squadron area. After this point the road became a narrow, one-way carriageway, which meant that to return from the 16 Squadron area to the south side was about a 5km drive!

When I asked someone about this he then asked me if I thought my room in the Mess was a bit small. This total non sequitur left me speechless and open-mouthed. It was then explained that the German construction company that, in the mid-1950s, had won the contract to build Laarbruch had 'shaved off' small amounts on all the tendered work on the base. The runway was 1m narrower than it should have been, each building's rooms were a few centimetres smaller in each dimension and the ring road around the northern, forested and not so often visited area was only wide enough for one 3-ton truck! The boss of the construction firm had pocketed the difference between the contracted price and his actual costs. His illegal profit was several million Deutchmarks. Of course the whole thing eventually came to light and, I was told, he was still languishing in a Federal German prison!

So the first challenge was to get over there; Geoff had driven out to Germany, so I hopped into his car and we made our way to the squadron. The first day went by in a whirl of meeting yet more people, getting given lots of publications and documents, filling out a plethora of forms and handing in our flying kit to the guys in the safety equipment (SE) section on the far side of the hangar. Of course, as part of the whole education process we were inculcated with the squadron's history.

The squadron was formed and numbered at St Omer in northern France on 10 February 1915. This meant that the following year, 1965, would be the squadron's Golden Jubilee. As with many squadrons in the first year of the First World War, it operated a variety of types until fully equipped with BE2s a year later. No.16's role was reconnaissance and RE8s replaced the BE2s in May 1917, which the squadron retained until returning to Britain in February 1919, finally disbanding at the end of that year. During the First World War No.16 Squadron was commanded by a number of officers who would achieve senior air rank in the future, including Hugh Dowding and 'Peter' Portal.[1]

Less than five years later, on 1 April 1924, the squadron was reformed at Old Sarum, near Salisbury in Wiltshire. It operated in the Army Co-operation role equipped at first with the Bristol F2b, then Hawker Atlases and Audaxes. In June 1938 the squadron became the first to operate a new RAF type, the Westland Lysander. The squadron remained in Britain until April 1940, when it moved over to France, but within days it had become obvious that the Lysander was not able to operate in the modern war environment and the squadron was evacuated to Lympne. However, it continued to use the Lysander for coastal patrols along the East Anglian coast and, later, the coasts of Devon and Cornwall. Training with Army units also continued, but it was obvious from the experience in France that, before undertaking active operations again, the squadron would need new equipment.

In April 1942 the squadron started to convert to the North American P-51 Mustang, although the Lysanders did not disappear overnight, some remaining in use until May 1943. The Mustangs were used on shipping reconnaissance and low-level interceptions of German fighter-bombers along the south coast. Spitfires replaced the Mustangs in September 1943, which No.16 Squadron used for photographic reconnaissance in preparation of Operation Overlord, the Allied invasion of Europe.

A year later the squadron was transferred to the 2nd Allied Tactical Air Force (2 ATAF) in the same role, which it continued until the end of the war. From June to September 1945 the squadron operated a high-speed mail service between Britain and Germany. In September 1945 No.56 Squadron, equipped with Tempest F5s at Fassburg, was re-numbered No.16 and the squadron then remained in Germany, moving to and from many Allied bases and operating Vampires and then Venoms in the day-fighter and fighter-bomber roles. After another brief disbandment the squadron ended up at Laarbruch, this time equipped with the then brand new Canberra B(I)8 operating in the low-level, day-night interdiction role. The squadron had an establishment of twelve aircraft and eighteen crews, as well as a share in the two or three dual-controlled T4s that were hangared on the south side of the airfield by Technical Wing.

The 16 Squadron badge is a pair of crossed keys, one black, one gold on a white background inside the usual crowned wreath. The squadron motto is *Operta Aperta*, which means 'Hidden Things are Revealed', referring to the early reconnaissance role that the squadron undertook. The squadron was informally known as 'The Saints' partly because of the place where the squadron was first formed, Saint Omer, and a possible reference to the keys, in that Christian tradition holds that Saint Peter was given the keys to Heaven and Hell.

Some of the aircraft even had the matchstick man with a halo painted on the fin: 'The Saint' figure used by the publishers of Leslie Charteris' novel and in the TV series of the same name, starring Roger Moore. All the aircraft carried the squadron colours, black and gold, adjacent to the

RAF roundel on the rear fuselage. However, unlike all other such squadron markings the band ran round the fuselage like a ring and not in horizontal panels each side. We were told that this was done as a mark of respect for one day in 1940, when virtually all of the squadron's pilots were shot down and killed while they were operating the Lysander in France.

The final part of the brief on the squadron and its history and customs had to do not with operational matters but with social matters. It was a squadron rule that all available aircrew were to meet in the Officers' Mess Bar at 5 p.m. on Fridays for TGIF (Thank God It's Friday) drinks. The obligatory neckwear was to be a plain green tie, purchasable from the Squadron Adjutant at a very competitive price. We were told that we must do this before Friday next or we would have to stand a round for the whole squadron if we turned up incorrectly attired. Geoff and I were actually in on this tradition via the instructors at Bassingbourn who had previously served on 16 Squadron.

The 'plain' green tie actually had lots of small, embroidered pink elephants all over it. The supposed joke on those not in the know was that when they asked why one had pink elephants on one's green tie, the response was, 'I haven't, it's a plain green tie.' Then one was supposed to turn to another 16 Squadron member and ask whether he could see any pink elephants on one's tie and he, of course, would deny it. All very silly in the sober light of day, but no doubt hilarious after an hour or so in the bar on a Friday evening! At one stage in the past squadron officers also wore the Arab Fez for TGIF; this apparently was no longer compulsory, but we were warned that we might see some of the older guys with them on.

So we integrated ourselves into the squadron and, along with Ken and Alec, were absorbed but, for the moment, we were not allowed to forget that we were the 'Junior Joes'. Our next job was to enter the squadron-training programme (yes, more training) with the aim of reaching the necessary 'Operational Readiness' standard. This meant learning to navigate at low level with precision, both by day and by night, and to drop practise bombs using the LABS delivery method, so that our average score on a single sortie of four bombs was within 50 yards of the target. We also had to prove ourselves in formation flight, low-level photography, high-level navigation and the use of several weapons ranges in Germany, the UK and France.

All these achievements were shown chronologically on a large board in the Ops Room; curiously the last column was headed 'Catch 22'. For the moment I didn't dare ask! Becoming operational would take us out of the

Junior Crew category, which was the good news. However, it also qualified us to go on the QRA roster, which was the bad news. That meant that for two weeks about every six weeks we would have to live for 24 hours in the QRA block and be ready to go to war, with a nuclear weapon, within 2 to 3 minutes. The two weeks were supposedly day on/day off, but we would find out that this was rarely the case!

One of the strange things in those first few days was that we didn't really get to meet the squadron 'Boss', Wing Commander Horwood. He was apparently away somewhere. In fact, we never saw much of him at all. A few weeks later we heard that he was posted, apparently prematurely and under some sort of cloud. We then got the news that his replacement was Wing Commander A.L. 'Trog' Bennett. We had met him at Bassingbourn when he was starting his conversion course. He had told us that he would indeed be coming to Laarbruch, but as OC Operations Wing. Obviously the premature posting of his predecessor had meant a switch, so he became OC 16 Squadron instead.

Trog Bennett would turn out to be a good and popular Boss. He was a talented pilot, he led from the front and knew how to connect and deal with people – especially young aircrew! How he got his nickname I never did discover. However, one of things that immediately struck one on first meeting him were the scars from burns that he had on one side of his face and his lower arms. He later told us that his injuries were received in an accident while he was flying Vampire fighters. Understandably, Trog was red hot on telling us off if he saw us walking out to our aircraft without gloves on or with our sleeves rolled up. He was married to a lovely, lissom, blonde lady who went by the sobriquet of 'Cubbie'. Again I never found out her real first name; she was Trog's nurse when he was being treated for his burns and her maiden name was McCubben (I think!). They were the right couple to lead an essentially young and vibrant bunch of aircrew on a squadron with such a great history. We couldn't wait to get started.

Notes

1 Air Chief Marshal Sir Hugh 'Stuffy' Dowding commanded RAF Fighter Command during the first part of the Second World War, notably during the Battle of Britain, and Marshal of the Royal Air Force Sir Charles 'Peter' Portal was the RAF Chief of Air Staff from 1940 to 1945.

9

The Interdictor

After spending Monday and Tuesday on the 'admin and org' we were finally allowed to go flying, but disappointingly only in the T4. My first trip was a familiarisation of the local area and procedures with another squadron pilot in the left-hand seat; I was just there to watch and learn. The next day I was on the receiving end of a Flight Commander's check, with the A Flight commander, Squadron Leader Dennis Atherley. He seemed a rather pernickety individual who would probably want everything done by the book. Having just left the OCU we were only too willing to oblige. He seemed happy enough with the result, so we were allowed to go off, again in the T4, with my erstwhile party host, Jim Seeger, patiently sitting on my right, while I got to grips with the airfield procedures and some local area familiarisation. Friday 5 June 1964 was to be the day when I would add another mark of Canberra to my repertoire and my logbook – the Canberra Bomber (Interdictor) Mk8.

By the Friday morning I had sat in and studied the B(I)8 cockpit (see Appendix) and been shown the few differences on the outside. It was different from the B2 in several respects. The most obvious, other than the camouflage and black colour scheme, was that the pilot's cockpit was at the back of the pressurised cabin, where in the B2 and T4 the navigators lived. In order to see out the pilot was placed higher and given a fighter-style canopy, which was slightly offset to the left. The canopy didn't open as one might expect, one still had to climb in through the same door on the starboard side. Below and to the right of the pilot's seat was a small seat that the navigator was supposed to occupy during take-off and landing; it was rather ominously referred to as the 'crash seat'.

Directly opposite the entrance door was a small desk, with an array of instruments, navigation equipment and controls. Above the desk was a window and below it a seat that could be folded out into the crawl-way. This allowed the navigator to sit sideways at the desk for non-visual navigation tasks. There was a Verey pistol mounted in the roof, with its signal cartridges of red, white and green in a rack on the wall. This was for signalling when either radio silence procedures were in use or the radios had failed in flight. As in the B2, there was a couch on the floor in the nose behind the transparent nosecone, but two extra Perspex side panels enlarged the nav's field of view. The nose was not equipped with a bombsight, but there were flight instruments and navigation equipment for use during low-level visual navigation operations.

In my part of the ship the view forward was excellent. At last, despite my short back, I could see out clearly ahead through the armoured glass, rectangular windscreen! The view to sides was also quite good but because of the offset, more so to the left than to the right. I could see both engines and the top surfaces of the wings and, via a rear-view mirror, the fin. Inside the cockpit the layout was similar enough to the other Canberras as to not be too disturbing.

However, there were a few things that marked out the B(I)8 as a war machine. In front of the pilot was a reflector gunsight and on the top of the right-hand yoke of the control column there was a gun-trigger, a camera button and a guarded bomb release button. Another change was that the bomb door selector switch, down to the left of the pilot, had three positions instead of two: open, closed and auto. I supposed that the purpose of this would become clearer when we got to the bombing exercises.

Being one of the 'second generation' Canberra designs, there were some more fundamental differences to get to grips with. First, there were two extra fuel tanks in the wings, carrying a total of over 6,600lb of fuel; they had associated switches and gauges on the fuel panel on the starboard wall. The Avon Mk109 engines had more thrust: 7,400lb as opposed to the 6,500lb of the B2 and T4 and they each had the triple-breech cartridge starters. Also, unlike the earlier Avons, these were fitted with an anti-icing system, which blew hot air from the engine compressor into the intakes to keep them free from ice build-up. After flying the B2 and T4 during an East Anglian winter this was a real bonus. The extra 1,800lb of thrust was needed because the aircraft weighed substantially more than the earlier marks: with a full fuel and bomb load it could reach a take-off weight of getting on for 50,000lb; but that was well below the maximum allowed weight of 55,000lb. However, the maximum permitted landing weight was 40,000lb and there was no system for jettisoning fuel, except by explosively separating the wingtip tanks, if they were fitted. The electrical and hydraulic systems were almost identical, but toe pedals on the rudder bar instead of a hand lever on the control yoke, operated the wheelbrakes. This feature was the one that brought the whole squadron out to watch each new 'JP' (junior pilot) taxi out for the first time. Apparently it took some time to get used to their response.

However, the biggest and potentially most important difference, especially for Geoff, was that I had the only ejection seat. The navigators had to roll out of the door. To help them with this were two additional features. B(I)8 navs had to wear a very special flying suit, which had an integral parachute harness with two large clips at the front, onto which the parachute could be attached quickly and easily.

The other feature designed to help them get out safely was a small vertical blast door, which opened whenever the main entrance door was jettisoned using a large black and yellow painted lever alongside it. The blast door did what it says on the label, it helped to reduce the speed of the slipstream past and made it safer as the nav dropped out. The nav's parachute was stowed in a container above the door and its ripcord was fixed to the aircraft wall. So, should the unthinkable happen and the crew had to get out, the nav would crawl to the door, clip on his parachute, operate the door jettison lever and roll out of the door. The static line would open his parachute and it would open almost immediately, except at altitudes above 13,000ft when a barostat would prevent the parachute opening until he had passed that altitude. What's more there was a small oxygen bottle in the right leg pocket of the suit to help the nav breathe on the way down. You had to be big and strong to be a B(I)8 navigator; the suit weighed a ton!

The minimum height for rolling out of the door was supposed to be 1,000ft above ground level. When I first arrived on 16 Squadron the Martin Baker ejection seat fitted to the B(I)8 was one of the earliest types. Unlike the ones I had sat on in the Jet Provost, Vampire and the B2 and T4 Canberras, it didn't have a leg restraining system; instead there were rigid metal stirrups fitted to the bottom of the seat into which you had to place your feet before pulling down on the face blind to fire the seat. The minimum height for doing this was also 1,000ft. It struck me that for a low-level, jet, fighter-bomber we weren't being given the best chance of survival. We would just have to trade excess speed for height by climbing and then I would hang on to let Geoff go before I pulled the ejection handle and disappeared vertically.

However, we weren't going to let such morbid thoughts put us off as we strode purposefully towards our impressive-looking flying machine. Sure enough there was a crowd out watching me as I nodded and swerved under the influence of the very snatchy toebrakes all the way out to the runway. I consoled myself with the thought that all those laughing pilots had gone through this humiliation before and they weren't having trouble now – so you must get used to them – eventually.

Despite the heavier weight I could feel the difference in performance on take-off. In flight the aircraft's flying controls, although still manually operated via the control yoke, felt that bit lighter and the aircraft seemed to respond more crisply. This was because the second generation Canberras had redesigned control rods that incorporated a sort of balance spring system, called a blow-back rod. It was all done to help reduce the forces and pilot effort at the higher speeds.

On this first trip I had been briefed to stall the aircraft, with flaps and undercarriage up and down, to check my 'critical speeds'[1] with each engine at idle and the other at full power, as well as try flying at speeds out to the maximum of 450kts. An hour and a half later we were taxiing back in, there were no watchers this time; that was a shame as I was already getting better at steering and braking. By the time we had shut down, signed in and got changed it was time for that long drive to the Mess and the famous 16 Squadron TGIF. I could feel another lost weekend coming up!

Notes

1 Critical speed was the lowest speed that one could fly on a steady heading with one engine 'failed' and the other at maximum thrust. One was allowed to use up to 10° of bank towards the live engine in establishing that speed. To be as near as possible to the most critical stage, immediately after take-off, this exercise had to be flown at about 3,000ft AGL. It was a high-risk exercise and one of the most important on the conversion course. Crit speed, as it was known, was particular to the circumstances and the strength of the pilot's legs and so varied; in the B(I)8 mine was usually about 130–140kts.

10

Finding Our Way Around

It was June and it was hot. The summer on the North German Plain was usually about 5°C hotter than the UK. The weather was mainly dry, sometimes punctuated by heavy showers or very impressive thunderstorms. Most of the time the winds were light and from the south or south-east. Once a high-pressure area was established it only moved away slowly and this brought about a phenomenon known in meteorological circles as 'Anticyclonic Gloom'. What it meant to us was that the industrial smoke from the Ruhr, only 50 miles or so south-east of Laarbruch, got stuck over the plains and reduced visibility markedly. As we did most of our flying at low-level, practicing for the avoidance of detection by enemy radar, this grey-brown murkiness brought what we knew as 'goldfish bowl' conditions.

The visibility was just adequate to see far enough ahead to navigate accurately, see any obstacles or rising ground in time to avoid it and pick your way around. The problem got worse at higher altitudes than the 250ft at which we usually flew. There was no perceptible horizon and above about 3,000ft we often lost sight of the ground, but we weren't actually in cloud. It called for absolute faith in the flight instruments and the discipline to ignore some of the disorientating sensations that came when manoeuvres were made. It was actually harder than flying in cloud, because you had to devote some time to looking outside into the murk for any other aircraft that might be coming your way doing the same thing.

The heat hit me during my second week on the squadron. Being the 'JP', I found myself being taken by the usual boneshaker RAF bus to RAF Wildenrath, along with Alec Wedderburn, to collect a T4 that was being allocated to Laarbruch for use by both squadrons. How Geoff got out of this one I can't recall – but he was probably playing his native land's sport of rugby! By the time we had arrived at Wildenrath, found the aircraft and signed the servicing document, known as the Form 700, it was late morning and the temperature on the concrete dispersal area was well above 30°C. Inside the cockpit, which had not been covered, it was probably a good 20°C more. Alec clambered into the back and I strapped in and got the engines going as quickly as I could. The Canberra was fitted with an air-conditioning device, called the Cold Air Unit, but for technical reasons it could not be used on the ground. Once airborne, when sufficient airflow was available to allow it to operate correctly, it could be selected to fully cold and then it was actually very efficient.

But there was one problem in the T4: the switch for selecting cold air was at the far right-hand end of the instrument panel, well out of my reach. I decided to take the risk of trying to operate it immediately prior to take-off and so, just before we rolled onto the runway, I loosened my shoulder straps and reached across. But I was too small! I just couldn't reach it. An equally sweaty Alec had by now, with the evidence of my grunts and bad language, worked out that we were stuck in 'hot'.

He passed his long navigation ruler forward to see if I could use that. It did reach the switch but to get it to the cold position I had to pull it towards me. Even using the hole in the end of the ruler I couldn't effect any change; it kept slipping off the spring-loaded switch. I decided that the best I could do was to leave the pressurisation off, then at least we wouldn't be roasted by hot air all the way home.

We got airborne and flew back as directly and as fast as was safe in the goldfish bowl conditions and landed at Laarbruch 20 minutes later. By the time I reached the hangar where our T4s lived, we had been in this mobile sauna for about 45 minutes. We were both soaked. Then a strange thing happened. As I came to a halt facing the hangar doors and applied the parking brake, I had the sensation that the aircraft was still moving forward. When I looked outside I could see that it wasn't, but when I looked down to put my ejection seat safety pins in and unstrap the sensation returned. My only thought then was, 'I must get out of here!' And when I did my legs just buckled under me and I found myself lying on the ground feeling ridiculous. The groundcrew rushed over to help me up and my laconic Scottish back-seater told them that we hadn't stopped at any bars on the way. The strangest thing was that my thought processes were totally normal and rational (well as much as they ever were) and, with help, I made it into the hangar and handed the aircraft documents over to their rightful owners. Someone brought me a large glass of iced water and I sank that in record time. After we got back to the squadron and I'd had a shower, I felt fully recovered. I found out later that what I had experienced was heat exhaustion and I didn't want to experience it again.

Having learnt that lesson, Geoff and I continued our work-up towards achieving 'operational' status; we were told that this could take up to five months. The first job was to prove that we were fit to be launched into the 2 ATAF Low Flying System (LFS) at 250ft. The LFS consisted of about eight geographical areas all over West Germany and a system of interconnecting 5-mile wide routes. All these areas and routes avoided major conurbations, civilian airfields and their associated control zones. The more minor towns and airfields we were supposed to miss ourselves by judicious and conscientious planning.

There were also many red blotches and circles on the maps that indicated other areas we should avoid for a variety of reasons. I noted with some disappointment that these included the Mohne and Sorpe Dams – so no reliving the Dam Busters! Another feature of flying in Germany was, of course, our proximity to the Soviets and their East German and Warsaw Pact allies. Fly directly east from Laarbruch at 300kts and you'd cross the border into 'enemy territory' within half an hour. The border was, as all borders usually are, not very regular, so wise old men in an ivory tower somewhere had smoothed it out and moved it an average of 10 nautical miles west. That was a line we must never cross in peacetime, whatever the circumstances: it marked the western edge of what was known as the Buffer Zone.

Even further west than that, but above 2,000ft AGL, there was yet another line; the airspace between that and the Buffer Zone was known as the Air Defence Identification Zone (ADIZ). Flight within this zone had to be, where practical, pre-notified and positive identification procedures were mandatory. Flight in the Buffer Zone itself was not permitted, except by Presidential Decree or a Declaration of War!

The squadron had a set of standard training routes and the most frequently used was known as Standard Route 9. So, for our first experience of low flying in Germany we were sent off on that, Geoff being overseen and helped by an experienced squadron navigator, Flight Lieutenant Trevor Carpenter. That seemed to go well so we were sent off on our first 'solo' effort on another route given to us by our bluff Navigation Leader, Squadron Leader Arthur Campey. We were expected to fly it at 500ft and bring back photographs of each turning point just to prove that we'd been where we were supposed to have been.

The B(I)8 had a forward-facing F95 camera in the nose, looking slightly down through a reinforced flat panel underneath the forward end of the navigator's couch. Both the pilot and the navigator could operate this camera, but it was usual for the pilot to do so. When the thing you wanted to snap had reached the lower half of the rectangular cockpit windscreen you just pressed the button. It was the one that wasn't guarded, so you weren't likely to drop a bomb instead! The photographs were processed at Laarbruch and they were usually available in your mail-box on the squadron by the next day.

We examined the route together, checked the weather with the Meteorological Officer and set off. All went well until about an hour into the sortie. We were right in the middle of the North German Plain, heading east. The weather was not great, the usual goldfish bowl punctuated by heavy showers. Out of the gloom ahead I could see a shoreline. It looked like a seashore, but we shouldn't have been anywhere near the North Sea. If it was the Baltic we were in big trouble!

I asked Geoff where he thought we were. He had to admit the he was temporarily unsure of our position – that was nav-speak for 'lost'. As we got closer to the beach we still couldn't see beyond it, as there was a heavy shower about 2 miles offshore. Geoff told me to turn right about 10°, as he couldn't believe that we were so far off track. I did so and we flew over the water and into the rain. The next thing to appear was what looked like a large boat, a grey boat in the grey rain. Geoff stayed silent – not a good sign. Just as I was about to press him for more ideas he said, 'I can see the far shore.' It wasn't the sea at all, it was a very big lake. Suddenly he asked for another change of heading, much more positively this time and, within minutes, normal navigational service had been resumed. We found and photographed all the correct turning points and went home.

The next day the results of our first sortie were decreed as satisfactory and we could fly the same route again, this time at 250ft without the need for photographic proof of our whereabouts. So off we went again. Overnight the weather had changed with a front passing south-east and clearing away all the murk and showers. It was a beautiful and not too hot summer's day.

We left the airfield flying east on the standard low-level departure route and at the Rhine we descended to our low-level cruising height of 250ft and told Laarbruch ATC that we were outbound. The next radio call we were scheduled to make would come in about 2½ hours time when we came back across that mighty river and called 'Inbound'.

Everything went swimmingly. We had discovered that the lake we had crossed yesterday was called the Steinhude Meer and we had been about 3 miles off track to the north yesterday. With today's great visibility it was so obviously a lake that my initial panic was completely misplaced.

As we flew past the lake Geoff suddenly said, 'Hey, that boat's still there, in exactly the same place.'

'That's not a boat,' I said, 'It's an island.'

'Well, that accounts for it being in the same place,' came the laconic reply!

Our low-level training continued apace. Geoff started navigating 'blind' by sitting at his desk and using a navigation system called the Decca Navigator. This was a very accurate system that used low-frequency radio signals from three stations, which the equipment in the aircraft picked up, and the human navigator could interpret using the controls and displays. But like all pinpoint navigation systems you had to be sure where you were to start with!

Over the next four weeks we did more low-level navigation and carried out several flying visits to other RAF Germany bases on what were known as Practise Diversions. We also flew a couple of high-level navigation exercises and one trip to the UK, on a flight profile known as HI-LO-HI because the transits were done at around 40,000ft with a period at 250ft in the UK Low Flying System (UKLFS). Now we were ready for some more challenges. Bring 'em on!

11

Learning to Throw Bombs

One morning I arrived at the squadron and saw that we were on the daily
flying programme to fly the T4 again, this time with an experienced 16
Squadron pilot. He was Flight Lieutenant Barry Nelson, the squadron's
answer to the Irish comedian Dave Allen. Barry was a jovial cove but
nevertheless very professional. The trip was aimed at re-familiarising us
with the LABS manoeuvre and to make sure that we would be safe to go
and practise them in the B(I)8. The sortie would inevitably include a couple
of simulated engine failures during the half-loop LABS manoeuvre. One
thing I had learnt was never to try to roll out at the top towards the engine
that was now running at full power. This was an important lesson because,
as Barry observed after my first few manoeuvres, like most pilots I tended
to prefer to roll always in the same direction, in my case to the left. So it was
important to practise rolling in both directions and, should an engine fail,
work out which was the correct way to roll at the top. Anyway, after an hour
or so of half-loops, the Irishman seemed happy so we were loosed on the
world to practise them, initially not below 3,000ft, until we were content
that the whole thing had become second nature.

Operationally the LABS manoeuvre was started from 250ft and 434kts
indicated airspeed and the target pull-up load was 3.4G. In the B(I)8 there
was a special instrument, right in front of the pilot, which had two needles,
one vertical and one horizontal. The vertical one was a very sensitive roll
and yaw indicator. If you kept that one exactly upright, by judicious use of
aileron and minimal rudder, the pull-up would be truly vertical. When it
was time to initiate the pull-up the horizontal needle would drop to the
bottom of the gauge and you had to pull it smoothly back to the centre to
achieve the correct G level.

There were two modes of delivery: Normal and Alternate. The Normal mode would be used when there was an easily seen feature on the final track towards the target. This feature was called the Initial Point or IP and was a calculated distance, and therefore time at a given speed, from the ideal pull-up point for the bomb to descend directly over the target. The navigator would pre-set the calculated time and at the IP the pilot would pull the trigger on the right-hand yoke of the control column. That would start the timer and when it ran down to zero the horizontal needle on the LABS indicator would drop and the pilot would initiate the pull-up. Another item that the nav would have pre-set was the bomb release angle, for a normal attack around 60°, and as the aircraft passed that angle the bomb should part company with the aircraft; it would then fly the couple or so miles downrange to the target.

The Alternate mode was used if there was no usable IP, or you missed it. That meant that the aircraft had to be flown over the target, the trigger pulled and, as the timer was by-passed in this mode, the pull-up would commence immediately. The bomb release angle this time would be about 110°. The bomb would then fly up to about 10,000ft before descending onto the target.

The recovery from both types of attack was identical. Once the nose had passed through the horizon, with the aircraft inverted at about 5,500ft, full aileron and a squeeze of rudder in the same direction was applied. The point at which this was done was critical. Too soon and the speed would decay further and, as it was already down to about 160kts, there was a real danger of a stall or even a spin. Too late and the nose would get very low and the ensuing dive could get dangerously steep. So to give us the maximum chance of getting it right there were several cross-checks of exactly when to start the roll-out. First, the time to the roll-out point was known, so the nav would monitor his watch and call it out. Second, the attitude on the Artificial Horizon, which remained accurate in inverted flight, would show the nose passing through the horizon. Third, the LABS indicator reverted to angular measurement once the bomb had gone and the pilot had released the trigger, so it read zero at the horizontal. Finally, at the inverted position the airspeed stopped decreasing and altitude stopped increasing. So, when all those things came together, it was time to roll out. During the roll, which took several seconds, the nose was allowed to drop and the escape was made in a 30–40° dive, accelerating to the maximum permitted speed of 450kts. It was then simply a matter of monitoring the height to level out as low as you dare; in peacetime not below 250ft above the ground. This 'escape manoeuvre' was aimed at putting the maximum distance between you and nuclear detonation that you had just hurled at the enemy. The atomic bomb's blast overpressure wave was the killer and you needed to be at least 10 miles away when it caught up with you!

After we were happy with the practise manoeuvres we were let loose on Nordhorn bombing range carrying four 25lb practise bombs, the same pretty, little, duck-egg blue ones that we had last dropped from the B2 at medium level into the Wash. The practise bombs were mounted in pairs on small bomb carriers on the wing pylons. The bomb release signals were passed to these carriers in turn so that one bomb came off each time that we made the right switch selections and carried out the LABS manoeuvre.

Nordhorn range was about 30 minutes flying time north-east of Laarbruch, close to the Dutch border. There was a set pattern for the approach from the north and a large square marker, painted white, was the IP. The range was operated by the RAF but used by all the northern-based 2 ATAF air forces. Squadrons were allocated 30-minute range 'slots' on a daily basis. The range also catered for single passes, known as First Run Attacks or FRA's, and these could usually be accommodated at any time; however, it was better to pre-book FRA's in order to get priority.

One thing that was very important to get right was the position of the Normal/Alternate switch. If the switch was in Normal when you did an Alternate manoeuvre over the target, the bomb went a couple of miles straight ahead out of the range area. A definite no-no! One of our pilots got it wrong and his little bomb hit and killed a cow, chewing her cud innocently a couple of miles away. The odd thing was that before joining the RAF he used to be a vet; he was devastated!

By the end of July we had dropped a good number of bombs reasonably near the target at Nordhorn and were ready to go on a week-long detachment to RAF Idris, just outside Tripoli in Libya; these were the days before Colonel Gaddafi overthrew the government of King Idris. There we would be flying two or three sorties a day on the nearby Tarhuna range, dropping bombs from LABS deliveries. We were supposed to achieve the required operational standard by the end of the week. That was four consecutive bombs inside an average of 50 yards. It sounds a long way, but throwing bombs up to as high as 10,000ft and expecting them to fall within 50 yards of the target was no mean task. Anyway the real bombs were going to make a hugely bigger hole than one only 50 yards in diameter!

So our next move was to be to pack our bags and go to foreign parts.

12

Gibraltar

However, before the trip to Libya, my first overseas trip on the squadron was to be a weekend away in Gibraltar. These mini-break Mediterranean holidays went by the name of Exercise SOUTHERN RANGER and the advertised destinations were RAF stations on Malta, Cyprus and in Libya, as well as 'Gib'. There were even longer-range destinations available on what were known as EXTENDED SOUTHERN RANGERS. These allowed, nay encouraged, flights to exotic places such as Bahrain, Aden, Nairobi and even Salisbury, in Southern Rhodesia. The longer trips were rationed to one per crew during their tour, but the normal Southern Ranger allocation was four per month per squadron. I'd no idea that life in the RAF was going to be this good!

We were going to fly to RAF Gibraltar via RAF Luqa on the island of Malta. There was only one problem with going to Gib: the management said that you weren't allowed to land there until you'd landed there. Was that why they wanted us to read *Catch 22* before we went into QRA? There was a bit of bad news: before I could go I was going to be fitted for a navigator's flying suit. That was because I was going to Gibraltar with an experienced crew to watch how they did it! There wasn't room for four on board the B(I)8, so Geoff was going to miss this one.

So, on the morning of Friday 7 August 1964 the adventure started. I spent most of the trip lying in the nose, watching Europe float by 8 miles below us; the Alps were particularly impressive. The crew, pilot Flight Lieutenant Don Betts and navigator Flight Lieutenant Trevor Carpenter, did their respective things and I listened to the radio calls to the various radar stations en route. After an hour and a half we passed over the Côte d'Azur and headed towards Sardinia, passing Corsica on the way. The two islands looked beautiful, the white of the waves breaking on their shores looked like they had been briefly dipped in sugar. Once we were south of Sardinia and Don was talking to the ATC Centre on Malta, he started the gentle descent towards the George Cross island. After 3 hours in the air we were landing on runway 24 at Luqa. Although I had effectively had nothing to do I wasn't at all bored, but I would now have sympathy, or even empathy, with all B(I)8 navigators who had to wear that heavy and uncomfortable suit; especially during the LABS manoeuvres when they were subjected to repeated exposure to 3.4G! Once we had disembarked, arranged for refuelling and filed the outbound flight plan to Gibraltar we were taken to the Transit Mess for lunch. It was mid-August in the middle of the Mediterranean so it was hot, but we had to stay in our flying kit.

After a disappointingly forgettable meal of nothing at all exotic we clambered aboard and set off on stage two, westwards to Gibraltar. This time it was to be about 2 hours at 40,000ft, so I crawled down the nose again. There didn't seem to be as much chat on the radio this time and there certainly wasn't much to see; only the sea. However, after about an hour a smudge on the southern horizon started to, very slowly, turn into a range of mountains – the Atlas mountains of North Africa. Not long after another smudge dead ahead showed up as Spain and, as we started our descent, the Rock itself started to emerge from the haze.

The reason I had to observe Don doing a couple of approaches and a landing was because of the unique arrangement of the airfield at Gibraltar in relation to the Rock and Spanish airspace, which we did not have clearance to enter. By international agreement the Spanish allowed UK aircraft the airspace to the west and south of Gibraltar, but that wasn't very big, especially as the centre of it was a 1,300ft-high lump of *terra firma*, which was often obscured by its streamer of cloud. The runway was 6,000ft long and stretched across the narrow neck of land to the north of the Rock, the land that joined Gib to the Spanish mainland. In fact that neck was too narrow for a modern landing strip, so at its western end the runway protruded, like a large aircraft carrier deck, over 2,500ft into the harbour.

At its eastern end there was a sea wall that was about 30ft high that prevented high seas from flooding the runway. At the western end there was nothing but water and lots of ships to each side. The only road off the Rock into Spain ran across the runway at its mid-point and road traffic was controlled via lights operated by the airfield control tower. However, the *bête noire* for the local controllers were cyclists and pedestrians. Although cars could easily be stopped well clear of the runway, the cyclist or walker who went through just before a red light often took several minutes to reach safety on the other side.

The runway at Gibraltar also had unique markings. The sloping surface from the sea wall down to the runway surface, on which we were not to land, was painted with black and yellow chequerboard markings. There were also two prominent yellow lines at about one-third distance gone in each runway direction; these were the 'last touchdown' lines. If the aircraft wasn't firmly on the ground before it crossed these lines then a go-around must be initiated.

So I had to absorb all this, as well as flying a strange circuit pattern during which the runway disappeared behind a huge lump of limestone. And the Rock itself caused another unique problem. It was not unusual, especially with southerly winds, for there to be a tailwind at both ends of the runway as the wind bent round the Rock.

This meant that very accurate speed control would be needed on the final approach, which would always be over featureless water onto what looked like an inadequately short runway. No pressure then! From my viewpoint in the nose I watched Don carry out a couple of circuits and low approaches before he landed. That was, of course, flawless and we taxied to our parking spot ready to have a relaxing evening in this Little Britain clipped onto Spain.

After sitting in the sun and drinking a cold beer on the terrace outside the Officers' Mess, we had dinner and then Don and Trevor took their young charge (me) on an educational tour of downtown La Linea, the first Spanish place you came to past the border. This tour included being introduced to the cocktail of Fundador (a type of Brandy) and Lemonade in a bar called Dirty Dick's. The next part of the tour was a walk down some narrow streets to find a place where we could view 'An Exhibish' – where my anatomical education of the female body was extended by watching two young ladies cavorting with each other and doing amazing things with candles and coins. I told them that they could keep the change. Although offered further services by the lady in charge I decided that discretion was much the better part of valour and we went back to the Mess for a nightcap. The next day we spent sightseeing in Gibraltar as well as a spot of sunbathing and swimming.

Gibraltar is a fascinating place to visit. I was totally overwhelmed by the view of the north face of the Rock when I opened my bedroom curtains the next morning. It was amazing that there could be such a huge, impressive obstacle so close to a runway. I could pick out the 'windows' that had been cut into the face from the tunnels and galleries inside it. There was also a cap of cloud being generated by the warm, moist southerly wind blowing from Africa.

I later learnt that the Rock had been populated since pre-historic times and afterwards by a whole series of peoples, representing all of the major historic Mediterranean nationalities, as well as the Spanish. Gibraltar seems to have spent most of its history under siege. It was in 1704, during the Spanish Wars of Succession and after the eleventh siege, that a joint British and Dutch military force next conquered the Rock. So 1704 is the year from which modern Gibraltarians take the colony's British genesis. But it wasn't until April 1713 that the Rock was formally recognised as British Sovereign Territory by the Treaties of Utrecht, when the perpetuity of British rule was first written down. In the year of my first visit there the Spanish had raised the whole question of the rightful sovereignty of Gibraltar at the UN, who had come down on the Spanish side. That was one reason that we had been told to be very careful not to fly into Spanish airspace. Indeed, during my time on the squadron, several pilots found themselves being escorted round the circuit by Spanish Air Force fighters, just to make sure that they stayed within Gibraltar's air traffic control zone!

There were lots of interesting things to see. I thought that the most impressive of these were the various tunnels and galleries that had been built over the years inside the Rock. There was also a magnificent natural cave named after St Michael in which concerts were often held; I would attend one of these some years later. The main street of the town was also worth a visit. It struck me as odd; here I was at the southern tip of Europe yet the shops and the buildings seemed more like an English market town. An impression enhanced by the Dixon of Dock Green uniforms of the Gibraltarian 'Bobbies'!

On the Sunday we caught the ferry across the bay to the Spanish town of Algeciras. More sightseeing followed, with an introduction to *tapas* and a reintroduction to Fundador and Lemonade. Then back across the bay in time for tea. No nocturnal expeditions this time: dinner, a couple of sunset drinks and bed. It was my turn to drive the next day, so I wanted to be sharp with these two old hands relying on me getting them home. As far as I remember that went well and we arrived back at Laarbruch in one piece, not long after lunchtime.

That wasn't my last trip to Gibraltar. I twice went there again and both visits have special memories. On one of them our new 'JP', Flying Officer Tom Eeles, was also due to do his first 'solo' landing at Gib and he was going to arrive about 2 hours after us. My landing was OK, although I was a bit tense as I came over the sea wall. Tom and I had both been told to make a couple of approaches with low go-arounds, just to get the feel for it before we committed to a landing.

By the time that Geoff and I had got to the Mess, changed and were sitting outside with our first drink we heard the approach of a jet. Sure enough there was Tom making his first practise approach. From our viewpoint the aircraft disappeared behind some buildings momentarily during the last bit of the approach and then reappeared as he climbed for the next circuit.

After two of these we expected that he would land and as he did so he stayed out of our view. However, when he did come back into our sightline he was crossing the road, going like an express train. I thought that he was going to take-off again. But then the nose went down as the brakes came on and both Geoff and I stood up because we were convinced that he wasn't going to stop. We were waiting for an almighty splash off the western end of the runway, rapidly followed by a Board of Inquiry.

However, Tom did stop, right at the end of the tarmac and then taxied in gingerly. The brakes must have been red-hot. We walked out of the Mess and across the road to meet Tom and his navigator, Flight Lieutenant Vic Avery, heading our way. When I asked Tom what had happened he said, 'I was so relieved to have got down before the yellow line, I relaxed too much and forgot to brake. It was when I crossed the road markings that I realised that I was still going far too fast!'

The second incident happened to me on another visit when I was leading one of the then latest 'JP's, Flying Officer Terry Newman, on a double Southern Ranger to Gibraltar via Malta. On our scheduled departure date we were lined up on the westerly runway for a stream take-off with me leading. Because of the short runway we would use a 30-second interval between my brake release and his; that meant that I could use full power. After only a few seconds the usual, very variable and strong crosswind was blowing me off towards the right-hand side of the runway. Because we didn't yet have enough speed for the rudder to be effective, I stabbed the left toebrake to straighten us up. Nothing happened. The brake pedal went fully down with no resistance and no braking. The aircraft was still accelerating so I applied full left rudder in the hope that it would steer the aircraft back toward the runway centreline, but to no avail. So I closed the throttles, called 'Aborting' on the radio and reached for the parking brake lever, which would apply equal braking to both wheels. I told Terry to carry on and return to Laarbruch as planned.

We were now charging off the runway edge towards the control tower! Thankfully, Gibraltar airfield is all tarmac and concrete, but there was a huge thump as we crossed a large drain. When I next looked out we were heading straight for a fire vehicle that was on a collision course. What I needed was more brakes, so I leant forward and pulled the little lever a bit more. As the aircraft finally came to halt I looked out and right in front of me was the fire engine. We were both stationary now. Then from out of it appeared a very pale-faced fireman. I shut down the engines and we disembarked, having briefly explained the problem to ATC and ordered a tow from a tractor.

When I finally reached the ground the pale-faced fireman explained that he could see that this jet was careering across the airfield, apparently out of control and, from his point view, without a pilot in the cockpit! This was all because this aircraft was one of the few on the squadron that had been recently modified to have its parking brake lever moved lower down the left side of the cockpit. And that was because previously it had been next to the similar-looking flap selector. Apparently some clown had put the parking brake on instead of raising the flaps and then he had landed with the brakes fully applied! Flat wheels and a very short landing run was the result. But for me, this meant that I could no longer look where I was going and simultaneously apply braking. As we were chuckling about the headless pilot syndrome, I saw that blood was pouring from Geoff's mouth. When we had hit that drainage channel he had bit his tongue quiet badly!

But that wasn't the worst thing for Geoff. Because of the fault in the toebrake unit we had to spend another two days in Gibraltar getting it fixed and the first of those days was his first wedding anniversary; yes he had joined the ranks of the crowd we regarded as the 'old married couples club'! He had promised his wife Sonia that, whatever happened, he would be home in time to take her out for a slap-up meal! Such is the life of the Cold War warrior!

13

Libya

The next stage of our journey towards the highly desirable status of 'operational readiness' was to practise dropping bombs until we achieved the magic 50-yard average. The work-up started with three sorties in two days when we dropped a dozen bombs somewhere in the vicinity of the main target at Nordhorn. But even in August the weather could be limiting, so we were briefed for a week's detachment to RAF Idris, a joint RAF-Civil airfield a few miles south of the Libyan capital, Tripoli. Ken Lilley and Alec Wedderburn, our classmates from Bassingbourn, who were also climbing the operational readiness ladder, would be going along with us. And just to make sure we didn't get into too much trouble, we would be overseen and authorised to fly by the experienced crew of Flight Lieutenant Ted Robertson and Squadron Leader Arthur Campey, the Squadron Navigation Leader. They'd drawn the short straws!

So I was now going to go to Africa – albeit just a part of the very northern edge of that vast continent – to the large nation of Libya. Libyan history was one of repeated colonisation by the Romans, Moors, Turks, the Italians and the British. However, in 1951, the UN finally gave the United Kingdom of Libya its independence under King Idris. In August 1964, Britain and the regime of King Idris were on relatively friendly terms; British and American companies were extracting most of the oil coming out of vast tracts of the Sahara Desert, which cover over 90 per cent of the country. The Libyans were getting huge tax revenues in return. However, things were going to change. A young Army officer called Muammar Gaddafi was waiting in the wings. As an admirer of Egypt's President Nasser, he was still developing his particular brand of Arab Socialism that would, five years later, see him head a military coup against the monarchy and establish a socialist Arab republic with its capital in the western city of Tripoli. We, however, were going to start our stay in Libya with an overnight stop at the eastern end of the kingdom: at RAF El Adem, about 20 miles south of Tobruk.

Ted Robertson flew the aircraft to our first refuelling stop in Malta; I hunkered down in the nose to watch Europe and the Med go by once more. After another mediocre lunch in the Transit Mess we got airborne again a couple of hours later. This time I was driving and Ted was consigned to the couch in the nose, while Geoff continued to navigate from his little desk. After the 3-hour transit from Laarbruch to Luqa this leg was relatively short and took just 1 hour and 20 minutes.

As we approached the north African coast near Benghazi, I was fascinated by the apparent change to the colour of the sky. The clear azure blue over the Med was gradually toned yellowish-grey as we came inland. I supposed that it was sand in the atmosphere and the reflection of the ochre landscape ahead. After our long descent from 36,000ft the landscape had changed only a little. There were pockets of grey, black and rusty browns, but precious little green. Geoff kept reassuring me that El Adem airfield was where it should be: right on the nose. I was blowed if I could see it.

As we descended the sandy haze got thicker and I was glad that we were flying down-sun and not into it. I was in contact with the El Adem Approach Controller and he had us on the radar, so he vectored us for a visual approach. The visibility improved a bit and I soon spotted the runway. It looked just like any other RAF airfield, except that there was a desperate shortage of grass. There were a few other aircraft on the large dispersal area, including a Transport Command Hastings and a flight of three straight-winged jets that I couldn't at first identify[1]. I got on with trying to make a good approach and smooth landing; there was a rather critical Scotsman downstairs to whom I didn't want to give the wrong impression! Taxiing in on a Saharan August afternoon was a hot affair. By the time we had parked the cockpit was roasting, even though Geoff had opened the door once we had cleared the runway. When I finally dismounted it was like standing in front of a hot oven. When we reached our single-storey accommodation block a shower was definitely the next thing on the menu, to be followed as quickly as possible by a glass of cold beer. It would be a scene comparable with the end of the film *Ice Cold in Alex*!

The evening was spent at the station's open-air cinema, with the balmy evening breezes wafting over our heads. As far as I remember the programme wasn't an intellectual challenge, even for aircrew. We watched, with great enjoyment, a series of Bugs Bunny and Road Runner cartoons, followed by an Ealing Comedy feature. It was odd sitting under a sky filled with stars as far as eternity and watching something so banal. And then, after a nightcap, off to bed. We had been warned not to leave our shoes on the floor. Apparently they were a favourite hidey-hole for scorpions.

The next day was to be a morning low-level transit to RAF Idris. This would take us more than an hour and a half at the usual cruising speed of 250kts. The route was across the southern part of Cyrenaica to the coast near Marsa-al-Burka and then following the coast road to a major junction, where we would carry virtually straight on to RAF Idris.

The minimum height was to be 250ft, but Ted dropped the hint that when we were flying over uninhabited territory he wouldn't mind if we went a bit lower.

'But not below 100ft, laddie,' he twanged. With the radio altimeter limit lights set to '100', we left El Adem and headed west.

An hour or so later we hadn't climbed above 250ft and had spent much of the time below it. By now we had picked up the coast road that ran from Benghazi towards Tripoli. It was easy navigation; just follow the black tarmac road. At one point I caught sight of a little lad throwing stones at us from the side of the road; another Arab anti-colonial socialist in the making? Not long after, near Sirte, the birthplace of Muammar Gaddafi, I could see what looked like a bridge over the road. But that didn't make any sense. As we rapidly approached it I could see that it was a monumental arch, like the Arc de Triomphe in Paris or Marble Arch in London. The road we were following was built as a military road during the inter-war Italian colonisation of Libya and it was called the *Via Balbo*. The road and the arch were built on the orders of Mussolini – *El Duce*; it was a bit prematurely called a victory arch. Whatever its history it was a bizarre sight; I climbed a little, not just to make sure I didn't hit it, but also to get a nice photo of it with our F95 camera in the nose.

The rest of the transit was fairly uneventful and once we were into Tripolitania there were more fields and villages so we eased up to above 250ft and when were about 15 miles from RAF Idris airfield I climbed to 2,000ft to establish radio contact and get instructions for our arrival. Idris had a single east–west runway with a length of about 7,500ft. We arrived from the east at 1,000ft and I broke into a left-hand circuit and carried out a visual approach and landing. It was just as hot here, so we parked and disembarked as quickly as possible. Eventually we found our way to the Officers' Mess and our accommodation was in twin-bedded rooms in blocks built in colonial style round a central courtyard, in which there were a few date palms. This was more like it!

When we went for dinner I was intrigued by what looked like a dish of small, white mints on each table. Being the naïve young traveller I asked what they were. The old hands told me that they were salt tablets and that we should make sure that we took a couple with each meal. Apparently, we were going to sweat a lot over the next few days and we would lose not only water, but also salt, and management didn't want us going sick. Naturally us juniors would do as we were told; we also decided to replace lots of our lost fluid in the bar every night. And it was there, over a few cans of Tennents lager, all the way from Bonnie Scotland, that we were briefed about the programme for the next four days. There was good news and bad news.

The bad news was that we would be making our first take-offs at 0700 hours, so up at 0530, breakfasted by 0600, brief and authorise by 0630 and airborne at 0700! The good news was that in order to have dropped at least forty bombs each by the end of the detachment on Thursday, we would be aiming to fly three sorties per day (virtually unheard of in Germany). And the really good news was that, because of the heat and the strong air turbulence it caused, the last landing would be made at or before noon. We could, therefore, have the afternoons off for sightseeing, shopping, sleeping or whatever we chose to do.

We were up early for our first day's work in western Libya. The first job was to fly a reconnaissance of the range, in the desert outside a small town called Tarhuna. It wasn't far away, about 5 minutes flying time, which we flew at about 1,000ft. RAF personnel ran the range and the radio communication and operating procedures were very similar to those we had got used to in Germany. Geoff had drawn the range pattern on a large-scale map and as the skies were cloudless and visibility unlimited we could follow the track easily. After 30 minutes we had found our way around well enough to go back to Idris and be loaded with four bombs. We had enough fuel to do this twice more, so all I had to do was shut down the engines while our friendly armourers loaded the tiny bombs, then start-up and fly back to Tarhuna. As the morning temperature soared, so the cockpit became hotter and hotter. Geoff could get out, but that was only into the baking air above the parking area, which would reach a local temperature of well over 40°C by early afternoon.

Fortunately, all these hot places had rather strange-looking shades for our aircraft; they were like small, curved, shed roofs on a stalky, wheeled frame that could be pushed into place over the cockpit as soon as the aircraft was at rest. The other trick that the groundcrews had up their collective sleeves was to wheel out a very large trolley and put it alongside the door. They then pushed a large flexible hose from it up to my part of the ship. This would normally have been attached to a special connection in the side of transport aircraft to which it supplied a continuous blast of refrigerated air to cool the passengers. It worked for me. In fact, it even got a bit too cold at times!

We soon got used to the heat and the next day we flew another three sorties. Our bombing average score was improving and we felt confident that we would reach the required standard before the end of the week. However, at the end of the second morning's sorties things would get even more exciting. I had been delayed by a small hold-up that morning so we returned a little later than planned. The turbulence was getting really bad and Geoff had been battered during our many high-speed, low-level attacks and the 3.4G pull-ups that followed. In fact, when he got undressed afterwards he had two large and colourful bruises on his chest where the parachute clips had repeatedly been pushed into his body. I was so glad that I hadn't continued with my desire to be a navigator!

As we came in for our final landing of the day, not long after midday, on the easterly runway with a stiff breeze blowing and a lot of turbulence on the approach, I must have made some sort of involuntary grunt as I struggled to maintain a safe speed and glide slope angle.

'Are we going to crash?' came the sarcastic question from below.

'I don't think so; but don't talk to me – I'm too busy,' was my reply.

Just then another great hole opened up in the air below us and we dropped onto the beginning of the runway like a stone. It was Geoff's turn for the involuntary grunt. But then I felt that the aircraft was trying its best to head directly for our parking area without using the taxiway. I applied lots of right rudder and brake to try to keep it on the runway; the sandy areas to the left didn't look particularly good for a 15-ton aeroplane to be running over. I thought that a tyre had burst and informed the tower of my diagnosis, as well as letting them know that we would need people to mend it and then tow the aircraft off the runway.

We came rapidly to a stop. I shut the aircraft down, made the ejection seat safe and then exited to find Geoff round the starboard side looking at the undercarriage leg.

'Well, boyo, you didn't burst the tyre,' he said in his usual dry, laconic way. I was surprised to find that he was right. The tyre was there, looking only slightly worn. The trouble was that it was round a bare oleo leg. The wheel itself had split into two pieces around its circumference and the two bits were behind the aircraft on the runway[2]. Just as we were taking this in, several Canberras loomed overhead and wheeled around for a while. Then a DC-9 appeared and disappeared just as quickly.

By this time we were beginning to wonder whether anyone was going to come out to see what was going on, whether we were injured, or even whether anything was on fire. A couple of minutes a later a single red Landrover, occupied by a lone RAF fire fighter, arrived. He inquired politely as to our health and, after we had told him that we were fine, but that our gallant steed needed some TLC, he seemed ready to drive off. We caught his attention long enough to gain a lift back to the parking area and our small briefing room.

Once there I told the groundcrew, Ted and Arthur, what had happened. This brought sidelong glances and an atmosphere that means that everyone had quickly come to the same conclusion as to whose fault it was. The problem now was that we only had one aircraft to service the needs of two crews. So the local management decided that Geoff and I would not fly the next day and that Ken and Alec would use the remaining serviceable jet to complete three sorties and then we would fly it on the following day. So Geoff and I had a day off in Tripoli to come. By mid-afternoon WT 344 had been towed back and was awaiting a new wheel. The airfield was back to normal operations with civilian aircraft coming and going.

The Canberras that I had seen overhead while I was contemplating the damage to our aircraft, turned out to be a detachment of four Canberra B15s from No.249 Squadron, based at RAF Akrotiri on Cyprus. Because we had blocked the only runway they had diverted to the USAF base at Wheelus on the north coast. Once our broken flying machine had been removed, they had flown over and were remaining at Idris for a few days range work on Tarhuna; I took a lot of 'flak' from them that night in the bar, but after I'd bought them all a beer we were the best of friends.

After quaffing so much ale it was quite fortuitous that the next morning Geoff and I had a lie-in. After that we met up with Ted Robertson and decided that we would take a look around Tripoli. A taxi was hailed and we set off in search of the mysteries of the *Kasbah*. The city had a very metropolitan and colonial look and the first place that our taxi driver dropped us was at the camel market. There were scores of the large, smelly, noisy and rather threatening beasts. We walked around trying not to get too interested in case someone tried to sell us one. The dust and dung-laden atmosphere was getting worse as the sun rose higher in the sky, so we decided to remount our taxi and go down to the harbour side.

There was another sort of market there: a trap-the-tourist market. The stalls were laden with lots of colourful materials, brass and leather goods, knives of all sorts – most of them highly decorated and curvy. I decided that I should take something back as a souvenir and started to look at one of a Worthy Arab Gentleman's large, leather, poof-style cushions. I thought that it might look quite nice squeezed into my tiny room and give me something to relax on while I was listening to music or painting. Of course, as soon as I picked it up, the aforesaid WAG was at my side telling me that I couldn't live without such a beautiful object.

I didn't say much, so he was soon plying me with other similar-looking and similar-smelling objects. It must be either goat or camel leather, I thought. With the aroma of the latter still relatively fresh in my nostrils I plumped for camel.

The WAG was still pressing his case for an extortionate amount of money for said object, so I was backing off. However, I had the advantage that he .didn't know that he was dealing with a Yorkshireman. I made a ridiculously low counter bid. This seemed to shock the WAG – he was probably more used to dealing with American tourists from the cruise ships, who weren't renowned for their bartering abilities. After he had recovered from my cheek (which took him only microseconds) his demeanour changed a little. He told me forcefully that the minimum that he could possibly accept was between extortionate and ridiculous. I counter-offered reasonable. At this point he suddenly changed from trying to sell me the cushion to showing me a large and very sharp knife. I smelled a very dangerous rat. I looked round for Geoff and Ted; they were still at the next stall, but when I called for them to come and help me they just laughed. So much for *esprit de corps!*

I made what I hoped would be a final offer for the leather cushion, which was much nearer ridiculous than reasonable. He put the knife away and reached for brown paper. I paid him and exited stage left as fast as I could, trying not to look too scared. Geoff and Ted were still laughing. Clutching my prize we made our way back towards the city centre and found a restaurant for lunch. This proved to be surprisingly good and the *spaghetti carbonara* showed that the Italian colonisation still had its acceptable echoes.

After more sightseeing we found a taxi to take us back to base. There I went for a walk and discovered that the garden areas all had chameleons clinging to the bushes. It was quite easy to break off a branch with the little creature still clinging to it; they weren't at all aggressive and I returned to the accommodation eager to show off my new little friend to the others. When I had got them all together, along with a few tins of the ubiquitous Tennents lager, I showed them my prize and put him down on the red tiles. He soon changed colour from green to a rusty red. When I put him on the sand sure enough he quickly changed again to match his background. At this point Alec Wedderbrun disappeared into his room. He came back with a tartan towel, no doubt the plaid of the Wedderburn clan.

'Right, put him on this and let's see if the wee bugger explodes!' he said. The Scots do have an innate cruel and sadistic streak – I blame William Wallace. However, after a couple of minutes, the 'wee bugger' had not exploded but had actually managed a mottled colour not too distant from the required background pattern and colour. By then I thought that he had given us sufficient amusement and took him back to his hibiscus.

Wildlife was also a feature on the following day. The overnight warning about shoes and scorpions had been repeated, so I asked one of the groundcrew whether they saw a lot of the little beasties on a daily basis.

'Oh aye, sir,' he said, 'haven't you seen any yet?' When I replied that I hadn't he said, 'Just ask one of our local cleaners, give him a couple of coins and he'll get one to show you.' I went into the hangar and found a likely looking lad and asked him if he could find me a scorpion.

He grinned at me with some of his teeth, took the coin and disappeared. I asked the sergeant to explain to him that I was going flying and would be back on the ground by noon. Sure enough when I next saw the lad he had a glass jar in his hand and inside it was a shiny black scorpion. It wasn't as big as I'd expected, but it still looked menacing. I took the jar and had a closer look and showed it to Geoff. Then I handed it back.

'Oh no, sir,' he said, 'it's yours now. Keep it *effendi*.' I didn't know what to do, so I took it with me. When I got outside the hangar I asked the groundcrew where I could dispose of the scorpion.

'Oh you have to kill it, sir,' I was told. I was beginning to wish that I hadn't started all this! Anyhow one of the groundcrew took it off me and, with that look that told clearly of his opinion of officers, he promised that he would dispose of it humanely.

And that wasn't the end of brushes with the local fauna. As we had taxied onto the runway for our first take-off, I was aware of some movement on the tarmac well ahead of me. I couldn't clearly make out what it was. Geoff thought it might be a herd of small deer or goats. I called the tower and the controller, no doubt having looked through his binoculars, informed me that it was a pack of feral dogs. He said that they often came onto the airfield at around dawn. I asked him if someone would come out and chase them off. It appeared that this was not normal practice. I suspected that asking folk to go and chase away wild and no doubt rabid dogs was deemed beyond the call of duty.

'Don't worry,' the controller said over the radio, 'they'll run away as soon as they see you coming. They usually do.'

Not very reassured I started running up the engines and as I released the brakes I wondered briefly how a report of damage to our sole remaining jet caused by a pack of dogs would go down. Birdstrikes are a normal hazard and I'd had a few of those by now – but a dogstrike? But the man in the tower was right; as soon as we got up some speed the dogs started to move off the runway and by the time we had reached where they had been milling around they had disappeared.

On the range we had often seen a man with a large herd of goats. On this day he had decided to move them to graze on the sparse grass and shrubs right beneath the run-in track. So every 10 minutes there would be a large jet, doing about 500mph, passing a couple of hundred feet over the herd's heads. I know they're only goats, but the poor chap spent all morning gathering them together again where he wanted them. He must have been the most persistent goatherd in the world! The only animals we now possibly had to contend with were the huge birds of prey that we often saw soaring over the desert.

Eventually, we were getting our bombs closer to the target until I heard those wonderful words, 'Delta Hotel': NATO phonetic language for DH – a direct hit! The next four bombs were well within 50 yards so we had done it. Our overall average for the week turned out to be acceptable, so this very large hurdle was over. We were ready to fly back to Laarbruch the following day for a well-earned weekend off.

However, the fun wasn't yet over. The aircraft that had had its wheel come off was going to be ready to go the next day, so Ken and Alec were to bring it back then. Our aircraft was the one fitted with the baggage pannier, a big wooden box that hung from the rear bomb-rack in the bomb bay. Ken and Alec had bought some watermelons and wanted us to deliver them to their spouses, so we had them loaded and our bags went in the pannier with them. After all what are mates for? *Esprit de corps* and all that! On the climb-out, at about 20,000ft, I heard a noise and the control column moved very slightly. I wondered what it was, but as nothing appeared untoward I forgot about it as we flew back at our usual very high altitude.

At least I forgot about it until we opened the bomb bay just before shut-down and I saw the groundcrew pointing under the aircraft. When I got out I could see what they were pointing at. It looked like we'd had a hydraulic leak: a pinkish liquid was dripping down the bomb doors and onto the ground.

The melons had obviously had a small amount of air or gas in them and, at 20,000ft, the air pressure drop was enough to make them explode. The mush then froze in the -50°C or so bomb bay temperature and then it thawed on the way down into Laarbruch. There were bits of melon and pips everywhere. Months later we were still finding pips stuck to parts of the bomb bay roof. My bag was never the same either.

Notes

1   I later found out that they were Hawker Sea Hawks being ferried to India.
2   It turned out that there were four fatigue fractures around the wheel and that our heavier than normal arrival had been the last straw. The wheel casing split apart and left the tyre spinning around the leg.

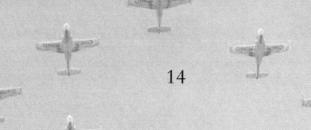

14

All in a Day's Work

After three months on the squadron we were starting to feel more settled. Some of the pressure to achieve set requirements was now over. However, there was still lots more to learn and we had yet to experience our first session of QRA. There was a sort of routine to the flying now. Most of it was done on single-aircraft sorties, flown at low level all over Germany by day and by night. The majority of trips included a First Run Attack (FRA) at one range or another and there were still regular dual checks to be endured in the T4. I was expected to upgrade my Instrument Rating (IR) from White to Green as soon as I had the appropriate number of flying hours. However, that would not be until March 1966, so in the meantime I had to undergo six-monthly renewals. The White IR meant that I was not to fly from, or recover to, any airfield when the cloudbase was less than 200ft above the minimum for the approach aid in use. In practical terms that meant a minimum cloudbase of around 500ft and a minimum visibility of about 2 nautical miles (nm). A Green IR would have allowed me down to 200ft and less than 1nm.

Low flying was our bread and butter and I got very used to the rate of flow of the landscape passing beneath me and to the best ways of climbing over ridges and following twisting valleys. We flew a number of sorties into the UK LFS and it was quite normal to carry out a stop to refuel, both the aircraft and us, at a UK RAF airfield, so giving us a 'day out'. The problem with this wide-ranging coverage was often the weather, but more of that later. Most low-level navigation sorties lasted between 2 and 3 hours.

The Canberra was often hard work to fly accurately at low-level. Of course it was all manual flying and above about 300kts the control forces became progressively higher. The rate at which the jet rolled wasn't great so to follow some of the tighter twisting valleys meant lots of two-handed application. With its big, fat wing the response of the aircraft to gusts and turbulence over the hills and trees was often bordering on the ridiculous, with large and sudden vertical movement giving us a very bumpy ride. On some occasions it could be just too much, especially for my Welsh companion lying in the nose, and when it got too much we would just pull up and go home. However, we'd press on whenever we could and a full 3-hour low-level sortie was about the equivalent of 1 hour in the gym!

Low flying at night was another novelty and it took a while to get used to it. For safety reasons we flew higher than by day, mainly because you couldn't easily see the ground and obstacles! Geoff used the very precise Decca Navigator in conjunction with a Doppler radar system that gave him accurate drift and groundspeed readouts and I helped, when I could, with visual position inputs. Although the Decca was usually extremely accurate, we were constrained to fly at a minimum height of 600ft above the highest obstacle within 10nm of our track. So we were often up at 1,000ft above ground level and higher in the hills and mountains, but over the North German Plain, we could often find ourselves at or near to 600ft.

In winter, after snowfall and with a good moon, it was feasible to fly visually well below 600ft, but you didn't talk about it afterwards! The radio altimeter had two scales selectable by a knob adjacent to the instrument: 0–500ft and 0–2000ft, so to fly at 600ft one had to select the higher scale. There were also limit lights that would indicate with green, amber and red bulbs when the aircraft was above, on or below the selected altitude; these lights could be dimmed at night.

One squadron pilot, who shall be nameless, went off on a night low-level sortie and forgot to change the scale on the radio altimeter from Low to High. As it turned out, the weather was not good for most of the first part of the route so he was flying his heights using the pressure altimeter. Part of the route went from the northern Schleswig-Holstein area west across the water of the German Bight to the island of Heligoland. At the coast the cloud cleared so he let down to what he thought was 600ft on the radio altimeter. It was as black as the ace of spades, so he concentrated on his instruments to fly accurate speed and height. After a while he became aware of lights flashing past in his peripheral vision, much faster than he thought reasonable and began to wonder what they were. So he looked out ahead into the blackness and saw more lights apparently rushing towards him. Then the realisation dawned. They were the masthead lights of a fleet of fishing boats and they were apparently moving so fast because he was at 60ft, not 600ft as he had thought. With an almighty rush of adrenalin he pulled up and changed the scale on his radio altimeter. He was still very pale and shaky when he came into the Mess later that night and sat down next to me at supper and confessed!

He was flying Standard Route (SR) 9. This was the most utilised of our standard routes because it gave a good variety of terrain and finished with a FRA at Nordhorn range. The most westerly turning point was the island of Heligoland, which had a large lighthouse on it. At night it was a disconcerting place to fly towards at low level. As you got closer the sweep of the light beam passing over the sea from left to right was very disorientating. You had to try to ignore the rather strange turning sensation that it gave. My trick was to lower my seat, which removed the sight from my peripheral vision, and then just fly on the instruments. At last I had found an advantage to having a very short back! I spent about 10 minutes like this because the same, but reversed, problem was there as we flew away from the island.

During the day there was obviously no such problem and the visibility over the German Bight was usually very good so this leg, from the coast near Sylt to Heligoland, was one of the easiest to get right. If we were aiming for a timed bomb-release, as we often did, this was the best leg on which to make speed adjustments.

One day our then new 'JP', Tom Eeles, was flying his first SR9 with his much older and wiser navigator, Vic Avery. As Heligoland hove into sight Tom said, 'That must be Heligoland. Have you seen it before, Vic?'

'Oh, yes,' replied the wise old head in the nose, 'But last time I saw it we were bombing it from 20,000ft.' (Vic wasn't that old; after the war, part of the island used to be a bombing range.) Tom didn't say much for the rest of the trip.

Another part of our work was high-level navigation. This was never popular, especially at night. Generally speaking it was boring. Just droning along at 0.74 Mach, usually giving a groundspeed of about 450kts, give or take the wind, and at heights of 40,000 to 45,000ft. Some of the routes we had to fly were 4 hours in duration. One such was a big square in the sky taking us north to Norway, then west to the Outer Hebrides, then south to Cornwall before the third and final left turn to head back to Germany. Apart from giving us a pain in the arse the only value of these trips was to push the squadron's hours up towards what was known as the SD98 value. In the days well before fuel crises (except the brief one during the Suez debacle) some wise man in MOD had worked out how much each RAF squadron should fly to maintain operational efficiency. This was all published in a Secret Document numbered 98 – hence SD98.

Because our role was predominately low level and 30 per cent at night there was no way that we could achieve the historic SD98 rate for a Canberra bomber squadron. So, every now and then, we would be sent off into the night sky, often in a stream of six aircraft around one of these tedious routes.

One night, in the summer, at about 2 a.m., we were coming south over Northern Ireland and were asked to call the next radar unit – Ulster Radar. I called on the published initial contact frequency and the sweetest-voiced Colleen answered us.

'MNA 36[1] Roger. Standby on this frequency for the controller,' came the dulcet response. Before I could acknowledge, Geoff pressed his transmit button and said, 'Oh never mind the controller, love, we'll talk to you.' This was followed by a short silence and then a deep masculine voice telling us to turn right for identification. He didn't need to do that as we had a fully functional IFF.

'There, that'll teach you,' I said to Geoff, 'Now you'll have to work to regain track.'

'Work at two o' clock in the morning – you must be jokin'!' There's little worse than a bored, demoralised navigator.

On another night, and setting off on a similar sortie, looking forward to another 4 hours in the dark, I was climbing over the Netherlands and had spoken to their military radar controller, callsign Dutchmil Radar. I was the third in a stream of four from Laarbruch. The silence was broken by a very public school accent.

'Dutchmil this is MPACG[2]. We are en route between Malta and the UK above your UIR[3]. This call is for information only, we do not wish a radar service.'

'Roger, Charlie Golf, continue on your track at your own discretion,' came the Dutchman's reply.

I imagined that MPACG was a Vulcan or a Victor, with a Cranwell graduate pilot who was just being polite by telling the radar controller that he was there and where he was heading. He was probably cruising at or around 50,000ft.

A few seconds later another, completely different, voice broke the silence. This one sounded just like the film actor Slim Pickens, who played a B-52 captain in the film *Dr Strangelove* – an American with a slow Texan drawl.

'Hey there, Dutch Military. This is USAF 55295. We're a B-52 at FL350 and we would sure like to start our descent into Wiesbaden, Germany.'

There was a long pause from below.

'Roger USAF 55295. We don't seem to have your flight plan. Can you give me your place and time of departure, please?'

'Sure, sir. Ah would be delighted to do so.' Then Slim started to read out the whole thing in detail, starting from Birmingham, Alabama and going on, and on, and on. He still hadn't finished when he paused for breath. As he did so, the very cut glass accent from way above us chipped in, 'Why don't you f*** off, Yank?'

Dutchmil now took to the airwaves.

'Aircraft using profane language on the air, identify yourself!'

'And you, Cloggie,' was the final word.

Some planned sorties included navigating low-level routes in France and using a USAF-managed range at Suippes in the Ardennes region. However, in June 1966 President de Gaulle finally pulled the French military out of NATO. This action led to the closure of French airspace to all NATO combat aircraft so our access to French low-level routes, airfields and ranges was ended.

This airspace denial also had the apparent effect of cutting us off from flying over France to the Mediterranean. The only alternative route for us was to fly to the south-west of the UK and then head due south through Portuguese airspace for staging into the Med via Gibraltar. However, someone soon realised that we could play the 'over-flight above 45,000ft' card.

Our first major detachment after De Gaulle's '*Non*' did just that, with eight aircraft flying in formation to Malta. The only change to our normal route was to fly initially over Belgium and Luxembourg to give us the time and distance to climb above 45,000ft. We therefore crossed the French territorial border in loose, high-level, battle formation at 47,000ft. It was very difficult to keep reasonably within sight of each other up there, but the oddest thing was that the French military radar stations would not acknowledge our information calls to them. That was until our lead nav, Flight Lieutenant Del Williams, tried his schoolboy French on them. After a pause a French-accented voice said, 'If you are going to talk to us in such bad French, I will talk to you in English!'

In fact the French military soon accepted these overflights, but we weren't supposed to carry any weapons with us. This gave the squadron an added logistics problem at times but, in the end, I got the impression that many ordinary French *Armée de l'Air* types were not that closely in step with their ex-*Armée de la Terre* President. We were often asked if we would accept fighter interception training; we usually did because it was quite amusing. The older French Air Force fighters just couldn't get up to our height and turn into attacking positions simultaneously. Although the then new Mirages did occasionally zoom-climb up and get a bit closer. Despite General '*Non*' de Gaulle, there was lots of sky left for us to fly in.

Another effect of the French withdrawal was that we lost the use of the bombing range at Suippes. However, someone up at HQ had negotiated the use of a range on one of the Dutch barrier islands called Vliehors. Geoff and I were the first RAF Germany crew to use it for LABS deliveries. We got hold of all the range maps, called a couple of Dutch ATC units and eventually set off to throw four practise bombs at their target.

We had to approach from the south-east, crossing the long causeway that separated the Zuider Zee from the North Sea. At the causeway we called the range and were cleared to run in. Because the run-in was over water there was no suitable IP; so we were confined to Alternate mode deliveries. That meant that we pulled-up over the target and the bomb came off when we were past the vertical, went up to about 10,000ft before it came down again. Obviously no one had briefed the Range Controller about this.

As per our usual procedures I called, 'Pulling up.'

'No bomb observed,' was the immediate response.

'It's still with us.'

'Do you want to report a hang-up?'

'Negative – just wait.'

A few seconds later I called, 'Bomb gone.'

'No bomb observed,' was again the immediate response.

'It'll be with you in about 50 seconds.'

'Say again.'

'Just wait!'

At last silence. It's quite hard to have a reasoned conversation when you're carrying out a half-loop and dive recovery in a Canberra.

'Oh yes, 36, we see it!'

By the end of the range slot he had got the hang of it. It was all in a day's work!

Notes

1   This was a Trigraph callsign. Each squadron was issued with a three-letter designator to add to the pilot's personal squadron allocated numeric identifier. The Trigraph changed at irregular intervals.

2   This is the five-letter callsign used for flights outside the UK. RAF Germany aircraft used these callsigns for sorties to the Mediterranean and beyond, but not for sorties from Germany to and from the UK.

3   UIR = Upper-airspace Information Region. In the 1960s the airspace above Flight Level 450 (approx 45,000ft) was regarded as free airspace so that aircraft flying above that height did not have to be controlled by the national authority of the country below them. There were very few aircraft capable of cruising above that altitude in those days. The U2, Vulcan, Victor and Canberra being the only ones in Europe.

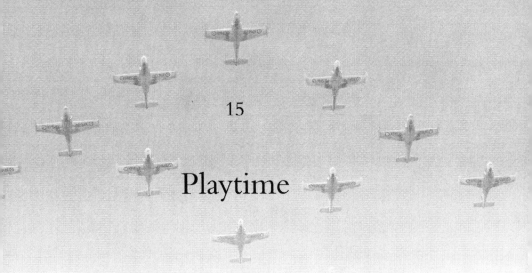

15

Playtime

All work and no play makes Jack a dull boy: me too. However, it didn't seem
to matter how hard we worked, and sometimes the hours we were on duty
were very long, we also played well. The wartime traditions of the RAF and
'The Few' were still only one generation behind us. Not only that but there
were still plenty of folk around with Second World War medal ribbons on
their uniforms. Within the life of any contemporary RAF Officers' Mess
there was plenty of opportunity for diversion and amusement. Attendance
at TGIF on Friday nights, starting at 5 p.m., was almost compulsory, much
lager was consumed and banter exchanged. Then there were the games that
went with the drinking.

There was Liar Dice, which was played with five poker dice and a leather
cup. The first player shook the dice and then had the option of two more
shakes, extracting dice as he did so, before passing on all five dice, covered,
to the next player and declaring what was under the cup. The second player
then had the option of accepting the call or, if he didn't believe it, lifting
the cup for all to see. If he accepted he also had two further opportunities
to improve on the called hand, all out of the sight of the other players. But
if the call was not accepted and the cup lifted then two further possibilities
arose. If a bluff was uncovered then the declarer had to buy a round, but if
the hand was true then it was one who didn't believe that had to buy. The
more the game was played the more ridiculous the calls became!

Then there was 'Seven, Fourteen, Twenty-one'. This was played with
three ordinary, numbered dice and they were rolled in the open. A bar
chit was also required. The players rolled the dice in turn and the one
who reached or first exceeded a running total of seven had to write three
different drinks on the chit. The player who achieved fourteen had to sign

the chit, so paying for it, and the player who rolled enough to first achieve a running total of twenty-one had to drink the 'cocktail'. This time the more the game was played the more ridiculous the ingredients became.

Another game was a challenge to drink 1 fl oz of lager or beer on the minute every minute for one hour. A small liqueur glass is about 1 fl oz, so it didn't seem much of a challenge. If the challenge was met, which turned out to be rare, the challenger paid for the drink; otherwise it was the rather chastened 'victim' who paid! The difficulty with this apparently innocuous game was that after about 30 minutes the build-up of gas was getting in the way of drinking the next tiny glass on time. If you missed the minute call then the game was lost, as it was if you had to leave the room for any reason or threw up, wherever you were!

Then there were the 16 Squadron drinking vessels: a 1-litre stein and a yard-long glass in the shape of a hunting horn, both of which were part of the initiation of new aircrew. The stein was kept in the Officers' Mess bar and the yard was brought out at joint aircrew-groundcrew events. In each case they were filled with Mr Amstel's best amber nectar and they had to be drunk not, thankfully, necessarily in one draft, but without the respective drinking vessel ever leaving the lips until it was empty.

This culture of apparently indiscriminate drinking was endemic throughout the RAF at the time, but I don't remember it ever spilling over into the working environment. If you did turn up the next day with a hangover, one of the best and most rapid cures was effected by putting on your oxygen mask as soon as you could and selecting 100 per cent on the regulator. By the time the aircraft had reached the end of the runway any headache and fuzziness had long gone!

Perhaps because the base was a piece of the UK dropped into the German countryside there were lots of on-base social functions: dining-in nights, both stag and with the ladies, as well as parties in the Mess and at various Married Quarters. There were two big annual events: the Summer Ball and the Christmas Draw. All social events were well attended and very lively. After my first Summer Ball at Laarbruch I well remember sitting outside the back door of the Mess Bar, looking over the fields as the sun was rising, with a glass of champagne and a freshly cooked *knackwurst* in my hands. The average age of the officers on an operational RAF Germany station was quite low and folk were always ready to dance, eat and drink.

There were also lots of opportunities for off-duty activities elsewhere on the station. There was a cinema, which doubled as a theatre; a four-lane

Ten-Pin Bowling Alley; plenty of sports fields and teams; a nine-hole golf course; a shooting range; an outdoor swimming pool; tennis courts; a whole raft of hobby clubs; hunting in the woods and a gliding club.

It was the latter to which I gravitated. I had started my flying by learning to glide and soar with the Air Training Corps and I was eager to try to gain some more expertise. I was one of only a handful of aircrew who flew with the gliding club. The majority of members were ground staff or family members. The Chief Instructor was Steve, a sergeant from Air Traffic Control. After a check flight with him I was allowed to fly solo in one of the less sophisticated single-seat sailplanes. After a while I was a regular enough member to be allowed to move up the ladder a bit. In time I achieved the gain of height required for my Silver C certificate.

On one occasion a cold front was due to come down from the north and being summer it was generating thunderstorms as it came across the plains. We had a good morning's flying and then Steve decided that we should fly all the aircraft one last time, each landing on the fifth fairway of the station golf course. That was the landing area closest to the gliding club hangar.

I was the last off in my little *B-Spatz* and soon found some incredible lift just ahead of the looming cumulonimbus clouds bearing down on Laarbruch. Soon, too soon, I had to give up and get the aircraft on the ground before it got torn apart in the storm's turbulence. So I selected the airbrakes out and made a rapid descent to the golf course. The heavy rain arrived as I came to a halt. I decided to stay in the cockpit, not only to stay dry but also to control the little sailplane if the wind should get up too much. I had been there a good 5 minutes, the rain hammering down on the small Perspex hood over my head, when two figures appeared out of the sheets of water falling from the sky.

At first I thought they were gliding club folk come to tow me in, but then I realised that they had golf bags over their shoulders. They came right up to the cockpit and I opened the small sliding ventilation panel in the Perspex canopy to speak to them.

'Do you know that you're blocking the fairway?' one of the dripping figures asked me, somewhat aggressively.

'Yes, we can't get on with our game,' splashed the other. Before I could either explain or apologise, sodden golfer number one said, 'You must be mad to fly in weather like this!' With which illogical remark they squelched off into the rain. My only thought was to wonder which of us was the maddest.

The gliding also gave me the opportunity to take part in the BAOR and RAF Germany annual championships. Most of my time was spent sharing the driving of our recovery car with a glider trailer in tow; my expertise in the glider itself was not deemed sufficient to warrant entry for the main competition. The whole thing was a lot of fun. Perhaps the best part was a passing visit to the Nürburgring motor racing circuit. When we got there we found that, for a modest fee, you could drive around one lap. Sadly they wouldn't let us go around with the trailer on. So straws were drawn and one of the four of us had to stay with the trailer. I drew the long straw and so I was the 'nominated driver' – we set the fastest lap ever by an Austin Cambridge Estate!

One day we were in the gliding centre clubhouse, discussing the weather forecast. It was winter and things were not looking good. Steve announced that it wouldn't get much better as there was a warm front[1] coming.

'Oh good,' said one of the members' wives, 'I think I'll change into shorts and sandals.' Well, she was renowned as a bit of a dizzy blonde!

Early in my time with the gliding club one of the members had sold me a 1949 Mercedes Diesel Saloon for DM500, which was the equivalent of £50. It wasn't a wreck by any means, although there were a few minor details that required attention. The matt sand paintwork and its body style made it look like a Second World War *Wehrmacht* staff car. The possession of this splendid means of transport opened up another way of spending my precious time off: touring the country. The valleys of the Rhine and Moselle could be reached in a few hours and there were plenty of *zimmer frei* (B&B) places to stay. This was an especially desirable area to visit in the autumn when the wine festivals were happening. Post-July 1965 getting about became even more fun when I bought a brand new, duty-free British Racing Green MG Midget.

Another diversion for Saturday mornings was to visit the markets in one of the Dutch towns, such as Nijmegen, Venlo or Röermond. When I was still a bachelor these visits could also provide the opportunity for a cheap lunch. The trick was to stop at the cheese stalls and ask to taste some of the wares; then do the same at the smoked eel stall. To round it all off one bought a paper cone filled with chips, doused in mayonnaise. This final prize was then taken to a nearby bar where one ordered a small, foaming *pilsner* to go with it.

But if a more substantial meal was required then a stop at the *Twée Brüders* restaurant for a *Nasi Goreng* was the best choice for a growing lad. One thing I do remember from my time at Laarbruch was that I very rarely felt bored. There was always plenty to do, even if sometimes it wasn't always good for my health, but in your early twenties you didn't really think of that. Playtime really was just that and this Jack had absolutely no chance of becoming a dull boy.

Notes

1 A warm front would bring grey skies and rain for the rest of the day. Being winter the actual temperature would not rise by much at all.

16

The Bucket of Sunshine

There was no doubt that Geoff and I were having a lot of fun. We were both doing a job that we would have paid to do, in a wonderful environment and with a great bunch of people. But there was no doubt either that there was a deadly serious side to it all. By the time that we had qualified as 'Operational' we knew of five fellow course members from our time in training who had died while flying the Canberra in Germany; all through flying into hard-centred clouds[1]. In fact, one crew had done so just after I had decided that the weather over the Teutoburger Wald, a sharp ridge that ran south-east from Osnabruck, wasn't good enough for staying low. Although not very high, the ridge's wooded upper slopes could generate their own wispy hill fog and that could, all too easily, blend into the overlying layer of grey stratus cloud. It was just too easy to be sucked into thinking that you could get through a gap and then, too late, find that you spent the last 2 seconds of your life watching the trees and rocks join you in the cockpit. That was what had happened to Harry and his crew, minutes after we had pulled up only a few miles away. Why were we doing this potentially dangerous thing every day? Well, to become as proficient as we could possibly be at flying very low in order not to be seen by enemy radar units, so that we had a reasonable chance of flying several hundred miles to the east and delivering our nuclear weapon successfully. That was if we were ever called upon to do it. Thinking any further than this was not a good exercise for morale!

So what about the weapon in question? When we had still been in the operational conversion training system, back in the UK, all three crews on our small course had spent three days at the Bomber Command Bombing School (BCBS), located at RAF Wittering, in those days a V-Bomber base equipped with Handley Page Victors. The school was set up to teach the principles and particulars of how each nuclear weapon worked. They then taught us the operation of our bomb prior to release and what we should do if it had any malfunctions. Most of the proceedings took place in the classroom, with lots of visual aids and countless frames of film showing the sky exploding. At first it was a sobering experience for young men like us. But after a while we went into nuclear overload and it all started to get a bit academic. But the thought was always in the back of our minds that it wasn't going to happen on our watch.

Just when the depression was reaching its worst, the whole thing went from the deadly serious to the farcically hilarious. That was when we were introduced to the BCBS Canberra Nuclear Bombing simulator. This was a dark room with the bare bones of a Canberra cockpit sat on a framework of steel, and a navigator's position was similarly simulated in rudimentary fashion. Behind the pilot's open seat was a bomb carrier with a large, black, rubber bomb hanging from it. The only things that worked in the two 'cockpits' were the switches and indicators related to bomb operation and release.

Each crew spent several periods in this darkened environment coming to grips with the switchery required to make sure that the bomb would go BANG when it should and how to cope with pre-release malfunctions. But the best was yet to come. The final session simulated the final part of a nuclear strike sortie, approaching our IP with full political clearance to make our target glow in the dark. Faults were simulated and overcome and finally we made our delivery manoeuvre.

I pulled back on the control yoke, which felt rather spongy, the LABS indicator showed the correct G level and as the simulated attitude reached the right release angle there was a *thunk* from behind me as the large rubber bomb came off and then proceeded to bounce across the floor. It was very hard to keep a straight face in front of our rather dour instructor. Humour will out in the end and it was during this phase of our training that the name 'A Bucket of Sunshine' came into our vocabulary. From then on in we would be able to keep a sense of reality in the rather unreal world that we were moving into.

But the Cold War was very much a reality. The Cuban missile crisis had taken us to the brink. The young, brave JFK had, perhaps because of his actions during those thirteen days, been disposed of and the bellicose 'Hawks' were back in charge in the USA. The military-industrial machine was cranking up as things in Vietnam went from bad to worse. The rhetoric flying back and forth across Churchill's Iron Curtain was getting more vitriolic and spying was a growth business. Indeed we were peripherally involved in that when we flew special sorties at high-level right down the ADIZ boundary. We would often spot East German fighters coming up to see what we were doing. This exercise was flown in coordination with monitoring stations in Berlin and along the border and, occasionally, with airborne electronic intelligence platforms from the RAF and the USAF.

When we finally got to Germany we found that the overarching principle was one of deterrence. The major, strategic nuclear weapons carried by manned bombers, such as the RAF's V-Force and USAF B-52s, and on various land and submarine-based ICBMs were the means by which each side hoped to convince the other that they would not attack first. This was known as the 'No First Strike' principle. However, mutual trust was not high. Over the postwar years the USSR had built up huge conventional forces in its European satellites. The West saw this as giving the Soviets the capability to mount a rapid, military-led expansion to the west, without recourse, at least initially, to nuclear weapons. The scenario was that enormous numbers of armoured columns would burst through the Fulda Gap, south-east of Kassel, and across the northern plains from Wittenberg.

This ground offensive would be supported by massive tactical air forces from airfields in East Germany, Poland, Czechoslovakia and Hungary. The NATO retaliation to this hypothetical offensive would probably have to include the use of tactical nuclear weapons, as our counter-offensive conventional forces were numerically inferior. Such tactical nuclear weapons were embedded in Short Range Missiles, such as Nike, special artillery and on tactical nuclear aircraft, including ours. A policy then evolved known as 'Trip Wire', in which no nuclear response would be taken unless the opposition forces reached a specific line in the German sand.

In addition to that possible tactical nuclear role was our part in the strategic deterrence posture of the West. That role was the one for which we were always prepared. The weapon that was available to all the RAF Germany Canberra squadrons was the American Mk7 'Thor'.

In 1957 an agreement called Project E had come out of talks between the governments of Harold Macmillan and President Eisenhower. Project E allowed the carriage and release of American tactical nuclear weapons by RAF aircraft, specifically the Canberra. The Mk7 was also to be carried by US Navy and USAF tactical bombers. So our 'Buckets of Sunshine' had 'Made in the USA' stamped on them and there was a small corps of USAF officers and men based at Laarbruch to make sure that we didn't steal them or go to war without US permission. So we were not part of the UK's Independent Nuclear Deterrent Forces; that was resident in the UK at the V-Force bases in eastern England.

The Mk7 was 15ft long and 2.5ft around. It looked 'chubby' and weighed in at 1,650lb. It was just a little bit too fat to fit in the Canberra with the original bomb doors closed so these had been modified to allow them to fit around our charge. The bomb bay length was sufficient for the Mk7 to fit neatly. However, because the final attack speed was nearly 100kts above the normal limiting speed for the bomb doors to be open, a special baffle plate was fitted to overcome this limitation. The bomb had Uranium 235 fissionable elements and it was possible to select a variety of yields in flight, before the final amount of uranium was inserted into the core, to achieve the critical mass in the chain reaction after detonation. The nose of the bomb contained a radar altimeter that would trigger the explosion at about 1,500ft above the target. This was called an air-burst, which gave the maximum damage to infrastructure for a given yield. We could select between 8 and 61 kilotons (KT) depending on the target; the Hiroshima bomb was nominally 20 KT. The maximum yield would be used against most fixed ground targets such as airfields. So we were armed and ready to go!

Notes

1   RAF aircrew-speak for a cloud-covered hill or mountain.

17

Quick Reaction Alert

We were now qualified to be sentenced to periodic incarceration in our local detention centre as guardians of a nuclear armed Canberra B(I)8. QRA was the only drawback of the whole 16 Squadron experience. Each qualified crew had to do a two-week stint about every six weeks. The roster was for each pair of crews to be there for 24 hours on alternate days, with the change-over taking place at 0900 hours. The more experienced crew would be nominated as the senior crew and for that privilege they assumed some additional responsibilities. One of four USAF officers was resident in QRA as the final representative of the US government authorised to release the weapons for operational use. Just to add to the penal ambience he was known as the Custodian.

The accommodation was a single-storey block split in half by the entrance door, with the groundcrew accommodation off to the left and the aircrew digs to the right. The USAF Custodian's office/bedroom was directly ahead. Each side had its own kitchen and cooking was DIY. The senior member of each group made out a daily ration order and the food was delivered from the Station Ration Stores by mid-morning (steak was usually ordered for Uncle Sam's man). Newspapers came over from the messes and there was a small in-house library. Each of the lounges had a radio and the groundcrew had a TV, but the only TV channels available in those days were either Dutch or German. On the radio we could get the British Forces Broadcasting Service (BFBS) from Köln, as well as the BBC World Service and Voice of America. There was a wardrobe in the aircrew room. Inside it were a Bren gun, several rifles and Colt revolvers, along with their ammunition in boxes. This mini-armoury was there in case there was ever a ground assault by invading forces or fifth columnists while we still hadn't gone off to do our bit for Queen and country; well, for SACEUR and NATO. A far-fetched contingency I thought, but it did have the bonus that we had to do regular live arms training on the station shooting range.

Before sentencing to my first shift in QRA I had fulfilled all my qualifying training requirements except one and that was to read *Catch 22* (Joseph Heller's novel about a USAAF medium bomber squadron based on a Mediterranean island during the Second World War). In a last ditch attempt to avoid my custodial stretch I pointed this out to the Flight Commander, alas to no avail.

'Well, there's a copy in QRA and you've now got the time to read it,' he responded. 'Tick it off on the board when you've done so!' I then asked someone why we had to read the book.

'Well, if you don't read it you won't understand half the banter that goes on in there. Anyway it's a great book and you'll enjoy it.'

I certainly did; its zany humour and wartime air force setting made it a good read and by the end of our first two weeks in QRA I had read it from cover to cover. I could now keep up with even the most obscure references to Yossarian, Milo Minderbinder and their buddies. Several characters in the book were allocated to certain personalities around the station. For instance, there was an administrative officer known as Major Major, because he was never in his office when you went to see him. One of the squadron pilots, Guy Pearce, picked up the sobriquet of Milo Minderbinder when he loaded some brand new tyres into the pannier of his jet before he set off on a Southern Ranger once. When quizzed about this it transpired that he had a weekend's trading and bartering in mind; he didn't disclose what he would return with!

On the mornings of our duty days, once we had arrived at the fenced QRA compound and gained entrance, the formal handover of each aircraft took place, with the oncoming crew making an inspection while the off-going crew watched. The first time I squeezed myself into the bomb bay with that big bomb hanging there menacingly was a strange experience. The knowledge that a huge amount of potential deadly force was just a few inches away from me was quite unnerving; but after a couple more handovers it became less so. In the cockpit I had to confirm that all the switches and levers were arranged in the attractive and eye-catching manner that would ensure that when I switched on the Battery Master Switch and hit the two Engine Start buttons simultaneously, the engines would fire up.

After the take-over was complete and the inevitable signatures obtained we could settle down to a morning's serious waiting. And that was what we did most of the time – just waited. However, there was usually something for everyone to do. First off, us new crews had to liberate our Top Secret target bag from the safe and study the route, the IP and the target. The maps in these folders were prepared by the Station Operations Centre from data passed to them from the MOD. The folders were regularly updated with the latest intelligence on things to avoid, such as enemy surface-to-air-missile (SAM) sites and other places that could be hazardous to our health. There were often black and white photographs of our IPs, some obviously taken covertly from a car or a train, and target photographs from reconnaissance overflights; some taken even before the Cold War had really started. By now Geoff and I already had another nominated war target, so at any one time we had to be familiar with the contents of two target bags. Most of the intended recipients of our buckets of sunshine were in East Germany, Poland or Czechoslovakia. They were, for the most part, airfields but large logistics areas such as rail marshalling yards and docks were sometimes included.

One fact that I hadn't really thought about came up when a reporter from a UK national newspaper came to Laarbruch to do a piece on the Cold War. He was brought over to QRA when we were on shift. During the interviews he asked me how old I was. I was by now used to this because I had a 'baby-face' and looked about sixteen. I told him I was twenty and so was my navigator.

'Oh, so you can go and drop an atom bomb but you can't vote,' he observed. He was, for the moment, right[1].

Reading, cooking and games of bridge were the main QRA pastimes. After a couple of shifts I finally gave in and let Geoff teach me bridge. Of course, I was then hooked and we often played late into the night. But we had to be ready to 'go' at all times, so we lived in our flying suits with our lifejackets and helmets close by. Our response was exercised at least twice in any two-week shift, usually once by day and once by night; this was a minimum because we would also be called out at the start of any station or command initiated exercise.

A call out was signalled first by a klaxon in the entrance hall sounding, whence the pilots, groundcrew and junior nav all rushed out to the aircraft. An armed USAF enlisted man guarded each aircraft and you had to show a special pass before crossing a yellow line into what was known in American military-speak as the 'No Lone Zone'. This meant that no person could be beyond that line alone. So if you were the first there the guard had to come with you until someone else came along.

During these practises we pilots had to climb aboard and strap into the ejection seat, however, we were not allowed to select electrical power to the aircraft. The nav meanwhile had grabbed the target bag, run out and, before he climbed aboard, cross-checked with the groundcrew that all the control locks and engine blanks had been removed. When we were satisfied that we could go to war, we then had to wait a few seconds for the word from the senior nav. He had, by then, been in contact with the Station Operations Room and received the coded release message – or instructions to stand down. So only a few minutes after we had been playing bridge, or reading, or sleeping we were back in the QRA hut again, ready to resume our previous activity. Well, we were once the adrenalin level had dropped back to normal.

After a few shifts of QRA duty it all became very routine, although the frisson of trepidation never totally went away, especially when we were called out during the early hours of the morning. Once, when we were the senior crew, Geoff stayed back to get the release message and then came running out to me and poked his head through the door with the words, 'We're off.' The surge of adrenalin was enormous and once I'd got my breath back, I shouted back, 'Do you mean we are off, or we're off?'

'That's right, boyo, we're off . . . we can stand down and go back to bed.'

Gee thanks!

To relieve the background stress and the boredom, we got up to all sorts of amusing pranks in QRA. Some involved telephones, of which there were two. One was supposed to be reserved for operational calls and the other for domestics. One good game was to get a metal waste bin and put the two phones in the bottom, speakers to earpieces. Then someone rang a random four-figure internal number on each phone. The subsequent conversations, amplified by the bin, were always amusing, with each respondent trying to establish why they were talking to each other.

Our support depended very much on being able to arrange motor transport (MT) to bring us all the things we needed on a daily basis: food, newspapers, weather forecasts, files from the squadron and so on. It seemed that the MT desk was run most of the time by a Corporal Jones who had a distinctive Welsh accent; he was probably known as 'Jones the Wheels'. One day, when the telephone had barely stopped ringing, the other pilot on duty, oddly enough called Pete Jones, picked up the phone and said, in perfect imitation, 'MT, Cpl Jones'. Of course, the person on the other end had rung QRA. So they rang off to try again and Pete had to do a repeat act. Eventually he had to start telling the people who were persistent in their attempts to get through to us that they should report a fault. Just as I was beginning to get a little worried that this prank might backfire the phone rang again.

'MT, Cpl Jones,' said Pete.

'Can't be,' said the Welsh accented voice at the other end, 'That's me!'

One of the irritations of being in QRA was the inordinate number of visitors we seemed to have to receive. All sorts of people visited RAF Laarbruch for a whole variety of reasons and every single one was brought across the airfield to see a couple of crews waiting to go to war. On one occasion, when we had already had our bridge tournament interrupted several times, we received the call that another worthy and very senior ranking person was coming over to be shown around. The senior crew was a couple of old hands, Flight Lieutenants Terry Frame and Doug Hall.

They hatched a plot. Doug had a wonderful knack for maintaining a deadpan expression, so Terry got him to step inside the wardrobe where our ground defence arms were kept. Then he 'hung' Doug by his collar over a coat hook and shut the door. When the visitor arrived, accompanied by the Boss and the Station Commander, Terry did the usual tour and as he came to the wardrobe he opened it, saying, 'In here we keep our ground defence arms – and a spare navigator.' Doug just hung there – expressionless.

Terry shut the door. The visitor opened it again, paused and then poked Doug in the stomach. There was no response. At that point the Boss said, 'OK, that's enough – Flight Lieutenant Hall you can come out now and stop fooling about.' Doug just hung there. I began to worry that the hanging had actually worked and that he had expired in the 15 minutes he had been in there. The Boss now really started to lose his cool, but he held back in front of the VIP. Terry whispered to the Boss, 'Don't worry, sir, we'll get him out when you've all gone.' The Station Commander wanted to give us all, Boss included, a rocket, but he too was inhibited by the presence of our visitor. However, thankfully it was the VIP that defused the whole situation by laughing uproariously and walking out of the door.

Then there was Charles Peace. That was the name of a notorious Victorian thief and murderer, whose twenty-four-year career of crime was ended on 25 February 1879 by his execution in Armley Prison, Leeds. Tom Eeles, who was off to fly Buccaneers with the Fleet Air Arm, had given this infamous name to his large green parrot; it was a name fitting the bird's murderous demeanour. Just before he left Laarbruch, Tom donated Charles to QRA where he hoped that the crews would look after the bird; at least that was the theory. We soon got used to the smell and providing all the needs of a parrot; some of the guys even tried to get him to talk. And that was the cause of the next incident with a visitor.

For reasons that could only be known to those in the ivory towers who sanctioned and arranged these visits, the next one was by the Moderator of the Presbyterian Church of Northern Ireland. When he turned up, obviously after a good and fairly liquid lunch at the Officers' Mess, he was accompanied as usual by the Boss and the Station Commander. The ruddy faced, white-haired old gentleman looked a bit like the Irish character actor Noel Purcell. He was dressed in his full regalia of black morning coat, breeches, buckled shoes and clerical tabbed collar. We had only just got started on the tour when he spotted the parrot.

'Oh, how amazing – you have a bird,' he said in his rich Ulster accent, 'Does it talk?' He then approached the cage, clucking and cooing at Charlie.

'Hello, bird. Who's a pretty boy then? What's your name?'

Charlie looked at him coldly with one beady eye and cocked his head on one side, '**** off! **** off!' he squawked. Then he proceeded to do his rather good imitation of the alert klaxon.

The Moderator obviously hadn't quite caught the rude words that Charlie had fired at him.

'He does talk, how splendid!' he enthused.

Before any further embarrassment could occur the Station Commander stepped in and made noises that suggested that they were getting behind the visit schedule and ushered the old gent towards the door. With a final benediction he left us in peace with Peace.

One summer's day when we were outside, lolling around in the sun like so many Battle of Britain pilots, one of the guys brought Charlie out in his cage. Of course it wasn't long before someone suggested that we should see if he could actually fly. He was liberated onto an arm and then launched. He knew what to do and flapped bravely, but all he achieved was a continuous left descending turn! Not surprisingly the landing was a bit of a shambles.

After this airborne failure we decided to write up what was called a Special Occurrence Report or SOR[2]. I was the Squadron Flight Safety Officer at the time so I wrote Charlie's bit and then coerced the Squadron Engineering Officer and the Boss to fill in their parts of the report appropriately. I also asked the Boss to similarly persuade the Senior Technical Officer and the Station Commander to do likewise. He agreed. The Station Flight Safety Officer let me see the final completed SOR before it went off to Command HQ. Everyone had entered into the spirit of it marvellously. The engineers between them had invented a wonderfully technical description of a feather and then concluded that there had been unauthorised modifications to the feathers on Charlie's port wing. This was the clipping that Tom had done before he handed him over to the squadron. Eventually HQ also joined in and a very amusing feedback piece was included in the Command Flight Safety magazine. The next thing we needed to do was to get Charles Peace commissioned.

Another day when we were on QRA duty we didn't have a four for bridge, so we all did other things. After a while I offered to make coffee and found Geoff slaving away over maps and charts.

'Are you planning our next Club Med weekend away?' I asked.

'No, I'm making a target folder for Charlie.'

And sure enough he had got hold of suitable maps and was making them up to look just like our wartime strip maps, with all the appropriate marks and symbols.

'What's his target?' I foolishly asked.

'A parrot food factory in Dresden,' came the surreal reply.

'And what are all those red circles?' (they looked like our SAM site indicators).

'That's where the crows and the buzzards are.'

This was getting too far out for me so I went to get the coffee. But it all backfired a bit later on. We were once more on shift when a team of senior officers from the Ministry of Defence appeared. These were the folk who made up our target maps and oversaw all the intelligence that went into them. When they arrived they asked to see our two target bags, which were duly fished out of the safe and handed over.

The more sharp-eyed of the said senior officers spotted another bag in there and pulled it out as well.

'What's this?' he demanded. Geoff paled a little.

'Oh, its just a bit of a joke, sir,' I hesitantly replied.

'What do you mean, Flying Officer? This is no joking matter!'

I supposed that you lost any vestige of a sense of humour if you had a job like his. So I thought it best to come straight out with it. Anyway our revered Flight Commander and the Station Senior Operations Officer were starting to fidget.

'We thought it would be fun to make a facsimile target bag for our parrot, Flying Officer Peace,' I said.

With a look that pleaded to be spared the immature minds of young aircrew he gave it back to me. He hadn't even looked at it – and it was a brilliant piece of work. A large sigh with a Welsh accent came from my navigator.

As our first Christmas in Germany approached, Geoff and I were told that it was usual for the single guys to 'volunteer' for Christmas QRA duty; so we did. However, we were off duty on Christmas Eve and I remember being in the Mess Bar when one of our company, which included a group of married guys and their wives, said that he'd just heard that one of the squadron wives had just had the baby she was expecting.

'It's a girl,' he said.

'Oh good,' piped up someone else, 'Now we can send those damn shepherds away.'

The next morning when I awoke and opened the curtains there was a thick blanket of snow over the tennis courts. A White Christmas! The bad news was that we had to walk down to the main road because the transport couldn't get up to the Mess. When we finally reached the QRA compound I hoped that the Red Hoards wouldn't decide to come over the border today. For one thing it was supposed to be 'Peace on Earth and Goodwill Between Men Day' and, for another, there was a foot of snow on the taxiways and runway. Inside we soon settled into cooking our Christmas dinner and playing bridge.

At least there would be no visitors today, not even Santa Claus, but there would be no wine either. On the radio BFBS were running a music request programme. We rang them and asked for a special record for all the other RAF Germany QRA crews: 'We've Got to Get Out of This Place' by The Animals.

QRA was a fact of life on a nuclear strike squadron. It was something to be endured, but there were plenty of self-generated diversions to make it a bit less arduous. It was also the one thing that made us realise just how fragile world peace was and that we were perhaps playing a small part in keeping that peace. We also knew that if we were called upon to hurl our buckets of sunshine at the other side we would do it to the best of our ability. And I think that we all believed that it would probably be the last thing that we would ever do.

Notes

1   In 1964 the minimum age for voting was twenty-one.
2   SORs were put in for any incident that could have or did affect flight safety. They later became known as Incident Reports.

1 This is what a one-year-old future RAF pilot looks like! Get the hair!

2 My dad with my brother Paul and me on the holiday when I took to the air for the first time.

3 After my first flight in the Auster, I take Paul flying on my favourite fairground ride at Southport.

4 From 4A at Pudsey Grammar School. Our Form Master was Mr Hallam, who was an ex-Fleet Air Arm pilot and influential in my choice of career. I am second from the right on the back row (still with an amazing head of hair!).

5   My first motorbike.
A 250cc BSA C15.

6   My Air Training
Corps friend 'Con'
about to launch on his
first solo in a Kirby
Cadet Mk3 glider at
RAF Linton-on-Ouse
in 1959.

7 Three ATC friends at Old Warden with a Spitfire of the Shuttleworth Collection in 1960. Little did I realise that thirty-six years later I would fly this very aircraft.

8 Two DH Vampires at RAF Shawbury in 1960, where I was given an air experience ride in one. Two years later I would be doing my advanced training on the same type.

9 Our party inward bound to the camp in South Wales during the Initial Officer Training Course. Officer Cadet John Sims in the lead.

10 The final objective. Our cold, muddy home for a week in the Brecon Beacons National Park, March 1962.

11   The official photograph of our Officer Training Course in May 1962. I am standing seventh from the right in the first row of cadets. Geoff Trott is fifth from the right in the second row.

12   This was one of a series of publicity photographs taken on a very cold winter's day in 1962. The instructor standing opposite me was a complete stranger from another squadron at RAF Leeming. Our eyes were streaming from the icy wind!

13   Another of those publicity photos. I am pretending that I know how to start a Jet Provost!

14   The formation flypast over our passing out 'Wings' Parade at RAF Leeming, 19 April 1963.

15   My RAF wings being presented to me by Air Commodore L.H. Snelling, CBE, AFC, a few days after my nineteenth birthday.

16 The official passing out photograph of No.5 Course at No.3 FTS RAF Leeming. Front row (left to right): Roger Hayes, Howell Davies, Colin Woods, Chris Blake, me, John Sims, Ian Cornish-Underwood. Back row (left to right): Graham Franklin, Mick Green, Sgt Jones (?), George Millington, Smudge Smith, Brian Jones, Tony Stafford.

17 The unofficial passing out photograph (Roger Hayes on the far right was, as usual, late on parade!).

18   The old Italian control tower at Idris airfield. (Gp Capt Tom Eeles RAF (Ret.))

19   Canberra B2 Prototype VX 165.

20 Production Canberra B2, WH 649.

21 My faithful 1949 Mercedes at Laarbruch – bought for 500 DM (£50) after many not very careful owners.

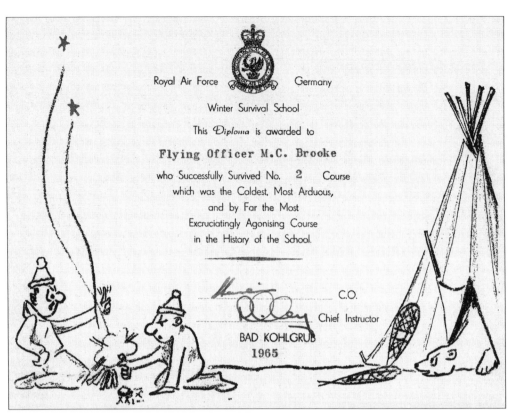

Royal Air Force Germany

Winter Survival School

This *Diploma* is awarded to

Flying Officer M.C. Brooke

who Successfully Survived No. 2 Course
which was the Coldest, Most Arduous,
and by Far the Most
Excruciatingly Agonising Course
in the History of the School.

C.O.

Chief Instructor

BAD KOHLGRUB

1965

LAAR RAF FLYING II SEP 64 PORT U.C. WHEEL HUB FAILURE
A.C.W.T. 330

24   Mike Kelly's Canberra B(I)8 leading four F-105 Thunderchiefs over the 16 Squadron site. The QRA area is prominent, with its two white sheds. The Canberra on the ground (just in front of the nearest 'Thud') is having a nuclear weapon loaded to take over from one of the aircraft on QRA. This happened on Thursdays.

Opposite:

22   The graduation certificate from the RAF Germany Winter Survival School, January 1965.

23   The broken wheel of Canberra B(I)8 WT 330 after our heavy landing at RAF Idris in Libya. The four old fatigue fractures are ringed.

26   B(I)8 XM265 of No.16 Squadron in conventional weapons fit with gun pack.

27   Canberra B(I)8 on approach to land.

Opposite:

25   The author's own 'artist's impression' of a 16 Squadron B(I)8 releasing a dummy nuclear weapon (a Shape) from a LABS manouvre at Nordhorn range.

28 The Boss leading in the returnees from the detachment to Kuantan, Malaya. His navigator, Squadron Leader Ian Suren, is flying the squadron Jolly Roger out of the door.

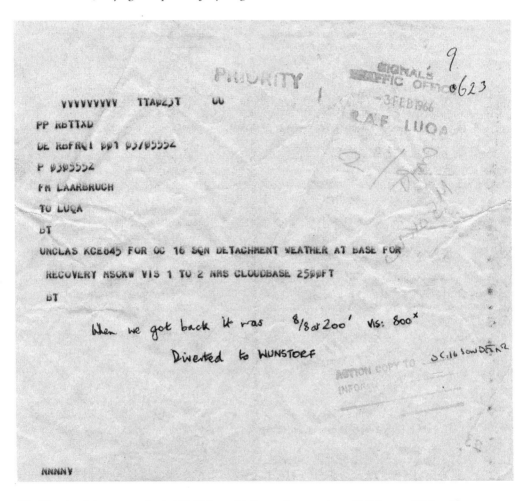

29 The signal that we received at RAF Luqa, Malta, on the morning of 3 February 1966, with my subsequent handwritten comment!

18

Surviving and Evading

In early 1965 Geoff and I were told that we would be going on the RAF Winter Survival Course at a place called Bad Köhlgrub in Bavaria. However, Geoff wasn't able to go on the same course as me; he was back in the UK on his post-Christmas leave. Another nav from 16 Squadron was going in his place and he was Flying Officer Harold 'Wedge' Wainman. How he got his nickname I never found out, but he was universally known as Wedge. He usually flew with a chap called Guy Pearce who, I believe, was also going to be away. So Wedge and I got all our cold weather kit packed and ready to go. It all started with yet another ride in a springless and very cold RAF coach, this time as far as the railway station in Mönchengladbach, about an hour away. There we met up with the rest of the RAF Germany contingent and boarded our sleeper train to Munich. It was a noisy night with not much sleep.

When we arrived in Munich we boarded another coach for the final leg of our journey to the school itself, which was in a typical Bavarian alpine village. The snow was, as expected, deep and crisp and even. The course started with a 'Meet and Greet' over coffee, with the students and staff all getting to know each other. I knew some of the other RAF Germany pilots and navs from training days and there was also a five-man crew from a UK Valiant squadron. Before the course was over they would receive the news that the whole Valiant force had been grounded for good, due to fatigue cracks in the old bombers' main wing-spar. The school's CO and most of the staff were RAF personnel, but the adjutant was an ex-RAF SNCO who had retired and settled in the local area. He had an Alsatian dog, called Fritz. Both Fritz and the Adj seemed to us even more German than some of the locals! There was also a USAF officer on an exchange posting; he looked and sounded like a wiry backwoodsman from deepest Tennessee.

We soon learnt that the programme would include some classroom work on the principles of winter survival and escape and evasion. But the good news was that we would spend most of the first week skiing. So we were issued with appropriate kit: skis, poles, boots, balaclavas, gloves and anoraks. On the second morning we boarded another bus and took the half hour journey to the slopes near Oberammergau. I had never skied before so I was looking forward with eager anticipation to trying it. We got ourselves out onto the nursery slopes and lined up. Those that had been downhill on planks before were taken off to the higher slopes and we novices were left with our lantern-jawed *skimeister* Hans. At first he took it very gently with us, just putting the skis on and not falling over was lesson number one. Then we were taught how to stop. A wise move I would learn later.

After lunch we progressed, or at least some of us did, to basic turns and speed control. It was all great fun; by the end of the day I'd started spending more time upright than sitting in the snow. I also had pain in muscles that I didn't know I possessed. Those were eased by an evening out in the village, testing various bars and their beers.

The first week went by in similar vein. Varying levels of improvement were being demonstrated on the slopes and some beginners, regrettably not me, had graduated to the upper echelons. I was still making star-shaped holes too frequently for Hans to let me go any higher. His rapidly receding voice from behind me shouting, 'Bend ze knees!' is what I remember most. If my skill on skis wasn't improving much my fitness was, which was the whole idea. I did finally start getting the hang of it and was allowed to graduate from the nursery to the 'primary school' slopes. This meant using a ski tow, which was another learning curve, an especially steep curve when there are queues of folk who've actually paid for their day's skiing behind you! And most of them seemed to be school kids. There was also one old boy who had a leg missing and who was zooming down the slopes on one ski like an Olympic champion. He had tiny little skis fitted to his ski poles.

By the end of our first week we were ready to go on the escape and evasion phase. This was started at the end of a day's further skiing, to simulate being shot down at night after a full day's work. We dressed in our winter flying kit, were searched for illicit items, like hip flasks or matches, and then issued with a normal European survival kit and a large knife in a holster. We boarded the bus and set off in the dark. After about half an hour the bus stopped and the first team of four were dropped off. Then it stopped every 5 minutes or so and a team despatched into the snowy darkness. We had been briefed on where we had to get to by midday the following day and one team member had a map. When it was our turn we were dropped off at the side of the road and headed across snow-covered meadows in the right initial direction. Wedge and I were teamed up with Frank Bebbington and Dave Rolf, a crew from No.3 Sqn at RAF Geilenkirchen; Dave had the map. Although there was no moon, the sky was clear and once our night vision had kicked in it wasn't too difficult to see where we were going. The worst thing was the depth of the snow, it was really hard work kicking a path through it, so every half hour or so we changed leaders.

At one point Frank was leading and we were going into an area with small fir trees sticking up through the snow. As he passed close to one of these he just disappeared! We all rushed over to the hole from which we could hear Frank's voice calling out that he was OK, but that he was halfway up a large conifer. These weren't small trees at all; they were tall trees with metres of snow around them. Getting too close had meant that Frank had fallen through the upper branches. After some effort we finally extricated him and went our way giving these 'small' trees a wide berth.

In the pre-exercise briefing we had been told that German Army Ski Troops would be out looking for us, and that at some point we would all be captured and taken in for interrogation. Like everyone else we had decided that we wouldn't be so dumb as to get caught. So, as we navigated our way across country we were also on the lookout for the 'enemy'. We walked for several hours and reached a small stream where it was crossed by a road. There was a gully underneath the road and as we scouted to see whether it was safe to cross the open ground a vehicle came around the corner and two white-clad soldiers jumped out, pointed guns at us and shouted in German.

The rules of engagement were that once a gun was trained on you that was it; you weren't supposed to run away. However, there were four of us and two of them, so Frank dropped out of sight into the gully. As the guys rounded us up I jumped over the place where Frank was hiding hoping that he wouldn't be seen. He wasn't; however, he was captured not long afterwards.

We were bundled into the back of the small Jeep-type vehicle and set off up the road. We soon arrived at a group of buildings that we took to be Enemy HQ. Sure enough it was and we were roughly manhandled off the Jeep and told to line up facing the wall. We then had to strip to our underwear and lean on the wall with our arms up and stretched forward and our feet wide apart. After a very short time it was agonising and very cold. Guards were watching us and they quickly and roughly put those who had moved back into position.

Every now and then someone would be led away, no doubt for interrogation. Occasional shouts and screams could be heard coming from inside. It was all very realistic and one couldn't help becoming a bit apprehensive. Finally my turn came. I was allowed to put my clothes back on, which was a real relief, and then I was frog-marched into a very brightly lit room where a member of the master race was sitting smoking a cigarette. I was pushed onto a bare wooden chair and he asked me which squadron I was serving on. As per the Geneva Convention rules, I told him only my number, rank and name. He repeated the question. I repeated my answer. I wondered how long this would go on. Not much longer was the answer. He tried then to engage me in conversation by asking about my erstwhile home in Yorkshire, for which he had the correct address.

I gave some sort of non-committal answer and he then started on another tack. After a while I had said nothing of any consequence and had got heartily sick of reciting my number, rank and name. I think that he was getting fed up too, so he said that I would be taken away and given electric shock treatment. Would I like to reconsider my answers now? I declined, so a floozy was called and I was pulled roughly from the room. The next thing I knew I was outside and being told to head off that way, so no electrical stimulation to warm me up.

Now I was on my own, but I soon found myself with Wedge. He had been released immediately after me. We met up with a couple of other guys and made our way toward the river, on the other side of which was our rendezvous and supposedly neutral territory. No sooner had we got up a steady pace than we came round a corner smack into another small patrol of troops. However, when we told them that we had only just been released and that we had been interrogated, they let us go on our way. If only war could be like that!

We then plodded on into the dawn. By now I was seeing soldiers everywhere, under trees, against hedgerows and crossing fields in the distance. When I pointed them out, nobody else could see them. I thought I could see camouflage netting spread over the hedgerows as well. Later on I found out two things: these were stress and fatigue-induced hallucinations and most of my fellow course members had suffered something similar.

By now we had reached the river, so we were getting close to the final rendezvous. There was a road bridge close by but we had spotted real, not imaginary, Army guards on it. So we decided to wade the river. It was flowing quickly but it seemed to be reasonably shallow, running over stones and rocks. I chose to take my boots off, remove both pairs of socks and then put my boots back on. It was freezing! But it wouldn't last too long. Once on the other side I took off my sodden boots, put my dry socks back on and then replaced the boots. It felt like heaven, all warm and soft. A brisk half hour walk later we were in sight of the rendezvous. As we covered the last couple of hundred metres there appeared to be lots of folk taking photographs and even film. Was I hallucinating again? Whatever, I decided that a cheery wave was in order and a quote from a long dead hero of Everest, 'We did it because it was there,' I declared.

Now all we had to do was survive another four days in the snow and well below zero night temperatures. To help us do that we were each given three panels from a parachute. Well, this was going to be a doddle, I thought sarcastically. It was now about mid-afternoon and we had until dark to make our camouflaged single-man overnight shelters.

As I selected somewhere to start building, I passed a couple of people who were already well advanced with their homes for the night. We had been told that the staff would search the area and if they could find anyone's shelter they would be turned out of 'bed' and have to start all over again, in the dark!

I found a tree, well away from the path, and remembering how Frank had disappeared into one just like it I dug down until I had found the base. I then went to another tree and cut off a whole load of branches to put underneath me as insulation. I then laid my parachute panels on top of that and proceeded to manufacture a sort of A-frame tent underneath the lowest branches of the tree. The next trick was to try to camouflage the outside with snow, so I did as much as I could from the outside and then retreated into my hole, all the while pulling snow onto the branches above me. I didn't know whether it would work but it was the best I could manage. Now all I could do was munch a couple of the Horlicks tablets from the ration pack and, using my aircrew torch sparingly, get myself wrapped up for the night. I had read or heard that it was a good, if not too apparently logical, idea to sleep with my boots off. So I removed them and put them under the excess silk at the top of my sleeping cocoon as a sort of pillow. It was dark and I was tired so I fell asleep quickly and spent a comfortable enough night, not waking until dawn. My feet weren't cold at all.

Once I had woken and got out of my hidey-hole, a member of the staff came round to tell me where to go for the briefing. I dismantled my bivouac and took my parachute panels with me to a large clearing in the woods, where very welcome hot drinks were served and our original groups were reinstated. We were then told to go and make shelters appropriate to the size of our group and start settling down for another three days.

So that's what we did. After a day's work we had made quite a good lean-to shelter, started a fire, boiled snow for drinking and were making a meal out of oatmeal blocks and Oxo cubes. You'll eat anything if that's all you've got. The first night went by quite well and by day two we were getting into the swing of it. It was still very cold and it was very easy to get dehydrated; in the cold, thirst doesn't trigger the need to drink like it does in the heat. The first sign of dehydration was a raging headache and when I started to get one I stopped all activity and drank as much as I could, as quickly as I could. One snag was that our water was limited by the size of our containers; also it takes about 10 litres of snow to make 1 litre of water.

Then everyone was summoned to go back to the clearing, where we found ourselves looking at several, sweet, furry bunnies in cages. This is when our Tennessee backwoodsman stepped into the spotlight. He was going to show us how to kill and skin one of the said bunnies and then some of us could have a go. If all this hadn't been serious enough, we now had to kill our dinner, and such a cute dinner. But we had a trick up our sleeves. Wedge's Dad was a butcher in Melton Mowbray and, before joining the RAF, Wedge had done the butchery course!

So, after the American had shown us how it should be done, he asked for a volunteer to 'do' another rabbit. We pushed Wedge forward. At first he acted the dumb survivor very well and we could see the staff all nudging each other expecting a bloodbath. But jaws dropped when Wedge gave the little furry creature an accurate *coup de grace* that worked first time. They dropped even further when Wedge expertly skinned it and then cut it into joints fit for hanging in a butcher's window. He then made sure that he collected the best bits for us.

After an afternoon of collecting snow for making water, adding more branches to the shelter, cutting wood for the fire and an abortive attempt at fishing in the local stream we settled down for the evening. But a survivor's work is never done and we had to prepare our rabbit feast. I got nominated for that and I managed to cook it long enough to make it tender and I added some more oatmeal to thicken and an Oxo cube to flavour the stew. Eventually I dished it up and we all munched away appreciatively. The funny thing was that we couldn't eat it all. Our stomachs had shrunk so much that they filled up in no time.

Life went on and before long a big German helicopter was there to give us the experience of being winched, but they couldn't fly us out because the weather at the other end wasn't suitable. So we walked to a road where the bus picked us up and took us back to Bad Köhlgrub. It was time for baths or showers and a party.

During the night I found myself running to the loo, shivering and feverish. By morning I was feeling very ill and the Medical Officer came to see me.

'You've got dysentery,' he announced. I thought that dysentery was a tropical disease, but not so. I blamed the rabbit; a sort of furry Montezuma's revenge. He gave me lots of pills and a bottle of foul-tasting liquid. However, I didn't miss the final day of the course, on which were the downhill ski races for the various ability groups; unsurprisingly I was unplaced! So that was all over; surviving in the cold, evading the enemy and getting dysentery. It was, in retrospect, a great experience and I learnt a lot. So back to the real world and flying again.

19

Huntin', Shootin' and Dive Bombin'

The Canberra B(I)8 was originally designed for conventional, not nuclear, warfare. Its gestation was via the first of the English Electric's second-generation bombers, which was given the mark number of B5. This model was to have had a two-man crew with a radar bombing system fitted. In the event the radar didn't materialise and so the layout of the B2 was resurrected, but with larger Avon 109 engines, additional fuel tanks in the wings and wing-mounted, weapon-carriage pylons; this was the B6. The PR7 was a similar update of the PR3, but without the weapons carriage capability. The original Mk5 prototype was then re-engineered by English Electric as the B(I) Mk8 for a new Day/Night Interdictor requirement. The fighter canopy, a gunpack in the rear half of the bomb bay and its overall black gloss finish were the distinctive features of the B(I)8 when it was first displayed in public by Bee Beamont at the 1954 SBAC Farnborough Air Show.

The (I) in the mark designation stands for Interdictor and gives a clue as to the specification it was designed to fulfil. Interdiction means that the targets to be attacked are usually well behind enemy lines and are usually those that affect the re-supply and logistic support of the front-line forces – targets like railheads, docks, bridges, major assembly points, airfields and military depots. The specification also called for the aircraft to have the ability to do that operational task by day and by night; hence the company painting the prototype black. Altogether English Electric built seventy-two of this mark and some were exported to several overseas air forces.

The B(I)8 could be fitted with a Boulton Paul gun pack in the rear half of the bomb bay. This pack was furnished with four 20mm Hispano cannons and a feed system that could be loaded with up to 500 rounds per gun. The muzzle velocity was relatively low and the firing rate was 600 rounds per minute. It was possible to select the guns in pairs from the cockpit, which gave the option of longer, on-range training times. In operational use all four guns would be fired simultaneously. Although two 1,000lb bombs could be carried in the front half of the bomb bay this was not the normal practice. Special carriers were fitted to take sixteen parachute flares; this option facilitated night attacks, more of which later. The two wing pylons could carry one 1,000lb bomb each.

By the time that the B(I)8 came into service in RAF Germany, where it was most needed, the Project E agreement had added a nuclear strike role to the squadrons. In the nuclear role the RAF chain of command answered to NATO, so all nuclear capable aircraft were declared to NATO's supreme commander, known by the acronym SACEUR. He was based at NATO HQ near Brussels and was a four-star US General. However, as part of the original agreement a period of national use was allowed, with the time to practise the conventional interdiction role.

So every year the RAF Germany Canberra squadrons were allowed to withdraw a number of their aircraft from the nuclear capability for a period of one month. This time could be extended if national priorities dictated; although I imagine that would have been a matter for negotiation at the highest levels within NATO. During these periods it was normal to hold four aircraft out of the establishment of twelve to maintain QRA.

In November 1964, No.16 Squadron's turn came and the conventional weapons Armament Practise Camp (APC) would be held in Malta, using the targets at Tarhuna in Libya and a big lump of rock off the west coast of Malta called Filfa. Geoff and I were selected to go, so we had a preliminary training session in the T4 with an ex-Hunter fighter pilot called Tony Hilton. It was all very exciting. We went to Nordhorn and flew dummy academic shallow dive bombing (SDB) and air-to-ground gunnery attacks. The academic pattern was flown at about 1,500ft, a bit like a large visual landing pattern. However, abeam the target the nose was pulled up and a roll towards the target was made. The top-out height was about 3,000ft and when the line-up with the target had been achieved, one over-banked and let the nose drop until the target was on the nose and the dive angle was at least 30°. It didn't sound much in the briefing, but it certainly felt a lot steeper in practice. The nav had to call out the rapidly reducing height and it was the pilot's job to maintain the dive angle and monitor the speed. The bomb had to leave the aircraft at 1,500ft and a 3 to 3.5G pull initiated immediately; we were supposed to clear the ground by at least 500ft. The gunnery circuit was similar, except that there was no pull-up at the turn-in point. After a level turn onto the attack heading, at an appropriate distance from the target, the aircraft was put into a dive of 8 to 10° and the wings were levelled. The aim was to fire at a range of between 600 and 300 yards. The minimum height on the pullout had to be 300ft to avoid ricochets or debris. Shooting yourself down was difficult to explain rationally to the powers that be. Even a few holes in your jet would not be received with joy!

When we were flying the B(I)8 the results of our attempts to drill holes in the ground were measured in two ways. In the port wing root there was a tiny circular window and behind that was a movie camera, so every time the trigger was pressed the film ran. This was then analysed by the weapons specialists, like Tony, at the debrief. The other way was that the gunnery targets were large white canvas panels, 15ft square, and after we had fired the range personnel went out and counted the holes we had made. They took with them a pot of paint and a brush and painted around the holes that they had counted. The number was sent to the squadron where it was converted to a percentage of the number of rounds fired.

Flying the patterns was all very busy stuff and it wasn't easy to achieve the right combination of heights, speeds and distances from the targets. Although great fun for someone like me, who liked throwing the jet around, it all needed real application and concentration to get anywhere near the right parameters. Doing it in the T4, with its comparatively poor field of view and different handling qualities, made it even harder work.

By the end of the one and a half hour sortie I was pretty tired.

'Wait until you do it in formation,' was the only consolation that Tony offered. The T4 didn't have a gunsight so all the aiming we'd done was a bit academic. The reflector gunsight in the B(I)8 had a ring and a central dot, known as the pipper. It was where the pipper was that mattered, although the ring was useful for giving one an idea of range.

Two weeks later Geoff and I, along with some other aircrew and a goodly contingent of our groundcrew, boarded a Transport Command Britannia and flew to Malta. There were lots of spare wheels and crates of other parts sharing the long cabin with us. For the next week we dropped lots of our

25lb practise bombs into the desert at Tarhuna from dive attacks. Some of them got fairly near the target and then we were allowed to get airborne with 800 20mm cannon rounds in our belly. The target this time was a 'splash target', the splash being made by a special board towed by an RAF Air Sea Rescue Launch, which was operating in an area of sea about 20 miles east of Malta. We were briefed to fire the guns two at a time, giving us about 20 minutes on the target. We found the boat with no trouble, the weather was perfect, and I tipped in for the first attack. It was a bit odd because we had to attack from abeam and so the target was actually disappearing stage right at 30kts. A bit of lead to start with and the judicious use of increasing bank to hold the aiming point was the way to do it! All that went out of my head as I pulled the trigger for the first time. I was expecting the sort of thing I'd seen in war films: shaking instruments, loud noises and the smell of cordite.

Of course it was nothing like that. Just a rippling vibration from the bowels of the aircraft and, a second or so later, splashes in the water – nowhere near the target! Geoff called the pull-up height loudly and off we went round again. By the end of our time on the boat we had thrown all our bullets into the Mediterranean and had actually started to get much closer to the splash.

By the end of the detachment we had got the basics of SDB and air-to-ground gunnery sown up, but we weren't in Division One yet. Our last two sorties were to be non-academic patterns; they were what were known as Operational Attacks or 'Pattern Whiskey'. On those the SDB pattern was flown at low level and 330kts, the pull-up was done using an increase in power and topping out at about 5,000ft.

Because we were practising for dropping the real thing the release height was higher, to allow us to pull-up and have at least 1,500ft between the bomb and us when it went off. The debris zone of a 1,000lb bomb was pretty big. I tried a couple of 'dry' runs to get the hang of it and then went round for a live attack. It all went very well and I got a reasonable score.

The next one didn't go at all well. Somehow I got the turn-in too far ahead of the dive so arrived on the attack heading with nowhere near the right angle of dive. So, with a warning to Geoff to hang on, I pushed. The negative G caused Geoff's navigator's bag to join me in the cockpit. He was floating above the couch in the nose. So, with my right hand trying to push the nav bag down into the crash seat and my left still pushing the stick forward, the target appeared in the gunsight.

Geoff was, by now, calling out the heights, which were rapidly approaching our release height. Thankfully the nav bag had disappeared and I could change hands back just in time to push the bomb release button. I checked the speed and height. Amazingly it was spot on. I pulled out and the range called me to announce that we had achieved a Delta Hotel – a direct hit! So that's how it was done? I don't think so. The remaining two attack patterns were much more conventional but there were no more DHs.

As we flew back in the Britannia I thought that it was sad that we might have to wait another year before we had another go at this conventional weapons stuff. It was much more fun than the nuclear role exercises. So was the detachment. When we got time off it was great to be on a Mediterranean island, even in November. We went to the beaches and even went swimming less than a month before Christmas. Then there was the squadron night out in Valetta that ended up with several groups of us hiring horse-drawn traps and racing each other to a nightclub in Floriana. Mind you, one group went a bit far: they paid the cabman enough for him to let them unbridle his horse and bring it into the nightclub. Management was not impressed!

Then there were all the other tourist sights like the Mosta Dome, the Blue Grotto and the skyline city of Rabat-Medina, all reached by hair-raising rides on the Maltese buses. In those days they were all ancient and driven over the rough Maltese roads at ridiculous speeds, especially downhill in neutral. It was no wonder that the driver's cabs were invariably decorated like shrines, with lots of crucifixes and Madonnas, and that all the passengers crossed themselves furiously when they got aboard.

As we got back to normal at Laarbruch little did any of us know how soon the squadron would be back in its conventional interdiction role – and not for practise this time.

20

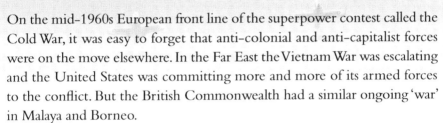

The Squadron Goes Into Battle

On the mid-1960s European front line of the superpower contest called the Cold War, it was easy to forget that anti-colonial and anti-capitalist forces were on the move elsewhere. In the Far East the Vietnam War was escalating and the United States was committing more and more of its armed forces to the conflict. But the British Commonwealth had a similar ongoing 'war' in Malaya and Borneo.

After the end of the Second World War, Indonesia had become progressively more anti-colonial. The Dutch had granted the country independence and that aspiration was contagious. Similar elements in Malaya had provoked conflict there, in which the UK armed forces had played a major role. In 1957 the British Government had granted Malaya independence and two years later it allowed Singapore to become self-governing. This was all a part of the UK's strategy to withdraw from its South-east Asian colonies. In May 1961, the UK and Malayan governments proposed the formation of a Malaysian Federation, which would bring together the peninsular states of Malaya and Singapore as well as the three states on the northern half of the island of Borneo: Sarawak, Sabah and Brunei. However, the Sultan of Brunei was not enthusiastic about joining the Federation and in September 1963, after a revolt there, he decided to remain independent. That was when the Federation of Malaysia formally came into being (Singapore didn't stay long either, becoming an independent republic in 1965).

The immediate reaction from Indonesia was furious, they saw the formation of the Federation as a neo-colonial threat, especially to their part of Borneo. The Malaysian ambassador was expelled from the Indonesian capital of Jakarta and riots broke out in Singapore and Kuala Lumpar. Tensions rose to fever pitch on each side of the Straits of Malacca and, by mid-1964, despite earlier attempts at forging peace, each side was involved in military conflict. In Borneo, border crossings were happening regularly and casualties were mounting on both sides. British and other Commonwealth armed forces had been involved for some years, but containment was not working. This was not a declared war; the Indonesians called it Confrontation and everyone else followed their lead.

In late 1964 attacks were being made by Indonesian insurgents on the Malaysian peninsula by sea and there was one rather abortive attempt at a paratroop assault; one of the two Indonesian C-130s involved in the raid crashed, killing all on board. UK, Australian and New Zealand air forces based in Singapore and Malaya were being drawn into the action. However, it was deemed that more air assets were required. So, in very early 1965, the British MOD was tasked with supplying more tactical aircraft into theatre. They were to be based on the peninsula to carry out attacks against any Indonesian forces that made incursions into West Malaysia, as well as being capable of interdiction into Indonesia.

So the New Year for 16 Squadron started with being put on notice to deploy to West Malaysia, specifically to an airfield called Kuantan. The squadron would be fully stood down from its NATO role, so QRA would cease while the deployment was on. Many cheers were heard around the place. Eight aircraft would deploy with a dozen crews. The management 'wheels' went into several huddles to decide whom they would choose to go. As Geoff and I hadn't completed all the conventional weapons training it wasn't a great surprise to find that our names were not on the list. It was still a huge disappointment though. There was also frantic activity in the navigation empire. The detachment had to fly out in formation and on the leg from Bahrain, in the Arabian Gulf, to the Indian Ocean Island base at Gan there were no decent diversion airfields. What's more, the aircraft were going to be operating at the limit of their range on the leg from Gan to Malaya. The merits of carrying tip tanks or not, flying level at maximum range speeds or whether to cruise climb at the optimum indicated Mach number were all exhaustively discussed. Geoff and I just got on with the usual flying.

After the majority of the squadron had departed south-east, and once the dust had settled, there was one task that needed doing: to go and get the two aircraft out of the QRA area. They had, of course, been disarmed and their bombs taken back to the weapons storage facility. Two pilots were to be detailed to go and bring the jets back to the squadron dispersals, from where they would be put back in circulation. Mike Gamble and I were standing in the wrong place at the wrong time, so we had to do the job. We asked the duty authorising officer if we could carry out a practise scramble, as long as we promised not to take-off (the aircraft needed some engineering action before they could fly again). He agreed so we briefed the groundcrew. We didn't have navs with us so we agreed that I would call the start-up. I also agreed to explain to Air Traffic Control that we were going to exit the QRA gate and enter the runway for a curtailed take-off, clearing at the first exit and taxiing back to the squadron dispersal area.

So, when I called for engine start I could, for the first and hopefully the last time, push both start buttons at the same time and watch the engines wind up. We were told later that it was quite impressive with four starter cartridges firing up simultaneously. Then it was out through the gates at a bit of a lick; I was first and Mike following.

ATC gave us immediate clearance to enter the runway and, as I applied full power, I noted that it had taken just over a minute from the 'Go' call. Pretty good! At 70kts I shut the throttles and braked to a safe taxiing speed, turned off the runway and taxied back to the pan. As I was getting out of the aircraft, I saw a fire engine dash past. It went round the corner to where the other ex-QRA jet was parked. It turned out that my colleague had got a bit carried away with the excitement of it all and had gone shooting past the exit, then had to hammer the brakes to turn off further up. The long taxi back didn't help and when he turned into his parking area the groundcrew had spotted flames coming from one of his wheels! I left him to explain himself to the Flight Commander.

Life soon settled into a routine of us practising more conventional weapons deliveries at Nordhorn range, picking up some of the tasks that always came our way, like fighter affiliation, where NATO fighters of various types tried to shoot us down. The only drawback from my point of view was that we weren't supposed to evade – just stooge along in straight and level flight, pretending that we didn't care. However, there were some fighters still in service, like the Dutch Air Force Republic F84 Thunderjets, that couldn't touch us when we were at or above 40,000ft. But the supersonic Lockheed F104 Starfighter was replacing them and that had no problem in getting up there, although its tiny wing meant that it wasn't too good at turning.

One of the things that I had to do was to supervise the 'JP' as he worked up his formation flying and leading a pair of aircraft at low level and on the range. It all went very well and he quickly picked up the right skills, except on his first sortie leading me as his number two. It was right at the end of the trip that it all went to pot. He had briefed for a departure and arrival on the westerly runway, which would require a right-hand break on arrival. But when we pulled up at the Rhine, Laarbruch ATC informed him that the wind had changed and that we would be landing on the easterly runway. Now that meant that it would be a left-hand circuit. So to make a break at a 3-second interval from close formation I had to be on the leader's right, in echelon starboard.

We flew around the airfield to position for this manoeuvre and my leader correctly called me into echelon starboard; that meant I was on his right about half a wingspan away. As we ran in for the break, at 350kts and 500ft, I tightened up my position to make it look good and 'JP' called, 'Breaking, breaking – GO!' At which point he broke to starboard instead of port! I pushed hard to let him fly over the top of us and then was faced with a view of the southern taxiway rapidly rushing up towards me, with a 31 Squadron PR7 taxiing along it.

So now it was a 4G pull and chase my leader around, but from a correct left-hand circuit. Needless to say, there was plenty of sarcastic comment from the PR7 and ATC. Although I was initially very angry that we had just so nearly been wiped out, I couldn't help feel sorry for him. He had briefed for a right-hand break and the runway change hadn't fully sunk in. He was still relatively new and I was glad that it wasn't any worse. In fact, he ended up going out to Kuantan when one of the pilots there had to come back prematurely. To say I was jealous was a huge understatement! But that, as they say, is the way that the cookie sometimes crumbles. The squadron was at Kuantan for about four months and, of course, we were regaled with many stories about their experiences when the crews got home.

These tales covered the following very varied topics: the high humidity and heat; leeches; mosquitoes; tents with uncomfortable beds; out-of-date maps; our Scottish Armament Officer blowing up old explosives to great effect; and enviable anecdotes about time on the beach and downtown Kuantan, some of the latter not being too savoury.

The flying was evidently uncomplicated compared with back 'home' – few airspace restrictions and very little ATC service. Just map reading your way about – although the maps were unreliable – and dropping bombs and shooting on China Rock range. One truly operational sortie was flown against a reported Indonesian incursion on the peninsula. The jungle there was liberally sprayed with 20mm bullets, but no one heard if it was effective. The real challenge at Kuantan was night operations. The single runway had poor quality and unreliable electric lighting, so that had to be supplemented by the old fashioned, paraffin-fuelled 'gooseneck' lamps, an object that looked like a very large oil-can with a wick shoved down the neck. The bad news was that there were only enough to light one side of the runway. It's a good job that the Canberra was fitted with a retractable landing light.

One crew, Paddy Carver and Mike Bush, had a very nasty experience one night when, at fairly low speed in the circuit, both engines started to misbehave badly. By dint of excellent flying by Paddy and support from Mike with the checklist, they managed to sort the problem out. They won a very well deserved 'Green Endorsement'[1] in their logbooks from the Commander-in-Chief.

The squadron arrived back in early June, in time for the squadron's fiftieth anniversary celebrations. As the saying goes, I counted them all out and I counted them all back; I just wish that I'd been with them.

Notes

1 A Green Endorsement was an accolade for exceptional ability applied to an emergency situation, written in the crew's logbooks, in green ink, and signed by the C-in-C.

21

NATO Exercises

To ensure that the squadron was well practised in all the possibilities that went with our NATO nuclear strike role, there were several nominated exercises that we had to complete. The most important of these was called TACEVAL, NATO-speak for TACtical EVALuation. This would normally happen about every two years and was the one exercise that could make or break the careers of squadron and station executives; but more of TACEVAL later.

Apart from the call-outs specifically for the QRA crews, which didn't seem to have a name – well, except for 'OHNONOTAGAIN' by those on shift – there were two major exercises that could be initiated on the instructions of HQ 2ATAF or by the Station Commander. They were Exercises MINEVAL and QUICKTRAIN. The former was a fairly regular event that usually lasted for 24 hours and was a recurrent practise of the station's ability to gear up for its war role. For 16 Squadron this meant getting all personnel not on leave into work as quickly as possible, then getting at least ten aircraft ready to go to war. Real weapons or dummies, called 'shapes', may or may not be loaded and any real ones would be downloaded before any flying took place. Exercise QUICKTRAIN was similar, but all the aircraft generated would be loaded with the real weapons and no flying was planned. The exercise ended when the final aircraft had been loaded and accepted by its aircrew.

The initial call-out of personnel was accomplished in several ways. The first was by the station 'hooter'. This was a very loud bass sound, just like a ship's whistle, which penetrated the air for a radius of at least 5 miles. After I got married we lived in a flat in a village just outside the wire. Our landlord was Laarbruch's Chief Heating Engineer and, although I had been woken already, he used to rush to the bottom of the stairs and shout up, 'Ees ze bloody 'ooter, ees ze bloody 'ooter!' Everyone on base usually heard the hooter, but to back it up the fire vehicles used to drive round the domestic areas with all their blues and twos going. For people who lived well away from camp there was a telephone callout roster.

Just how much the sound of the hooter became a part of life was well illustrated when we were once in Gibraltar. By early evening there were several Canberra crews from Germany in the Officers' Mess bar. It was, as usual, warm and all the doors and windows were open. When a ship in the harbour sounded its whistle about ten pint glasses were slammed down on tables and the bar and their owners all started to get to their feet and head for the door. Then we all realised we were not in Germany and relaxed, laughing foolishly.

After the station hooter sounded the 'wacky races' followed, as everyone drove around camp at breakneck speeds, doing the macho thing of trying to be the first one in! Once at the squadron we aircrew first had to change into flying kit and then report to the operations room to be allocated our aircraft. The mission number and order of departure would be the same as for our real targets. Then it was retire to the crewroom and do what we were so good at: waiting.

Tedium soon set in for us aircrew, as the groundcrews and armourers sweated away outside getting the aircraft ready. This was the only time that I recall wishing I was on QRA; those guys would be back at the bridge table or in bed by now. I'll never forget arriving at the squadron one night and hearing our squadron clerk walking down a corridor singing with gusto and real sincerity, 'This is a lovely way to spend an evening, can't think of anything I'd rather do.'

If there was to be flying then we had to plan a sortie. The stream take-off that we would do had a specific and rather complex pattern to make sure that we were quickly separated from each other as soon as practical. Working up from crewroom standby to cockpit readiness and then to release could be quite exciting, although a couple of hours strapped in waiting for the war to start, before you were going to spend another couple of hours in flight, was tedious and, literally, a pain in the arse.

The stream take-offs and departures were challenging as we had to sort ourselves into mission number order. On one exercise one of the guys in the middle of the stream had accelerated and then, without a word, braked and turned off the runway. As the rest of the stream took off the local controller called, 'Mission 405, why have you not got airborne?'

Silence.

'Mission 405, why have you aborted your take-off?'

More silence.

In a louder voice and with an impatient edge, 'Mission 405, the Station Commander wishes to know why you have aborted your mission?'

This time one of the guys in the outbound stream could stand it no longer so he called, 'Laarbruch, this is Mission 405. I have had a total radio failure.'

'Ah, Roger. Understood, 405, total radio failure.' Then the biggest 'thinks bubble' you ever saw rose above the control tower.

There were other NATO exercises that didn't involve pretending to wind-up for our war role, but did involve us exercising other people's jobs. ROULETTE and KINGPIN were air defence exercises in which we played the part of enemy bombers who had to be shot down. Because we could fly very high that was usually where we were for these sorties; we sat up there and watched various air forces' fighter pilots coaxing their aircraft into an attacking position from astern. I once actually observed a swept-winged fighter depart into a spin as he tried to climb and turn at the same time. I was at 48,000ft at the time!

Exercise ROUND ROBIN was a good one. We had a day out, landing at another NATO airbase, usually with lunch thrown in. This exercise was to make sure that everyone in NATO could turn round another air force's aircraft. Re-arming was rarely exercised, but refuelling and checking all the usual after- and before-flight items was. We were supposed to stay with the aircraft, to make sure that everything was done correctly and that the refuelling started with the forward fuel tank and not the rear one. One of our guys, at a French base, got called away and when he got back to the jet he found that the rear tank was being refuelled.

For a moment he thought that the refuelling was, therefore, coming to an end; then he noticed that the young Frenchman was actually bending over progressively on his ladder as the refuelling point was, very slowly, moving away from the nozzle. The pilot then spotted that the nosewheel leg looked unusually long.

'STOP – er – ARRÊTE!' he screamed, running towards the refueller and waving his arms dementedly. The man stopped and looked round to see what all the fuss was about. As he did so the aircraft settled even further onto its haunches and was on the point of overbalance. Our intelligent pilot realised that there was now only one thing he could do. He ran to the nose and leapt in through the door, bashing his shins on the sill as he did so. The momentum of his weight stopped the tail-down movement in its tracks. The snag now was that he could no longer communicate with the man on the ladder – in any language. His navigator was in station operations filing his outbound flight plan and getting the weather forecast. Thankfully, the man with the *carburante* had the presence of mind to come forward and find out what was going on. Eventually all was clear and the refuelling recommenced in the correct order.

One day Geoff and I went to the French airbase at St Dizier for an Exercise ROUND ROBIN. Everything went well and before we left we found our way to the aircrew restaurant where we had a very acceptable four-course lunch with several local Mystère pilots. However, we were astounded to see that they were all drinking wine with their *déjeuner*! Although it was not much and sometimes watered. We were offered wine and I admit that both Geoff and I had a drop of *rouge* in a glass of water, mainly to keep the RAF end up. Our usual rule was '10 hours from bottle to throttle'; it seemed to us that the French didn't fly *until* they had 60 milligrams per centilitre of alcohol in their blood! When we were taxiing out for take-off we were asked politely if we could do a low pass over the airfield before we set heading. We duly obliged with a fly-by at 250ft and 350kts. *Vive la vie Française!*

Exercises PLAYBOY and SPREADEAGLE were flown for ground defence units and Forward Air Controllers (FAC) to practise their war roles. These trips usually involved finding a camouflaged or partially concealed target or targets and carrying out a single level pass or a simulated gunnery attack on them.

On one occasion I was leading a pair of our aircraft and my number two was one of the newer guys. Because he had not yet done pairs attacks I briefed him to break off at a predetermined point, carry out a 360° turn and follow me at that distance. The FAC would then talk him onto the target. Everything went well as we approached the target, I was in radio contact with the FAC and my number two had checked in on the same radio channel. I told him to break off and then I continued with the FAC giving me directions.

Usually FACs picked some very prominent feature on the landscape in the general area of the target and used that as an easily identifiable IP for us.

So the conversation went something like: '36, can you see the single pine tree on a mound about a mile dead ahead?'

'36, affirmative.'

'36, from that tree the target's at ten o'clock[1] and 3,000 yards. A group of armoured vehicles by a brick building.'

'Roger.' By now we were pulling up and turning left with two pairs of eyes looking for the target. Once it was acquired the gunnery dive attack was completed and I called, '36 off target.'

My oppo got the same treatment. However, the next thing I heard on the radio was, 'NO, you bloody fool . . . that's us!' The last words were almost drowned out by the noise of his jet going over the FAC's head. We rejoined formation at the previously arranged rendezvous and flew home. The poor lad had got his ten o'clock and his two o'clock mixed up!

There were other national, as well as NATO, one-off or annual exercises that we got involved in. They were all usually a bit of a challenge, often involving a high-low-high profile with an intervening attack on some target, like a dam or a missile site. Sometimes, but not often enough for my liking, we in turn were attacked by fighters that we *were* allowed to try to evade.

But that happened *ad lib* in Germany. If you were just navigating your way around at low-level the fighter guys regarded you as fair game. Once I was flying as number two in a pair and we were in open battle formation, about 1,000 yards apart at 250ft, when I spotted an F-104 Starfighter, no doubt a German Air Force one, heading towards us at about 500ft. The F-104's smoky engine gave it away well before we could make out the tiny needle-shaped fuselage. He seemed to spot the leader first, so he started a turn towards him. Then he spotted me and reversed his turn. Then the leader called for us to reverse our direction using a crossover turn and, as we did so, he just didn't know which way to go! Because of its tiny wings, the F-104 had a very large turning radius and by the time we were going in the opposite direction he was back in front of us. He obviously then gave up and went on his way, no doubt *Gott unt himmel*-ing to himself.

On another occasion we were flying back to Laarbruch at low level after a range sortie at Nordhorn. Geoff called my attention to an aircraft pulling up at two o'clock.

'It's a Javelin,' he said. I was actually watching a distant Javelin on my left, so I responded, 'Don't you mean ten o'clock?'

There was a miniscule pause while he looked at his watch.

'No, I mean two o'clock, boyo. I think he's going to have a go at us.'

I stayed low and straight and put the speed up to see what happened. Sure enough the guy on our right was pulling over to attack us from right astern. I looked left and the other Javelin was now doing the same on our left. I started to hope that they were talking to each other. By now we were flying as fast and as low as I dared, so I twisted round to see how things were developing behind us. Then I looked in the rear-view mirror just in time to see two fighter pilots taking violent avoiding action on each other! Two-nil to us.

Notes

1   This is the Clock Code; it is much used in flying whereby twelve o'clock is dead ahead and six o'clock directly astern, etc.

22

Rivalry and Helping Out

The only other operational squadron at Laarbruch in the mid-1960s was No.31 Squadron, equipped with the PR7 Canberra. Their role was tactical, day and night photographic reconnaissance. They inhabited an area in the south-west quadrant of the airfield, diametrically opposite No.16 Squadron's hangar and dispersal area. There was a healthy rivalry between the two squadrons, mainly because there was no one else to be rivals with. The two roles were not really comparable and the only thing that we had in common was that we flew the same type, if not mark, of aircraft.

Photo-recce has always had a dubious name among the bomber and fighter communities, despite the fact that we couldn't do a lot of our work without the photo-recce that was put in beforehand, and that the intelligence community would be blind without it. We combat crews saw the PR boys as somewhat emasculated. We reckoned that they went to war and flew about going, 'Click, click . . . F8 at 100th!' We thought that they saw themselves as the aristocrats of warfare, not getting their souls dirty by actually killing people and damaging property. Moreover, a recce pilot would never tire of telling you how difficult it was to fly in a straight line and take a series of pretty pictures.

Of course much of 31's work was, like ours, done at low level, predominately using side-facing F95 cameras. So they used to sneak off on their own to do their nefarious work all over Germany and the UK. Sometimes they even flew in the dark, using n-million candlepower photoflash flares. The flares made an enormous bang and a brilliant flash that lit up the ground for miles around, but not for long. However, it was long enough to get good photographs of target ground features, if you were in the right place.

A phrase that we got used to hearing from the recce team was 'last photo-light'. This meant that, when 31 wasn't in its night fit, they were all usually down well before the sun or our squadron was, especially in the winter. So many a time the first folk in the bar were the recce boys! But, in reality, it was all banter and we mostly got on with them and our separate tasks without trying to get in each other's ways.

Although on one occasion we were flying along at our usual 250ft when I spotted a Canberra ahead of us, flying slightly higher on a similar heading. We were both following a canal to our left. As we were cruising at 300kts we were steadily overhauling the aforementioned Canberra. As I watched, it occasionally dropped a wing for a few seconds and then I realised that it must be a PR7 taking photographs of bridges and locks with its sideways-facing cameras. As we got closer, he still didn't know we were there (the rearward view from the PR7 was appalling) so I upped the speed to around 400kts and aimed to fly right through his photographic line of sight as close as I dared. As we appeared from under his left wing there was a sudden lurch and he broke away in shock! Gotcha! I wondered whether he would have a photograph of us before we scared him off. Even if he did I wouldn't be asking anyone for it – that would be really foolish!

However, there were some occasions when we were called in to help the south-side flashers complete their tasks. One was for an annual photo-recce competition called Exercise Royal Flush. The 31 Squadron crews would be given fairly short-notice recce jobs to do and the squadron's performance was judged on the final results: how many targets they actually photographed and the quality of the piccies.

To help them out during Royal Flush our squadron used to fly early-morning weather survey trips over their likely target areas and report back by radio as we flew around. This meant very early take-offs for us so that they could be in their target areas at 'first photo light'. On two consecutive mornings in May 1965, Geoff and I flew over to the UK to report on the weather in northern and eastern England.

It was odd to be flying around at 250ft across a very misty Lincolnshire and East Anglia, with the power line pylons sticking up out of the fog, long before most people down below had breakfasted. There was a mystical quality to the light as the sun rose out of the North Sea. Less than an hour later we were back in the squadron crewroom having coffee before most of the other crews had arrived for the day's flying.

We again helped out 31 when two of their crews had been unable to locate a camouflaged, mobile, anti-aircraft Surface to Air Missile (SAM) unit in a field somewhere on the North German Plain. They now didn't have another aircraft and crew available to go have a third look. So they swallowed their pride and asked 16 Squadron if they could cover it. This was because their in-house photographic interpreters were also being assessed and the exercise umpires wanted them to look at this target in particular. Geoff and I had been to the Mess for lunch and had returned not expecting to fly again, so we just happened to be hanging around the Ops Room when the phone call came in. Talking on the phone to his opposite number on 31, our revered Flight Commander had just said, 'Well, Jim, I'm not sure if we have a crew either.' When he turned round he spotted us, just standing there drinking coffee.

'Ah, just the chaps. Get yourselves over to 31 Squadron for a briefing, be back ASAP and I'll sort you out an aircraft and film for your camera. Don't just stand there – GO!'

So we did. The target coordinates and all the maps they had used earlier were turned over to us. The brief was to get a photo of the unit's vehicles and, if possible, its Thunderbird missiles. We rushed back to the squadron and got airborne as quickly as was safe. Less than 2 hours later we were back with a film full of shots of the SAM unit, which we dropped off at 31's dispersal area and then taxied back in triumph to our parking area. The photographs turned out to be exactly what was required and we were stood drinks that night. I couldn't work out why they'd missed it. Although fairly well camouflaged there were enough clues to there being something there other than cows and tractors. It just confirmed my high opinion of my Welsh steering advisor.

Another task that fell into the 'helping out' category was that of going to pick up aircraft that had been left in various places and in various states of health by other people. There were several ways of getting to the now serviceable flying machine, dependant on how far away it was. If it was on one of the 'clutch'[1] airfields then a bus was requisitioned; further away, but still in West Germany, then a lift in the T4 was usually arranged and, if in the UK, then the services of the Command Communications Squadron was called upon. This meant a trip in the back of a clattering Percival Pembroke.

Geoff and I did one such trip to collect a Canberra from the Maintenance Unit (MU) at RAF Aldergrove, north-west of Belfast in Northern Ireland[2].

First, yet another bone-shaking bus ride to RAF Wildenrath then aboard the Pembroke to Ulster, but on that day via Boscombe Down. We parked there for a short stopover, right outside the biggest hangar that I'd ever seen. We had about an hour to wait so we took a look around.

There were all sorts of RAF aircraft parked all over the place and inside the hangar I noticed enormous metal plates on the floor and wondered what they were; then I remembered that someone had said it was called the Weighbridge Hangar – they were huge scales for weighing aeroplanes! Little did I realise then that I would be back at Boscombe in ten years time to do the test pilots' course and then spend three more tours there. On the last of those tours, nearly forty years later, my office would be overlooking the airfield from this huge hangar.

We were soon called to reboard our trusty transport just as someone arrived with a very nice wooden box. Inside it was a very strange object. It was tubular and had fins, like a small bomb, but the front end had a flat plate protruding from it, mounted on a concentric rod. When asked what it was the recipient said that this was the first of our new practise bombs. He explained that it would be the one we would use when we changed from the LABS delivery to Laydown. It was all Greek to me, but only a few days later we would find out what it was all about. So it was back to our seats, the newspaper and another cup of the disgusting in-flight coffee. We arrived at Aldergrove that afternoon, found our rooms in the Officers' Mess and made contact with the MU. They said that the aircraft wouldn't actually be ready until late morning on the following day.

The next morning at breakfast I couldn't help remarking as to how good the bacon was. A fellow breakfaster told me that it was local, from a butcher in Crumlin.

'It would be great to take some of it home,' I said.

To my astonishment he said, 'If you've got the time I'll take you down there and you can buy some.' So I accepted thankfully and with alacrity. By ten o'clock we were back with bundles of smoked pig in our bags.

When we arrived at the MU we were told that we would be able to take over the aircraft in about half an hour, so we had a nose about. There were lots of guys working on several aircraft and we did our best to keep out of their way. At one point my waggish Welsh navigator said, 'I dare you to run into that hangar and shout, "Are you here, Paddy?"' I ignored him.

When we went to collect and sign for the aircraft we discovered several modifications had been incorporated. The first was very obvious: the undersides of the jet were painted silver-grey and not black. Apparently this was the new colour scheme for all our aircraft. Then there was a much-improved, new French gunsight, in which the sightline could be depressed; this would help with all our future weapon aiming. There were also newer UHF radios; well it was about time. Finally, there was, for me, a more recent ejection seat – the Mk2C. This seat could be used at sea level, as long as the speed was above 90kts.

This gave us an immediate ethical problem. Instead of us both being affected by the same limitation for escaping safely from the aircraft – i.e. at a minimum speed of 120kts at or above 1,000ft – I now had the only option of leaving safely above 90kts from ground level upwards. Geoff, and the rest of the navs, did not have that option.

After discussion we decided that if we ever lost an engine on take-off and I couldn't get us safely above 1,000ft I would do the best I could and then I would pull my ejection seat handle. Geoff decided that he would still jump out of the door and take his chances. Thankfully the flight out of Aldergrove back to Laarbruch went without incident.

One of the latest Army weapons to arrive with the BAOR at the time was the radar-laid, anti-aircraft gun. Although Geoff and I didn't get directly involved, one of the in-theatre proving trials was held at Laarbruch with a 16 Squadron crew attacking the airfield from various directions and in various way, while the guys on the gun simulated shooting them down. I think that it all went well from the gunners' point of view. I just hoped that the Russians weren't that well equipped or trained. We did quite a lot of cooperation with the Army in various ways, such as flying attack sorties on Sennelager range with all sorts of army stuff going on in the dirt below us.

For some reason that either I can't remember, or I never knew, we struck up some sort of relationship with one of the BAOR cavalry units. It had lots of numbers, like 16th/18th, and either Lancers, Hussars or Dragoons in its title. I do remember that they came to visit Laarbruch and Geoff and I were 'volunteered' to stand by a B(I)8 in the hangar, with a dummy nuke and all the possible conventional weapons laid out on the floor in front of it. The cavalry chaps arrived, looked around and chatted and guffawed in their cut-glass accents. Then one of them came to look in the open door and up at the cockpit.

'I say, do just two of you fly this thing?'

'That's right.'

'And you're both awfficers?'

'That's right.'

'Do you mean to tell me that you're going to go to war without the help of a reliable Senior NCO?'

'That's right,' I sighed. Spare me from the cavalry!

Later there was a return invitation for a crew to go to observe an exercise that some of our aircraft were taking part in. Straws were drawn and Terry Frame and Doug Hall got the job. When they finally arrived near the range, after a train journey I believe, they were picked up by an Army Land Rover and taken to where the cavalry squadron was living in tented accommodation, including a marquee that was the Officers' Mess. The Landrover pulled up outside the Mess tent and the young subaltern, who had drawn their short straw to look after the RAF chaps, came out to meet them. Terry was alighting from the front and Doug from the back with their baggage.

'Oh good!' said the subaltern gleefully, 'You've brought your man.'

Terry winked at Doug, who immediately picked up on this misunderstanding; it might, for the moment, be worth perpetuating. So Doug stood in the background while Terry was introduced to the Colonel. They were then taken to their tent, with Doug being shown where to go after he had carried out his valeting duties. Thankfully the tent was equipped with two camp beds so our heroes settled in.

The first event was a dining-in night; the lads had been briefed about this, therefore they had their Mess Kits with them. So, shower and change to be at the Mess by half past seven. Spruced up and ready to go they both arrived at the entrance to the marquee, to be met by their young escort with a very open mouth. You could see 'My God, he's brought his man to dinner!' written all over his face! Nevertheless, after introductions and explanations, they had a good evening with their flamboyantly turned out hosts.

The marquee was furnished with large tables, groaning with silver, lead crystal and all the trimmings. The top end of the Army is amazing at retaining tradition; the RAF is in its infancy in comparison! But one thing that they both noticed was that the beautifully polished and, no doubt, antique tables had deep scratches all round their edges. The reason became clear after the Loyal Toast. The President stood and called upon Mr Vice to toast the unit. At this Mr Vice leapt onto his chair, put one foot on the edge of the table and called out the name of the unit. At which bidding the rest of the assembly, with the exception of two baffled officers dressed in light blue, also leapt onto their chairs and stuck one spurred foot on the table. By the time Terry and Doug had got up there everyone else was sitting down. They got a round of applause. The edges of the tables were scuffed by countless points of spurs being dug into them over many, many years!

Another time that Geoff and I tried to help out was in North Africa. We were on yet another Southern Ranger, this time at RAF El Adem in Eastern Libya. On the Saturday we were to fly a long-range, low-level sortie over the Sahara, south to a place called Kufra Oasis, returning via Benghazi to make a 3-hour sortie. The B(I)8 was due to receive a modification to give the crew air-ventilated suits, in fact two of the most recent jets out of update and refit had come back to the squadron with all the fixtures and fittings in place. But, as usual, the blanket stackers[3] hadn't got the suits to us yet. However, our sortie was designed to scientifically analyse the effects of the heat *before* the suits were trialled on an identical sortie at a later date. Unhappily, the science was to see how much weight we lost on a low-level sortie in hot conditions. So we had to log the outside air temperature (OAT) at regular intervals and follow a strict protocol for the use of cabin cooling. So just before we walked out, we each had to be weighed (without urine!) and then weighed when we got back (again after our post-flight pee).

To give us the required range the flight was to be made with a full fuel load and the take-off was planned for 0900 hours. However, after start-up, there was a minor technical problem that we couldn't fly with, so we got out and handed the jet back to the engineers.

It was fixed and ready again about 2 hours later. So we were weighed again and we boarded our steed. Although it was October it was very hot. I could barely touch anything metal in the cockpit because we had not been allowed an air cooler, just a shade over the canopy. Then, as we taxied out, Geoff piped up with more potentially bad news.

'I planned our take-off for 28°C and now its 35°C[4]. I'll have to recalculate our take-off run distance, acceleration and stop speeds. Ask air traffic what the surface wind is, please.'

'OK. Let me know if there's a problem,' I replied, thinking that the boffins will be really unhappy if we don't go now. A few minutes later Geoff came back with the answer, 'We should be OK, but we'll use a lot of runway and your stop speed is ever so low.'

When I got departure clearance I taxied on to the runway and turned left instead of right. There was about 100 yards of concrete there that I could well use. Normally we only opened the engines up to about 90 per cent of full power before we released the brakes, but today I went to full throttle. Because of the heat the thrust was less than normal and the brakes held. When I was satisfied we were getting all that Rolls-Royce could give us, I released the brakes. We crept forward. There was acceleration but, as Paul Daniels says, not a lot.

However, we achieved the correct speed at the acceleration checkpoint, although it was 20kts lower than we were used to in Germany. The take-off run went on and on; I was seriously beginning to hope that Geoff hadn't misread the graphs in the Operating Data Manual. We were now well past the speed and distance where we could stop without entering the arrestor barrier and the jet was still firmly stuck to *terra firma*! I eased the control yoke back and the nose started to lift. Then I could feel the lift easing us into the air, but not as swiftly as I would have liked. I was watching the arrestor barrier, like a large horizontal fishing net coming towards us I called, as calmly as possible, 'Tower, 56, please lower the barrier!'

It started to bow downwards as it went out of sight under the nose. The wheels were now airborne, but not by much so I stabbed the toebrakes and hit the UP button. We were now over the scrubland off the end of the runway accelerating slowly, but we still hadn't achieved our single-engined safety speed. However, not far off the end the El Adem runway was a downward slope, where the land fell away towards Tobruk and the coast. I eased down that at a couple of hundred feet and we achieved 175kts. Phew!

From then on it was going to be 250ft all the way – well officially anyway. We turned left and set off south to try and find the green dot of Kufra Oasis on this vast canvas of yellow ochre. The maps didn't help much, they were as featureless as the world outside. Geoff was working on dead reckoning, helped by the readouts of drift and groundspeed from the Blue Silk Doppler radar. At least the cockpit temperature was coming down. It fell quiet as we bowled along, skimming the desert, each with our own thoughts.

I was wondering what all the long straight lines that we kept crossing were; perhaps desert 'roads' to the oilfields? Cruising over this unchanging landscape was almost hypnotic, especially after we reached the Great Sand Sea. It was like flying over water, difficult to judge height; I kept checking the radio altimeter. About 30 minutes into the trip, it having been silent for quite a while, I heard the click of Geoff's microphone being switched on. Here comes a track correction, I thought.

'Do you know something, boyo?'

'What?'

'There's more sand here than there is on Barry Island.'

His microphone clicked off and Saharan silence reigned again.

A bit later on, as I was scanning the horizon for any features other than sand, I noticed what looked like a plume of black smoke off to the right. Without thinking I said, 'There must be a train over there, I can see its smoke.'

With deserved derision the reply from below came back, as quick as a flash, 'Don't be daft. If there were trains out here I'd be following the railway lines, not just guessing where we're going!' Oh yes.

'Well I wonder what it is,' I replied sheepishly. To see smoke in the midst of all this desolation must mean something. I asked Geoff if there was any feature on his map over that way.

'Not a sausage,' he replied. That made me suddenly realise that I hadn't had anything to eat since six o'clock and it was well past noon now.

'Shall we go and take a look, or will that put us too far off track?' I asked.

'As I've no real idea where our track is any more, we might as well,' he responded. I thought I detected a slight despondency in his voice. Geoff was a first-class visual navigator and map-reader, so it must have been disheartening for him to be map reading over a featureless part of the world. A bit of interest might cheer him up.

As we got closer to the smoke its source became clear. There was a large fuel tanker with its back end partly buried in the sand. In front of it was a barrel with smoke issuing from it. There was one man standing up waving at us and another lying in the tiny bit of shade under the front of the tractor unit. They'd obviously fallen off the 'road' and become stuck in soft sand. We wondered how long they'd been there and what we could do to help. We had a spare survival pack, but apart from jettisoning the door we couldn't get that to them; I briefly imagined the Boss's reaction to getting a signal that told him that the jet was stuck at El Adem without a cabin door!

As usual Geoff came up with the right answer.

'Why don't we climb up overhead here until we can talk to El Adem on the radio and get a bearing from them[5]. I'll give my best estimate of position now and then we'll fly back to their overhead and I'll calculate the distance.

That'll give us a fairly accurate location for those poor guys and we can tell someone.'

'OK, but so much for the trial, the boffins won't be too pleased. What's more you won't get the satisfaction of finding Kufra Oasis,' I replied. But we agreed that the plight of those two human beings down there was much more important than either of those considerations.

'Anyway,' added my modest nav, 'we would probably have missed the oasis; I've no real idea of where we are now.'

So we climbed up until I made contact with El Adem. We were too far away to get a radar position, but they did get a bearing. We explained what we'd found and asked them to alert anyone who might need to know. Then we headed back directly for El Adem at low level once more. On the way back we saw lots of rusting vehicles from the Second World War and also passed over a large military cemetery. After we had landed we went to the operations room and I spoke by phone to a man from the Shell oil company in Benghazi.

'Oh yes,' he said, 'That truck's been overdue for a couple of days now. We're planning to send our aircraft out to find them tomorrow and drop water and food. Then we'll send a surface team out to recover the oil.'

I asked him if he would like us to fly out and circle overhead so that they could home in on us. He obviously saw pound signs popping up in front of his eyes for the payment of a couple of hours flying by a Canberra, because he turned down our offer with indecent haste.

On the Sunday afternoon, I asked the Station Ops Officer if he knew whether they had found the truck and its crew.

'I rang the Shell man earlier,' he responded. 'He said that they had flown to overhead the position we had given him and they couldn't find anything.'

I wondered whether they would bother again. Sometimes you offer to help and people just won't let you. We let the boffins know that we had failed to do the full trial; they didn't seem that bothered. That evening we thought we might go to the open-air cinema.

'What's on?' asked Geoff.

'*Lawrence of Arabia*,' I replied.

'I think I'll pass on that – I've seen enough sand this weekend. Let's go to the bar instead.' I was in full agreement.

Notes

1 The four westerly RAF Germany airfields of Laarbruch, Wildenrath, Bruggen and Geilenkirchen were collectively known as 'the Clutch'.
2 Now Belfast International Airport.
3 'Blanket stacker' was the aircrew nickname for RAF Suppliers; they thought of themselves much more highly as 'Logisticians'.
4 The increased temperature meant that the thrust from the engines would be reduced, so slowing our acceleration and making the take-off distance longer.
5 All military ATC units had automatic direction finding that gave a bearing for each radio transmission that they received.

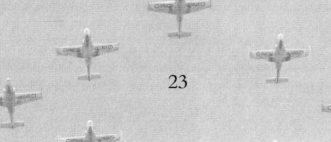

23

Visits To and From Friends

Another part of life in 2ATAF was the regular exchange visits we made with other NATO squadrons. These exchanges were officially sanctioned and encouraged from on high to extend the principles of Exercise Round Robin in our understanding of how other air forces worked. There were, at that time, no serious attempts at interoperability and exercising jointly, as is all the rage now (and, in my opinion, correctly so). Exercises with 'Flag' in their names were still a while away.

My first experience of a squadron exchange was with a USAF F-105 Thunderchief outfit based at Spangdahlem in the Eifel Mountains. Because we were still in our first few months, Geoff and I were not in the party that went south to the F-105 base. On the appointed day, their five 'Thuds' arrived in neat formation and broke into the circuit. When they taxied into our dispersal areas they turned out to be enormous for a single-engined, fighter-bomber. Their fuselages were just a few inches shorter than the Canberra's, but they sat impressively high on the ground. We all accompanied the Boss to meet the American pilots by their CO's aircraft. As he climbed down the long ladder everyone had the same thought, 'Isn't he small? How does he fly that great big airplane?' We soon learnt that he was in fact very proud of his diminutive stature and had, some time ago, started a worldwide, informal organisation called the Midget Air Force. To qualify you had to be active aircrew and less than 5ft 6in tall. It wasn't long before the Colonel spotted one of our navs, the small but perfectly formed George Nettleship, measured him and enrolled him into the Midget Air Force. There was a certificate and all sorts! Although I have a very short back, thankfully my legs are not quite in proportion, so at 5ft 7in I didn't qualify.

As on all squadron exchanges the visitors operated on their normal schedule, but using Laarbruch as their base for about a week. Our guys would be doing the same thing at Spangdahlem. Some of the silverbacks got given rides in the two-seat F-105; all returned with sweaty brows and big grins. Us junior Flying Officers were obviously not going to get a go. After three days the two-seater came back with a problem that required the engine to be changed. As it happened one of our jets needed an engine change, so the two lots of groundcrew had a friendly race; ours won!

Before the Thuds left Laarbruch a photo call was arranged. Mike Kelly flew a B(I)8 leading the four single-seat F-105s past the squadron dispersal area and a 31 Squadron PR7 took a very nice picture of the event. Looking at the photograph in detail it can be seen that it was taken on a Thursday; there is a third Canberra in the QRA enclave having its nuclear bomb loaded. That happened on Thursday mornings.

Our first trip away on a squadron exchange was in September 1965 when we flew to the German Air Force (GAF) base at Pferdsfeld, also in the Eifel Mountains. We were exchanging with *Jago 42* who flew F-86 Sabres in the day-fighter and attack roles. The trip down was flown in two sections of three and we were number two in the lead section.

We flew in battle formation at low level, coming into close echelon for the break on arrival. The airfield was at some altitude on a flat-topped hill. Once we had cleared the runway all the parking areas were downhill; 'this is going to be fun,' I thought. Eventually we parked, on a bit of a slope, then the second section arrived and we were greeted by the German guys with bottles of beer. This *was* going to be fun. The welcome party in the evening was as good as the earlier arrival had promised and I went to bed in my rather spartan room well prepared to sleep.

We flew low level and conventional weapons sorties every day, flying much further south than we did from Laarbruch. We used a range, new to us, at Siegenburg, not far from Munich, and we flew close to the Swiss and Austrian borders. The German guys had a nice story about one of their pilots who strayed very close to the Austrian border. The Austrian military radar made a radio transmission on the 'Guard' channel, which everyone listens to all the time.

'German aircraft heading for Austrian airspace, turn away or we'll send up our interceptor fighters.'

'One or both?' was the Teutonic reply.

Towards the end of the detachment I was offered a flight in the German squadron's trainer, which was a Republic T-33 Shooting Star; there were no two-seat, dual-controlled Sabres. The T-33, or T-Bird, was a straight-winged jet with a long bubble canopy over the two ejection seats. I sat in the back and *Oberfeldwebel* Häker gave me a ride around most of the flight envelope, including aerobatics. The performance and handling of the T-33 reminded me very much of the Vampire, although rolling it was much easier because it had power-boosted ailerons. One thing that did take me by surprise was that when I operated the airbrakes for the descent there was a huge rushing noise and my cockpit filled with dust and detritus from the floor.

'Ah, zat alvays happens,' I was told, 'You're sitting right above where ze speedbrake comes out.' Despite that I really enjoyed flying what was the fourth type of aircraft I'd got my hands on. The detachment was a good experience and we learnt a lot about how another type of NATO squadron operated and what the German view of the alliance with their former combatants was: overall an enhancing experience.

In the following year, 1966, because of the detachment to Kuantan we didn't do a spring squadron exchange, but we did another one in the autumn. This time it was again to a GAF squadron, *Jago 52*, who flew Fiat G-91 day fighters from a famous old Luftwaffe airfield at Leipheim, near Ulm in Bavaria. The G-91 was, like most Fiat cars, small and didn't go very far on a tank-full. Being Italian in origin it was a pretty little aeroplane, but not that good as a fighting machine.

There was the usual welcome and then we discovered that the German Base Commander and all the officers were going to throw a big party for us all. The detachment boss decided that we ought to reciprocate and decided on a whiskey-tasting evening. He called Laarbruch and arranged for as many different whiskeys to be boxed up and charged to the squadron's bar bill.

Then Terry Newman and I, and our navs, were detailed to fly two formation sorties that would go via Laarbruch for lunch and the whiskey pick up. It was odd flying the return leg with several boxes of *uisge beatha* strapped into the crash seat. It was well stirred and shaken when it got back to Bavaria; I hoped that it had travelled well!

Both parties were a riot, especially the whiskey tasting, as just about everyone with a German accent got severely wasted. The Base Commander, who had lead from the front the previous evening, declared the next morning as a no flying period. The big surprise was that the party that he had arranged was a celebration of the Battle of Britain. Once over our amazement, the evening was very amicable, although there was one young, blond Aryan blade who definitely acted like a member of the master race. At the party he was heard to say, in a strident voice, 'Next time vee vill not vaste a veek invading Holland – vee vill do it in a day!' However, we had a convivial time and took his outspoken remarks as just a bit of booze talk. After all, as a famous German fighter pilot once said, 'We're basically the same. We all fly planes and chase girls.'

Although we didn't have any more exchanges, I remember one incident when 31 Squadron were having an exchange with a Norwegian fighter-recce squadron. They flew the reconnaissance version of the Republic F-84 Thunderjet, which they operated with four underwing tanks fitted. On one hot summer's day, while they were at Laarbruch, I was taxiing out for a westerly departure and a Norwegian four-ship formation was coming up the opposite taxiway all the way from 31 Squadron's dispersal. The leader beat me to the draw in calling for departure clearance and got permission to line up on the runway. As his three companions arranged themselves around him he asked ATC for the latest air temperature. I was steaming gently in my cockpit; it was 29°C outside and about 40° inside. Then there was a long pause.

'Laarbruch Tower, I'm sorry, it's too hot for us to get airborne at this weight,' the recce leader said, 'We'll have to taxi back and get some fuel taken off.' Then ATC, as is their wont, cleared them to taxi all the way down the runway. Hey, I'm burning up here! There's a saying: if someone built a runway all the way round the equator, then the Republic Aircraft Company would build an airplane that would get airborne with 6ft of runway to spare!

24

Picking Oranges

Exercises ORANGE GROVE and CITRUS GROVE were the names for RAF Germany Canberra squadron detachments to the Mediterranean for conventional weapons delivery practise camps. Our first one was to Malta in November 1964, which I've already made mention of. The next was to the real home of oranges, the island of Cyprus, in January 1966. It was great to fly away from the snow, the cold and the grey gloom of the North German Plain to the sunny, sparkling skies of the eastern Med. We were to occupy the temporarily vacant No.6 Squadron buildings and dispersal areas; 'Shiny Six' were away down the Arabian Gulf at RAF Muharraq, on the island of Bahrain, doing the same thing as us.

After the usual settling-in period and recce of the two ranges we would use – Episkopi for bombing and Larnaca for shooting – we started the serious business of flying weapon delivery sorties. We would be at Akrotiri for the whole of January so we should be able to achieve a lot. Geoff and I still had to complete our conventional weapons qualifications by dropping live 1,000lb bombs, doing operational pattern shooting (op-shoots) and dropping flares at night, then bombing and shooting by the light of them. We started with the usual academic patterns and soon graduated to operational patterns with the 25lb practise bombs and guns. The squadron conventional weapons leader started a status board for each event, arranged like a ladder, on which each crew's names were placed. There was a trophy for the winning crew. After three days the more experienced crews were naturally moving to the top, with us beginners following up like also-rans. Then the Boss came out of his office and stared at the ladders.

'Get your kit on, Del,' he called to his navigator, Flight Lieutenant Del Williams, 'we're going flying.'

An aircraft was arranged, refuelled and armed and off they went. A couple of hours later he was back and moved his crew's names to the top of the two academic ladders. He then turned to the assembled motley crews and said, 'Come on you lot. Get your arses in gear – you can't let the old man be top of the table for long!'

He did the same thing about every three days. Now that's leading from the front! It was a lesson I carried throughout my subsequent career – never ask your guys to do anything that you can't do and, if possible, do it better than them. The flying was absolutely great. It was challenging and tiring at times, but the weapons delivery practise gave instant feedback of how we were doing; which wasn't too bad at all, especially with the shooting.

Time off was fun too. Hire cars were cheap, there was a super beach called Ladies Mile on the bay north-east of Akrotiri and the whole island was there to be explored. Because it was winter there was quite a lot of snow on Mount Troodos and it was possible to water ski in the morning and snow ski in the afternoon, but you had to drive flat out up the winding road to the slopes! Some folk went up there and stayed in the lodge for the weekend.

Although some years had passed since the EOKA troubles there was a partition between the predominately Turkish north and the more Greek south. It was called the Green Line and manned by the UN; it ran through the middle of the capital, Nicosia. As British service personnel, we were allowed through, so a few of us hired a car and set off to see the port of Kyrenia on the north coast. The town, its harbour and its castle were beautiful and we spent the day sightseeing and eating delicious seafood. The hire car broke down on the way back and we had to go into a Greek Cypriot bar to find a telephone. It was populated by several swarthy men with only a normal mouthful of teeth between them. They looked at us suspiciously until they had assessed that we were at least not Turks. We asked for a telephone and offered drinks and cigarettes. By the time the nearest mechanic had arrived we were all getting on famously.

As long as one didn't mind a bit of goat, another great thing about Cyprus was the food. The favourite meals were the 'kebab' or 'mezze'. The kebab wasn't shaved meat in a pitta bread, it was a multiple-course meal that seemed to come at you in bits for the whole evening. It was accompanied by multiple glasses of a thick, red Cypriot wine called *Kokinelli* and finished off by a glass or two of *retsina* and thick black coffee.

We had another evening out with the groundcrew, as we had done in Malta; however, no horses were involved this time. After the kebab at Niazi's Restaurant, which at that time was outdoors near the petrol pumps in a village not far from RAF Akrotiri, some of the by now rowdy crowd went to downtown Limassol and to a nightclub in Eros Square. There the boys had settled in and got their drinks when the owner came onto the front of the small, brightly lit stage to announce his special act for the night. It was to be a genuine Egyptian Belly Dancer. The lights went down, there was shimmering noise as she got into position and then the spotlights came on. She was a well-built lady with a considerable belly to dance with. There was a momentary silence that was immediately broken by one of our company shouting, 'Mother!' Unsurprisingly, the raucous laughter, whistling and shouting that this impolite remark had triggered got everyone involved ejected. It seemed to be another squadron tradition that we hadn't been told about earlier.

By now Geoff and I had graduated to the 'operational' stuff. We were not yet top of any of the ladders, but we weren't far off. Our next major event was flare dropping. The briefing was reasonably clear, but gave pause for thought. We had to fly in formation, in the dark, at 12,000ft heading towards the target. The leader then opened his flare doors and gave a countdown to the point where he would start dropping his eight flares. At this point the number two had to turn away through about 45°, descend to 6,000ft and then turn back onto a parallel track. When the number two could see the target he then had to turn towards it and start his 30° dive to drop a bomb. Once he had done so he called the leader, who by now was making a descending turn to achieve the 8–10°, shallower, gunnery attack dive underneath the still descending flares. Meanwhile the erstwhile number two became the leader, climbed back to 12,000ft and waited for the new number two to catch up.

Then the whole thing would be repeated until four attacks had been made and all the flares, bullets and bombs were littering the desert. I thought that this was probably going to be the most challenging flying I had done to date. For one thing we had to fly to RAF El Adem and its nearby range, in Libya to do this exercise, because we weren't allowed to drop our parachute flares over Cyprus. That meant that it would be really dark over the target out in the desert, with nothing in the way of cultural lighting. We would also have already flown for well over an hour to get there before carrying out this demanding work. We had to land at El Adem afterwards to refuel for the journey home. The good news was that we could have the mornings both before and afterwards off.

We took notes of all the details and went off to mull it over. On our first night attack sortie I was the number two to start with and we got airborne at a time suitable to arrive at the range at least 30 minutes after sunset. Because of the easterly wind we taxied out in a westerly direction down Akrotiri's long southern taxiway. The sun was setting above the leader's cockpit canopy. As it started to disappear over the horizon we were ready to go. It wasn't too dark yet to do a formation take-off and once airborne we started a left turn onto a south-westerly heading. The sun had risen again. We climbed in battle formation to around 36,000ft in glorious sunshine and not a cloud in sight. We were chasing the sun and, because of the glare, I had my tinted visor fully down. When we got to the descent point I closed up from about 1,000 yards to what was known then as attack or arrow formation, in a swept position at about 100 yards from the leader. As we descended I saw my second sunset that day. It got dark very quickly. As we levelled off at 12,000ft I thought that this was going to be even more difficult than I'd imagined; I could hardly see a thing. Then I realised that my tinted visor was still down. Dolt! When I'd lifted it things were better – but not much!

We ran in, the leader called, I turned and started my descent. There was no discernable horizon so every manoeuvre had to be done using the dimly lit instruments. Then I turned back on my parallel track and saw the flares dangling and twirling on their parachutes. But instead of the neat line that the briefing diagram had shown, they were all over the place and a couple weren't even there! Now what?

Well, I could actually see the target so I tipped into the 30° dive angle. The sight picture looked good and Geoff was counting down the height to bomb release. Once that had happened, I pulled up and went straight back onto the dials. Once we were the other side of the flares it was like suddenly being frozen in black aspic. All sense of motion was suddenly and very rudely removed. Concentrating hard I levelled off at 12,000ft having turned left again onto the outbound heading. I called to the other pilot to let him know and waited for him to tell me that he was ready for the inbound turn. This time we had to drop the flares.

Geoff released them and reported that his indicators up front showed that they had all gone, so I closed the flare doors. After the turn-in call I had to do a turn through 270°, while descending quite rapidly to 3,000ft above the ground. During the last part of the turn I allowed myself a look outside and saw my flares; they were no tidier than the last lot. We now had to make our 10° dive and all the while the flares were coming down on us. In we went, 600 yards, open fire, 300 yards or 500ft – cease fire and pull out. Now we were number two again. Now do it all over again – twice!

When we had finished I had used about a week's worth of adrenalin, my legs were hurting from the unconscious tension and I was feeling both elated and exhausted. And we still had to fly back to Akrotiri. First off, back to El Adem airfield, only 5 minutes away and land to refuel and check that we weren't still carrying anything we shouldn't be. That night we weren't, but the next time we went over to do this we suspected that one flare had not released. So after shut-down, during which I didn't open the flare doors, Geoff got out and I pumped the doors open slowly with the hydraulic hand pump next to my seat (placed there for operating the undercarriage). I heard a muffled 'STOP!' and got out. In the small gap between the two doors there was a flare, looking like some menacing mole. It had not come off when selected but had fallen off later, probably during our last 3G pull-up. Fortunately there was a safety wire attached to the flare that would inhibit its illumination before it had cleared the aircraft by the length of that cable (I think that the cable was about 12ft long). The armourer came and took over, talking to it gently while he removed it from the flare bay. Back at Akrotiri and after a late supper and a couple of 'wind-down' drinks, I really slept well that night.

The next thing we had to do was to drop live 1,000lb bombs. Because of the explosive power of the bombs we had to use the range over at El Adem, but at least this would be in daylight. It was a different target as well, otherwise the practise target might have been totally destroyed. It all went well and the dust plumes that our two bombs generated were really impressive. We just had the op-shoot to do now. So we flew back to El Adem and picked up 400 rounds of live High Explosive (HE) 20mm cannon rounds. After a very quick lunch we were back on the range, barrelling around at 250ft and 330kts. On this occasion there were no panel targets; there was a pile of old debris in the middle of a cleared circle in the sand. We could use the rounds sparingly ensuring that we got lots of practise, so I made a good number of passes. Just after I opened fire I could see the effect of the HE kicking up dust; it was fascinatingly dangerous to watch. It is easy to get what's called target fixation and get too low. Some folk have hit the ground suffering from that; it's always fatal.

Later in the week we got to do it all again but this time with non-explosive bullets on the range at Larnaca where our efforts could be scored. It was hard to get more than 50 per cent during academic practise and the op-shoot had an added challenge. The score would be taken against the number of bullets loaded and we were only allowed two passes. This meant that we had to open fire at maximum range, but not come below the minimum height and range. So you had to aim high to start with and then push the gunsight pipper down to be in the middle of the target at 450 yards and at the foot of the target at 300 yards. Once we'd done it on our own we then had to go back and do it in formation.

That really was hard work and it was, at first, a bit disconcerting to be firing with another jet not far away doing the same thing. The probability of ricochet damage increased during these passes. Our best scores were 27 yards with four bombs and 62 per cent with guns. The latter put us momentarily at the top of the shooting ladder, but the Boss went out the next day and beat it!

So now we were fully operational and Combat Ready in all the squadron's possible war roles. They had said it would take five or six months and it did. The detachment was wrapped up after the final party at which the trophy was bestowed; the Boss didn't win it because it was for the best overall scores and he didn't fly last: again an excellent leadership lesson. A Britannia turned up to take everyone to Laarbruch who wasn't flying a jet home. Eventually they were all loaded, along with all the spares and lots of bags of fresh oranges.

We flew back to Laarbruch, via Malta, in Canberra XM 272, feeling very satisfied with ourselves. It had been a great detachment and I was still pinching myself that I was living the dream. All that euphoria was quickly quashed when we arrived back at the squadron. There was Squadron Leader Ian Suren, our Squadron Leader Operations or SLOPS, with the joyful greeting, 'Ah, Brooke and Trott. Don't bother to unpack your bags – on Monday you're off to Idris for the week!'

25

What's the Weather Going to be Like?

Meteorology is a word that is too long for aircrew, so it's always abbreviated to 'Met'. There's the Met Office, where you go to see the Met Man (or Lady) and get the forecast for the day or for your overseas flight. The Duty Met Man is the person who comes to the Morning Briefing every day to give his forecast, complete with charts and cross sections of the atmosphere. The duty Air Traffic Control person is also there. He or she outlines the state of all the airfield navigation and landing aids, as well as which airfields are the nominated diversions (another long word always abbreviated to 'divs') for the day. There are always two divs; one in case the weather deteriorates below limits for recovery to base and one in case the runway gets blocked; the latter is usually the closest.

Forecasting the weather is a science, but an inexact one. It was even more so in the 1960s. There were precious few satellites, no hugely powerful computers nor the worldwide web. Instead the Met Men had to rely on reports from ground stations, three weather ships in the Atlantic and cross sections of the atmosphere taken by radiosondes, carried aloft by balloons. Then he had to collate and interpret all that data and come up with a forecast, always flavoured by his experience and knowledge of local effects. No wonder they got it wrong so often!

As an aviator one becomes quickly aware of atmospheric conditions and how they might affect what you are trying to achieve. Met is one of the major subjects taught in flying training schools and that knowledge soon gets turned into wisdom by direct experience. Nevertheless, the weather has never ceased to fascinate as well as occasionally frustrate me. It has also often impressed me and sometimes frightened me. Its ever-changing and unpredictable qualities are, I think, what interests us all and turns it into a daily topic of conversation.

Generally speaking, the Met Men (and Ladies) rarely get the weather in their forecasts horribly wrong; it's usually the timing that they don't get right. The other most frequent error that has caused me problems during my career is that the bad weather often turns out to be worse than was forecast. One winter's night snow showers were forecast, with a minimum cloudbase of 500ft and minimum visibility of half a nautical mile. But when we started our recovery to Laarbruch we were told that the cloudbase was less than 200ft and visibility 300 yards in heavy snow. So we were diverted to the USAF base at Spangdahlem, quite a way to the south.

However, when we got there they too were in the midst of a snowstorm. We didn't have enough fuel to get safely back to Laarbruch, especially if they were still having similar weather. So we had to try and land there, despite the driving snow. American airfields have very bright strobe lights that light up in sequence leading to the beginning of the runway, so when we got below 500ft on the radar-directed approach I could just make out the sequential brightness passing below me.

I carried on with more confidence, but at my decision height I still couldn't make out the runway touchdown area. We had enough fuel to make another couple of approaches so I put the power up, retracted the undercarriage and flaps and started my climb away. Halfway down the runway we popped out of the snow into clear air. I immediately asked for the radio frequency of the local controller, selected that and asked if I could make a visual approach to the opposite runway. My terminology wasn't the same as that used by the Yanks, so after a bit of a pause I received, 'Sure, 36, help yourself. Nobody else is fool enough to fly tonight.' We turned around and landed in the clear, running back into the snow as we slowed down.

Sometimes the weather is awe inspiring, if a little scary. One night we were flying back to base at about 15,000ft and there were a lot of thunderstorms about; in fact that's why we were going home at medium altitude. We had avoided a huge storm during our low-level sortie and Nordhorn range was unfit for bombing for the same reason, so we'd decided to give up, go home and have a night flying supper (always a treat) and a couple of beers. There was a full moon and I could see the towering cumulonimbus thunderheads all around us, but ahead there was a convenient gap between two of them. As we got closer, with the clouds occasionally being internally illuminated by the lightning, there was an enormous bolt of blue-white lightning that flashed back and forth several times in the clear air between the two clouds. It was blindingly bright and it appeared to be at our height and very close. I wondered whether to climb or change heading, but in the end decided to carry on. Thankfully it didn't happen again.

We were struck by lightning more than once in flight, but one occasion is etched in my memory. There were four of us flying in battle formation at low level from RAF Idris in Libya to RAF Luqa on Malta. As we progressed north over the sea there was a cold front between us and our destination. We could see quite clearly the clouds and the curtains of rain hanging down from them. The leader called us to close into arrow formation and then he picked the lightest-looking patch and flew towards it.

When we hit the rain the visibility dropped markedly, but by closing up a bit more we could still see each other. After a few minutes there was an almighty flash. I watched a bolt of lightning hit Mike Gamble's jet amidships. I asked him if he knew about it; I got a gruff, affirmative response.

After we had landed and gone back to the Officers' Mess I received a message to call our Engineering Officer. He asked me if I knew that we had received a lightning strike, and if so, why hadn't I reported it. He sounded a bit miffed.

'No, Jim, it wasn't me it was Mike Gamble. I think he was flying 344,' I said.

'Well, you just come over here and have a look at your aircraft.' He still sounded grumpy, so I thought I'd better. I grabbed the squadron aircrew transport and drove up to our dispersal area. We walked out to my jet, XM 268, and he pointed at the tailplane. There were several small, black-rimmed holes in the end of the elevator. He then marched me around to the other side and pointed to a similarly adorned wingtip.

'Oh,' I said, 'I didn't feel a thing. What about 344?'

'Oh yes. That's even worse, but he reported it.'

I felt a certain sense of injustice, but apologised anyway. I really didn't know we'd been struck. The last time it had happened I had heard the bang and felt a shock from the cabin wall onto my left hand, which was holding the throttles. The compass had, on that occasion, gone a bit haywire – a usual effect of a lightning strike.

Another peculiar weather-related effect was St Elmo's Fire. This was long renowned for frightening the crews of sailing ships, when the effects of static electricity used to make the masts and rigging glow with an eerie blue light. Well it happens in aeroplanes too and quite often. Usually St Elmo lights us up when we fly through high-altitude cirrus clouds, which are made of ice crystals. The passage of the aircraft through the thin ice generates static electricity and ethereal blue fingers of wispy light start running up and down the windscreen. Sometimes it builds up to such a level of ghostly activity that it affects radio reception and you can hear it hissing on the intercom. It is a bit disturbing the first time you see it, but after a while it becomes a fascinating phenomenon – a bit like the Northern Lights!

But there are two weather effects that were potentially deadly for the low-level Canberra crew. One, that I have already alluded to, is low stratus cloud clinging to hillsides when the sky above is overcast. It really was difficult at times to make out where the earth stopped and the sky began. That sucked crews in to going too far before pulling up and then hitting the ground hidden by the cloud.

Once, when we were flying south at low level from northern Scotland down the eastern half of the UK, we ran into deteriorating weather ahead of a warm front. Geoff had told me to look out for a valley to follow that should get us through the Cheviot Hills without taking us high enough to go into the lowering cloudbase. Unfortunately we picked the wrong valley and not long afterwards all I could see ahead of me was rising ground meeting a layer of scrappy grey cloud: hill stratus. I pulled up hard, full power, 30° nose up. As we entered cloud I saw the radio altimeter going up as we moved away from the ground, but then it started to descend again. I held onto the altitude and the radio altimeter bottomed at 300ft. We levelled off in thick cloud, initially at about 5,000ft, before contacting the area radar station and getting permission to climb higher and go home. About a month later I read an accident report of a Vulcan crash, which had killed all five crewmembers. The Vulcan had just clipped the top of the hill at the end of the same valley. I wondered whether the pilot had watched the radio altimeter winding down as well; that's if he had one.

So low cloud was something we didn't want to see in our weather forecasts, especially in mountainous areas. But there was one humorous occasion when we were on our squadron exchange to Leipheim in southern Germany. Each morning a short, stout, bespectacled Met Man, whom everyone German addressed as *Herr Doktor*, gave the weather briefing there. He used to come in and commence his briefing briskly and in a very authoritative way; this amused the more irreverent members of our squadron hugely.

However, one day he strutted in, everyone stood (which is an honour the RAF reserve only for the Station or Squadron Commander) and he announced in accented English and in his usual aloof and strident manner, 'High ground will be extensive in Southern Germany today.' So nothing new there, then. What he really meant to say was that *low cloud* will be extensive *over* high ground, etc! I suppose that we should have been grateful that the *Herr Doktor* was doing the briefing in English especially for us; but even if we were, his remark generated lots of giggling and banter.

The other problematic weather phenomenon was icing. Although the B(I)8 had an anti-icing system for the engine air intakes, it had no similar system for the leading edges of the wings or tailplane. The recommendation was to avoid icing conditions whenever possible, which was hard to do in Northern European winters, and, if one couldn't, then the advice was to switch on the engine anti-icing system as soon as possible after entering icing conditions. As I alluded to earlier, we also had to modify our engine settings to help minimise the effects of ice formation on the engines' performance.

One grey winter's day we were recovering to Laarbruch from high altitude. There was a continuous layer of cloud, called stratocumulus, over most of northern Germany and the slightly bubbly tops of that sort of cloud, which are usually at or around 5,000ft, are normally below freezing. On days like that there is rarely any high-altitude cloud above the lower layer and from on high the world looks like an immense cauliflower spread out below you.

As we were descending for our recovery to Laarbruch we called the area radar station, callsign 'Clutch Radar', only to find that every Canberra that had got airborne that morning was trying to get home at the same time. The radar controller was trying his best, but he was getting overloaded. So, to ease his task, he started stacking us and asking us to go into elongated orbits, while he sorted out the guys at the bottom of the stack. He told us to level off at 5,000ft; when we got there it was just below the cloudtops. Within seconds the ice started to form on the windscreen, then the leading edges of the wings. I had switched the anti-icing on about 2 minutes earlier, so that should have been working its magic on the engine air intakes. I had set the correct power with the throttles and we started our holding pattern. About 2 minutes later the ice build-up on the bullet-shaped starter housing in the centre of the engine air intakes was easily visible. I was about to ask if we could hold 1,000ft higher, above the cloud, when I heard the controller ask the aircraft descending behind me to level off there. Oh well, I thought, we won't be here that long, surely?

Twenty minutes later we were still going round and round at 5,000ft. There was a lot of ice on the wings and the ice on the starter housing had built up to about a foot ahead of the engine. Enough! I was just to put out an emergency call when I heard my callsign. On responding, the controller gave me a heading to fly and asked me to descend to 3,000ft and call the Laarbruch Approach Controller. I'd never been so glad to go down.

At 3,000ft the temperature was just positive and I saw the ice starting to melt. Some of it fell off in big lumps and some of the ice in front of the engines must have gone through them, but there were no untoward symptoms. When we came out of the cloud at 2,500ft the world was uniformly grey, but I was very glad to see the ground.

Another weather problem was the same one that nearly caught us out at Bassingbourn: the weather being passed to the ATC controllers not being the real weather. On one trip to Malta, when we were fitted with a gunpack and not carrying tip tanks, we had to check the weather before starting our descent because, once we were down there, we would not have enough fuel to reach our diversion airfield on Sicily.

We were told that there was a very small amount of cloud at 500ft and more at 1,500ft; so down we went. They also said that they were having trouble with their radars. As we levelled off at 2,000ft over the sea we couldn't see the island for cloud. Then we were informed that all the radars had become unserviceable and that the ILS was off the air, being serviced. As we had an aircraft with a radio compass we elected to fly overhead the radio beacon, let down over the sea and then make a visual approach from the north-east to runway 24. We went into cloud and I descended quite slowly, watching the radio altimeter carefully. At 500ft we broke cloud over the sea; that would make the cloudbase at Luqa airfield about 300ft. I turned around and aimed for the island. As the Grand Harbour soon came into view, I slowed down, dropped the wheels and carried on. As we entered Grand Harbour at 300ft I could see the runway approach lights ahead. I flew level at the cloud base until I was on the correct glide slope then dropped the flaps and landed very shortly afterwards. As we parked, I was asked politely to report to the Wing Commander Flying at my earliest convenience. I did so, supported by my loyal nav, and explained why we had crept up on the airfield using all available cover and upset some of the natives. He accepted the explanation with a wry smile.

Another similar incident happened on a return journey from Malta to Laarbruch. When we went to the Operations Centre to plan the homeward trip and get the weather forecast we were given a Priority Signal Message (like a military telegram). It said 'Weather at base for recovery of MSOKW (our callsign) – visibility 1 to 2 nm, cloudbase 2,500ft.' When we got there, about 4 hours later, the visibility was 800 yards and there was complete cloud cover at 200ft! How could it possibly be so much worse than forecast? At the time it was well below the limits for me to even attempt an approach. We were diverted to the GAF base at Wunstorf near Hanover and came back to base the following day. Our allies looked after us very well.

In the depths of winter Laarbruch received its fair share of snow and ice, so there was a reasonable selection of snow-clearing equipment. One of these machines was a peculiar Heath-Robinson device: a wheeled platform with two jet engines and a cab mounted on it. This was known as the Blacktop De-icer and it had to be operated by a pilot. So, we were asked to volunteer to do the short training course then we could be available for shifts of about 2 hours in this wonderful machine while snow clearing operations were taking place.

The two engines were de Havilland Ghosts, as fitted to the Gloster Meteor. The jet pipes were modified into wide, fishtail shapes and they could be moved up and down a limited amount. It was great fun to be ensconced in the little cab operating the throttles and the tilt levers to get the hot jet to lift the frozen snow and ice off the runway. The de-icer was pushed along by a fuel bowser, which was also providing the fuel to the engines, and there was a radio link to the bowser driver. Sometimes using too much power caused the whole assembly to stop, with the bowser driver calling for us to ease off a bit! One dark and snowy night I was doing my bit when the OC Technical Wing's RAF Mini hove into view on my right-hand side. He was keen, despite the fact that it was two o'clock in the morning, to see how things were going. Just as he came into position, slightly ahead of the rig, a huge sheet of ice lifted off the runway, performed a graceful parabola and landed plumb on top of his car. He drove off not to be seen again!

The weather is a part of an aviator's environment and its effect is dependant on what the aviator is trying to do. It is essential that everyone who flies understands the weather, how it works, how it is forecast and, most of all, to always respect it like sailors respect the sea.

Geoff told me a story about a private pilot who landed on a fine and sunny Sunday afternoon at the airfield where he was doing his advanced navigation training. Geoff was the Station Orderly Officer that day, so he had to go and find out why this civilian 'puddle jumper' had landed at a military airfield without permission. The pilot said that she had got lost and was worried, so she landed at the first airfield she came across to find out where she was. Geoff asked to see her map and weather information; the latter was for the previous Sunday! When asked whether she was aware of this she said, 'Oh yes, but the weather today looked just the same, so I used that.' Well, the weather was about the same, but the winds were about 180° different. She was 25 miles off track!

26

Air Displays

I think that it all started with a misdemeanour. We had gone on another Mediterranean mini-break, that is Exercise SOUTHERN RANGER, this time to Akrotiri in Cyprus. We had to leave there on the Sunday to fly to Malta and then leave there on Monday morning to arrive at Laarbruch before lunchtime. Having arrived on the Friday evening, we spent one day and two very pleasant evenings at Akrotiri. On the Saturday evening we had renewed our acquaintance with Pete Balding, one of our fellow Basic Flying Training Course members, who was now an Air Traffic Controller. There were also other folk in the Mess that we knew. By bedtime we had been persuaded to give the local beach a flypast as we left on the Sunday morning. Pete had said that he would be on duty in the tower as the local controller and that he would be happy with that.

So, after take-off I held the height down to about 500ft and flew round the south of the Akrotiri peninsula, avoiding the domestic site and the military hospital, and then turned west to re-enter the bay where the Ladies Mile beach was. There was someone on waterskis in the bay, so I aimed to fly between them and the beach and dropped down to about 50ft and put the speed up to about 350kts. Once past the beach I pulled up sharply and climbed away steeply. I thought about a roll but then discarded the idea; that would be showing off too much! Pete called me and told me to check in with Nicosia Centre. When I made contact with them they asked me to call the Akrotiri local controller again. I did so and received the following call from Pete, 'Hey mate, I've turned the recording tape off. I've just received a call from the Station Commander who sounded hopping mad. He wanted to know whether you were authorised for that fly-past and, if so, what minimum height you were cleared to. Don't worry about the answer now

– I told him that you were already with the Nicosia Controller and that we couldn't contact you. All the best, my old!'

Phew! What bad luck. I wondered whether the Station Commander had been the guy on the waterskis. The whole trip home was flown in a quiet, contemplative sort of mood. I spent most of the following week expecting some sort of comeback. By Friday morning I said to Geoff, 'Looks like we got away with it.'

I had spoken too early. I was making my first coffee when the Boss poked his head round the crewroom door. He looked at me seriously and said, 'Noddy, my office, now, and put your hat on.' That was code for, 'I'm going to give you a bollocking.' I went to his door and knocked.

'Come in.'

I approached his desk, saluted and stood to attention; I knew the form by now!

To my surprise he handed me a letter.

'Read that.'

It was from an Air Commodore North-Lewis, OC RAF Akrotiri. The Air Commodore went on to outline his view of my lack of maturity, airmanship, flying ability, officer qualities and general prospects of a continued career in Her Majesty's Royal Air Force.

The final sentence was something like, 'If this officer was under my command I would have him court-martialled; however, I will leave you to do what you think best.' It was pretty damning and I really took exception to the lack of flying ability bit.

The Boss said, 'Think yourself lucky. I'm not going to have you court-martialled. However, you will spend two weeks continuously in QRA over the period of the squadron's fiftieth anniversary celebrations. You are an idiot and I'm disappointed in you. Now get out, get your coffee, make me one and come back, this time without your hat.'

As I made the coffees I wondered what the Boss was up to now. When I went back into his office he invited me to pull up a chair. A bit like Max Bygraves, he said, 'I want tell you a story. There was once a young Vampire pilot who thought that he was a bit of an ace. There was a squadron detachment to El Adem and when the squadron left to fly home this young man's jet went unserviceable, so he had to stay behind. A couple of days later he finally set off and decided to beat up the airfield as a parting gesture. By the time he reached his base the Wing Commander Flying at El Adem had called his boss and told the latter what he had witnessed. He was obviously upset and the young pilot got a severe rocket from his boss. Now the bit that you might find hard to believe, I know I did. The young pilot was me and the Wing Commander was called Lewis; yes it was the same chap. He adopted the 'North' later, probably to go with his career aspirations!'

That coincidence had perhaps saved me from a worse fate; although the punishment was bad enough. It was also a salutary lesson and, in retrospect, I needed pulling down a peg or six. After less than two years on the squadron I had received above average assessments from the two tests I had flown with the visiting CFS Agents and, mainly because Geoff was a first-class navigator, we had achieved some very good results in all our 'operational' flying. We had represented the squadron in the annual bombing competition and acquitted ourselves well. I had also been recommended for, and received, a Permanent Commission – in short, I was doing very well, but I was on the slippery slope to overconfidence and that can be a killer.

A month or so later, the Boss once more poked his head around the crewroom door and caught my eye.

'Noddy, come in and see me; I'll have a coffee.'

This was the friendly invitation – no hat. I went in and the Boss asked, 'Do you think that you could design a 10-minute, solo Canberra flying display and bring it to me when you've done it?'

'I think so, sir,' I said, 'Who's going to do it?'

'You are, you chump; if I approve it I'll send it up through the Group Captain to Command HQ.'

Wow, I thought. I'd never done a flying display before but I enjoyed aerobatics and flying my aircraft to the limits. So off I went and thought about all the many displays that I'd seen over the years and devised a routine. There were two variations: one for a flying arrival start and one starting from take-off. The routine contained wingovers, high-and low-speed passes and a gradually tightening series of 360° turns, during which the bomb doors were opened and then, as the speed reduced, the undercarriage and flaps lowered. At 140kts with full power and the flaps down the Canberra can turn impressively tightly. There was also a barrel roll and a LABS manoeuvre to finish. When I took it to show the Boss he asked a few good questions, changed one part of it and then asked me to redo it for sending up the line. He also told me that 16 Squadron had also been given the task of producing a formation display for the Hanover Air Show in early May that year, 1966. I would be involved in that as well.

About ten days before our slot at Hanover, we started the formation practises. The team was six aircraft and the plan was that we would arrive in an arrow shape, with two jets in echelon each side of the Boss and me in line astern. As we made our first pass I would drop out of the arrow and perform a tight 360° turn in front of the crowd. That would give the rest of the guys time to turn around and form another shape. As they ran in I would then pass beneath them pulling up behind them as soon as it was clear. After another couple of passes, with more solo bits in between their turnabouts, I would carry out a LABS manoeuvre immediately following the penultimate opposition pass. The flying spare aircraft would then join the other five in the slot I had vacated for the final pass. We would all join up to the west before going back to Laarbruch.

We flew five practise sorties and by lunchtime on 3 May we had got it stitched up; that was good because the afternoon of that day was when all seven of us departed for Hanover. The transit was made at a couple of thousand feet in a battle formation of two sections. About 10 minutes out from Hanover Airport the Boss called us into close formation; the spare flew above us and acted as a 'whipper-in' to make sure that it looked good. I tucked myself under the Boss's tail and waited. At about 2 minutes to go, Geoff said, 'He's lined up with the wrong runway!'

'Are you sure?' I asked.

'Yes, the air show is happening on the south side and he's lined up with the northern runway.'

'OK, I'll tell him.'

Just as I was about to press the transmit button to call the Boss he called, 'Hang on men! Turning right – GO!'

I had the easy slot. The guys to the left and right of the Boss were working very hard to hang on. We only had 30 seconds to go. As the turn was reversed I was aware of the airfield passing beneath us. Geoff called when we were abeam crowd centre and I departed to the right. The rest of the display went to plan. It was just the recovery at base that was going to be different now. The Boss had said that we would rejoin the circuit via LABS manoeuvres. We had to fly in an extended line astern at low level and 430kts. Each aircraft would then pull up abeam the control tower and complete a half loop. From that we would then all descend for individual run-in and breaks to land. I thought that this might be a bit over-ambitious and had the makings of possible chaos. In the event it worked out quite well and the assembled crowds in the squadron gave us a round of applause!

My full solo display had been viewed by the Station Commander and approved by the Commander-in-Chief, so we were ready to go off on our own. Our first display venue was in Denmark. We had to fly to an airbase called Tirstrup for the Royal Danish Air Force Air Day on 19 June 1966. Sergeant Brown was coming with us as our technical supporter and we had a pannier in the bomb bay for our weekend bags, a spare wheel, other bits and pieces and the appropriate tools.

We flew north to Tirstrup at low level and skirted a storm over the North Sea, just off the western coast of Denmark. It was a dark, turbulent-looking thing and there were several waterspouts coming up out of the sea. It was the first time that I'd seen such a phenomenon.

When we got to our destination we were parked between a Royal Navy Sea Vixen and a USAF Phantom. I'd never seen either of these types up close before. There was also a RN Buccaneer and a GAF Fiat G-91. We were told that our accommodation was off-base and we would be taken there in a bus. Once everyone was ready we boarded and set off. One of the Fleet Air Arm pilots was a larger than life character who reminded me of Captain Haddock from *Tintin*. He had a big black beard, a booming voice and a huge laugh. His name was Pete Sheppard – little did I know that our paths would cross quite a few times in the future. Once we were on the bus he pulled a cardboard box from under his legs. It contained several bottles of gin, one of which he extracted and opened. The problem was that there were no glasses, so he filled the bottle cap and passed it around like that. This turned out to be fortuitous because our Danish liaison officer announced that the hotel that we would be staying in was a Temperance Hostel and there would be no bar! Whoever heard of putting aircrew in a dry hotel? My esteem for the purveyors of probably the world's best lager and bacon took a tumble.

After a couple of sneaky gin snifters we went to Aarhus, the nearest town and found a decent restaurant and bar. But there was more bad news to come. At the briefing the next day the Display Director, a RDAF officer wearing four stripes, told us that we would make flypasts at the four main RDAF bases and then land back at Tirstrup, where the final flypast would happen. They gave us a route to follow and timings to achieve. I was disappointed that all my display practise had, for the moment, been wasted. It turned out that some years ago a RDAF jet aerobatic formation team had crashed at one of their Air Days and the political response was to stop all aerobatic routines and just have lots of different types of aircraft make flypasts.

There were other types from all over NATO that would join the stream from other bases, so it was all rather complicated. We were told to fly round at our usual cruising speeds and then adjust our route to take in any differences. We all agreed to fly at 330kts to make it easy; however, the Fiat G-91 said that he didn't have enough fuel to do the whole route, so he was excused one flypast. Italian car-makers shouldn't be asked to make jet fighters!

It all went well until we got to Karup. We were behind Pete Sheppard and his observer in the Sea Vixen and the timing seemed to be going to plan. But then we received a call that asked us to slow down and arrive at the display datum a minute later. At the time they called us we only had 3 minutes to run and we weren't allowed to orbit because someone else was following us. So I slowed down as much as I dared; the big fat wing of the Canberra came into its own and we floated along at 150kts. I'd only just retrimmed and settled when the controller called us again, 'Canberra, I'm sorry we got that wrong. Please now get here as soon as you can.'

OK. Full power and accelerate. Geoff was busy helping me locate the runway and I started to drop down to the 200ft they wanted. As we crossed the airfield boundary I glanced at the airspeed indicator and saw it passing 350kts. I now concentrated on flying at the right height and waited for the other end of the runway to pass under us before pulling up. As I did so I looked at the airspeed indicator and saw the speed reducing past the maximum allowed indicated airspeed of 450kts; I must have misread the twin-needled instrument at my last check! Anyway, no harm done and we got back safely as did all the other jets. We all passed another riotous evening in our temperance accommodation and set off home on Monday morning!

We did get to do our full show several times that summer, but the most memorable was over the airfield at a place called Straubing-Weidmuller, which was way down south in eastern Bavaria, not that far from the Czech border. We had to get special clearance because the location was inside the Buffer Zone. We were warned that Czech or Russian radio intercepts may be made and that we should not be drawn in by false directions to head east; they were just trying to get us to cross the border. I didn't realise that being an air display pilot could get this complicated! We planned carefully and set off from Laarbruch on Saturday 11 September in XM 274. The airfield was specially opened for us; I'm afraid that we stopped my erstwhile gliding club friends from flying for a while.

To conserve fuel we flew down at high level and got a radar service to watch us descend. The weather was glorious and we located the airfield from a good distance away. We were asked to call Straubing on their published VHF frequency, but when we did two voices answered in sequence. So the intelligence chaps were right. One of the voices kept telling us to continue on an easterly heading, even though I was now positioning to the north of the airfield for our high-speed arrival. I ignored Boris and stopped talking on the radio. In those days we were allowed to arrive from behind the crowd, so we came to the display datum at 440kts and 200ft. I closed the throttles and opened the bomb doors. For those on the ground this made an impressive noise; the effect was a huge version of the noise you get when you blow across the top of an open bottle. After that we went into our usual collection of turns and wingovers, a slow flypast and the LABS manoeuvre to finish. The barrel roll had been deleted by HQ RAF Germany! Then it was home, James, and don't spare the horses.

I think that my very short time flying both solo and formation displays was a highlight of my time on 16 Squadron. I also think that Trog Bennett was both courageous and farsighted in choosing me for the task. Although he thought, rightly or wrongly, that I had the required talent, he realised that the responsibility to do what I enjoyed, but very publicly and keeping it safe was something I needed to learn. He was right. Later in life I would become a regular air display pilot on the historic aircraft scene. What I learnt on this first encounter with the discipline stood me in good stead later.

27

Aden

Most crews were allocated one Exercise **EXTENDED SOUTHERN RANGER (ESR)** trip on their three-year tour. Before Southern Rhodesia's unilateral declaration of independence on Armistice Day 1965, there were options of flying as far south as the capital, Salisbury. After the Southern Rhodesian Prime Minister, Ian Smith, removed that item from the itinerary, and until mid-1966, Nairobi was the ultimate destination. We missed both of those, but in July 1966, we were allocated an ESR to RAF Khormaksar in the Protectorate of Aden, by then a part of the Federation of South Arabia.

In December 1963 a grenade attack against the British High Commissioner in Aden had triggered an official State of Emergency and the threat level had not diminished since. Before we went we were made aware that it was essential that we did not night-stop in Aden, but left before sunset. When asked why we were told that the Big Chief, SACEUR, didn't want his nuclear assets left where they might be open to mortar attack or sabotage. That meant that we would have to fly from a base in the Arabian Gulf into Khormaksar by mid-morning, get downtown to do any shopping over lunchtime and then get airborne during the late afternoon, to return to the Gulf by evening. Of course the prime purpose was not the acquisition of such 'goodies' but to experience long-range navigation to a new part of the world. However, while we were there ... why not?

The 'goodies' available were things such as gold, fine china and cameras, and the savings we would make would be worth our long day to get them. I had not long been married and had found out that Noritake china was very cheap in Aden, so I got hold of the squadron's copy of their catalogue and we made our choice. Geoff had the purchase of a camera and a hi-fi in mind. So we started planning. We would have an aircraft with tip-tanks and two panniers fitted; we were also due to pick up things for other folk. We planned to fly from Laarbruch to Akrotiri, on Cyprus, direct, then on to RAF Sharjah on the southern Arabian Gulf the next day. The third day would be the two flights from Sharjah to Aden and then the return, across the Empty Quarter of Southern Arabia, direct to RAF Muharraq in Bahrain. We could then have a day off. However, we had heard about Bahrain in July, with its oppressive heat and humidity, so we elected to have two days off in Cyprus instead, flying back, via Malta, on the last day of our week away.

It was a lot of work for Geoff and I ensured that all the required diplomatic clearances and international flight plans were done and ready for submission at each stop. We packed all our kit, including our Khaki Drill (KD) shirts, shorts, socks and desert boots and our shopping list. Geoff had a navigator friend in Aden, Bill Campbell, who was on the SAR helicopter flight, and he got in touch with him to arrange transport for our trip downtown.

On the morning of Friday 15 July we were all ready to go. At about eleven o'clock we lifted off from Laarbruch for the 4½-hour epic to Cyprus. We had never flown to Akrotiri direct before, so it was going to take some special techniques to get that range out of our jet and still have enough fuel for the possibility of a diversion to Turkey.

However, the forecast for the route was excellent all the way, with clear, blue skies on the island, so we didn't really expect that to happen; as long as no one crashed and blocked Akrotiri's only runway! The plan was to fly to the toe of Italy, at 45,000ft and then do something called a cruise climb above Greek airspace, as far as a place in the sky called West Point, not the US Army College, but the high-level western entry point for Cyprus.

The cruise climb was a way of optimising fuel consumption by accurately setting an engine rpm, calculated by the nav, and flying a fixed indicated Mach number. We would then have a very slow climb rate and, as we got higher, we would periodically adjust things depending on the air temperature outside, which would be something in the region of -56°C. It was going to be a long ride, we had no autopilot so the accuracy, which was crucial, was down to me. We had, as usual for these sorts of trips, in-flight meals, which was a very overblown title for a white cardboard box of ham and cheese sandwiches, an apple and a can of fruit juice. They never gave us a can opener for the latter, so Geoff opened them with the crash-axe down in his hidey-hole. The axe was really there to help us break out should we have survived a crash and there was no one to let us out. It was best if the hole in the can was made before we got too high, otherwise there would be an explosion of sticky liquid all over Geoff's maps and charts.

All went boringly well to our cruise climb point. By then I had consumed my sandwiches, which at a cabin altitude of 23,000ft went as dry as British Rail fare in an instant! I'd drunk my juice to help the cardboard sandwiches go down and was saving the apple until we got abeam the island of Crete. We slowly climbed and, as we were no longer talking to any air traffic service, Geoff had tuned our radio compass to the BBC World Service. Then a hand came up from down below with a small piece of paper in it. I took the proffered scrap, which turned out to be a tiny world map, in those days found in the lid of tin boxes of Benson and Hedges cigarettes. On it was a fine line showing our track and a small red cross.

'What's this?' I asked.

'It's just in case you wondered where we are,' was the reply. Then he said, 'Don't hang on to it, I need it back to work on the rest of the route.' For a moment I thought that he was serious. Save me from loony navigators!

By the time that we had passed Crete, well over 8 miles below us, the blue of the sky had deepened quite noticeably. I looked ahead and saw that the dark blue above faded to a yellowish haze at the horizon and then the blue of the sea mirrored it, getting deeper below. I then made a big mistake. I thought that this sight could easily convince me that I was flying upside down. And that was enough! The thought had triggered a psychological response. Suddenly there was a very large butterfly pounding my insides and I instinctively tightened my grip on the controls. The more I then told myself that it wasn't true, the more the effect took hold. It was not nice. I lowered my seat so that I couldn't see so much of the Mediterranean blue and the effect slowly faded. After a few more minutes it had gone. I told myself to get a grip and not do it again.

Much later in my life I was talking to an American astronaut and he told me that when he was in the Spacelab and he had to change workstations inside the tubular spacecraft, he actually used that mind over matter effect to establish his own up and down.

When I'd got my head back in order, I noticed that we were approaching 50,000ft. I wondered whether we would actually get above it before we reached West Point where we would start our descent. We did, by 50ft! Once we had made contact with Nicosia Air Traffic Control Centre I pulled the throttles back to flight idle and we started our long, glide descent into Akrotiri. As we got closer I could see the island and then the airfield. It was a beautiful afternoon down there; no cloud and a gentle westerly breeze. I was able to make a visual descent and positioned us for a descending run in and brake. The throttles were still closed so I brought them up slightly to give the required minimum of 4,500rpm on the final approach. That was the first time I'd increased power since we left 50,000ft!

We spent a pleasant evening in the Mess, but not a late night . The next day we were up and away by ten o'clock for another 4-hour flight to RAF Sharjah. Because of diplomatic clearance requirements our initial heading was an illogical northerly one because we had to avoid Syrian airspace. We headed north until we reached a point about halfway between the cities of Ankara and Van. Once there it was a right turn to overfly Lake Van, heading for Tehran, then the capital of Persia, now Iran. That was about halfway and it was easy to see the huge city nestling beneath the mountains to its north and east. From there on we took a south-easterly track direct for Ismir, then down the middle of the Arabian Gulf to Abu-Dabi and Sharjah. Because we had once more changed time zones, we had lost another hour. As we descended into the sandy-coloured gloom and goldfish bowl conditions over the featureless water I had to fly by sole reference to the instruments, even though there wasn't a cloud in sight.

The temperature outside rose quickly and the high humidity showed itself by hoar frost forming on all the cold surfaces of the aircraft. That soon melted as we dropped lower and we were steered by the radar controller at Sharjah until we could see the airfield and make a visual approach and landing. Sharjah was another desert airfield to chalk up on the 'places we have been to' list. In fact, it was so much so that we were parked on sand, thankfully very solid sand. As we walked to the Officers' Mess two chaps wearing shorts came round a corner carrying golf bags; it was a surreal sight. It turned out that they played their game in the world's largest bunker. Oil was poured on the sand at intervals to make the 'greens', except that they were called 'browns'!

After another hot and steamy night, under mosquito nets and fans, we arose early and were airborne by 8 a.m. The first track took us due south to meet the coast of the Gulf of Aden overhead the RAF airfield at Salalah. As we set off I could see a huge, anvil-shaped cloud towering into the sky; it appeared to be just left of our track. As we climbed it became clearer, jutting high above the dusty layer of haze that went up to about 20,000ft. By the time that we levelled off at 40,000ft the top of the colossal cumulonimbus was still at least 10,000ft above us. It was undoubtedly being fed by hot, humid air blowing inland from the sea into the Al Akhdar Mountains.

After that there was little to do, no one to talk to, not even much to look at. Half an hour later I could make out the coast ahead and Geoff managed to get a signal from the radio beacon at Salalah; that gave me something to steer towards. Over Salalah, a remote RAF staging post, we turned right and headed directly for Aden. From our altitude I could see the mountains and hills where some of my friends from flying training days, now flying Hunters based in Aden, were occasionally shooting rockets and bullets at the Radfan rebels. Beyond those rocky hills lay the sands of the Empty Quarter. That reminded me that we would be flying over that truly deserted landscape this afternoon. I wasn't looking forward to that much.

We arrived at Khormaksar almost 3 hours after we had taken off from Salalah. We parked, carried out the post-flight servicing and asked the groundcrew to arrange a full refuel, with the usual warning about starting with the front tank. By now Geoff's friend Bill had turned up and took us to Base Operations, where we filed everything for the return flight and ordered the route and terminal weather forecasts. After a quick change of clothes and coffee in the SAR Flight, we headed downtown on our shopping spree.

We managed to get everything except my china: the delightful man in the shop didn't have it in stock. However, he said that he would order it and could have it shipped to my German address for his price, which was ridiculously cheap, plus 10 per cent. So I paid him a deposit and we agreed that I would post the rest by traveller's cheque when I had received the goods; it worked, about a month later we had our lovely set of china.

With everything else on the list stuffed into Bill's car we set off back. After a quick, light lunch we changed back into flying kit, loaded our loot and started up to head for Bahrain. The temperature was now 33°C and it was very hot in the cockpit. We left the door open until the last moment before lining up on the south-westerly runway. That would take us out over Aden Bay after lift-off. The last 300 yards of the runway stuck out into the water, a bit like at Gibraltar. I applied full power and we accelerated sedately. Geoff called out the acceleration check and the stop speed. As we reached about 125kts I raised the nose wheel and a few seconds later she lifted, a bit reluctantly, into the air. As I pressed the undercarriage UP button four red lights came on instead of three: three for the undercarriage being unlocked and the other one right in front of my face. It was the port engine fire warning light! I shaded it from the sunlight with my hand to make sure it was actually on. It was!

'Geoff, we've a fire warning light on.'

I then put out a brief emergency call. The tower acknowledged and then another voice said, 'Ready!' It was Geoff, who had already clipped on his parachute and was kneeling by the door, ready to go on my call.

'Stay where you are, we're still only at 200ft,' I said. I had a brief image of Geoff doing a ducks and drakes impression across the bay if he jumped out now.

Long ago I had decided that if an engine caught fire on take-off, but below safety speed. I would not do anything until we had achieved that speed. That wasn't strictly by the book, but a fire indication comes from around the engine – the inside's already on fire and still producing full thrust. I had also decided that if the engine was going I would control the aircraft better if I shut the throttle first and then cut off the fuel with the high pressure (HP) cock. Again this wasn't by the book, but like my decision about the speed, it was designed to give me the best chance of recovering safely and climbing away. After all I had my best friend on board and he couldn't get out until we were at 1,000ft.

So at 175kts I closed the throttle and reached for the HP cock. The fire warning light went out. I didn't shut the HP cock immediately and opened the throttle again. It could have been a rare electrical fault with the fire detection system. But it wasn't; at about 60 per cent power the light came on again. It was a hot gas leak, probably from around the turbine joint. No choice now – shut down drills completed.

'You can relax,' I told Geoff, 'We're stuck here now.'

We were about 5,000lb over our maximum landing weight so we had to burn that off before landing and it would take about an hour. I apprised Khormaksar ATC of our situation and cancelled the emergency. We were asked to hold over the sea at not above 4,000ft. That suited me fine. But half an hour later I had run out of lateral trim and was holding the port wing up with a constant pressure on the yoke. The left wingtip tank had refused to feed. They often did that, but usually only at high level. I expected that once the right tank was empty the left one would start to fill the rear tank; it was just a case of waiting. But 15 minutes later the contents in the rear tank started to reduce so I was beginning to suspect that we had a real problem. One tip tank was full of fuel and that could seriously jeopardise my control of the aircraft during a single-engined landing. Anyway, my arm was getting tired, but I was willing to wait a bit longer. Then ATC called us.

'MPACG we advise that you return to the airfield and land immediately. Rising sand has been observed coming across the bay towards us.'

I told them that I was still overweight for landing, especially at this high temperature, and that I also had fuel hung up in one of our tip tanks, which was giving me an additional control problem. I said that if we had to land any time soon the best course of action would be to jettison our tip tanks. After a short pause he told us that we could do that 10 miles off the coast, on a south-easterly bearing from Aden, as long as we used clear range procedure. That meant that we had to make sure that our tanks weren't going to fall on someone's boat. We went to the assigned area, descended to 2,000ft, looked carefully around and in straight and level flight at 250kts I pressed the jettison button. As I did so I watched the left tip tank. It flipped up and over the wing and rapidly disappeared from view. I turned the jet around to see if we could spot the splash: we didn't.

Now it was time to head back. We were probably just coming down to our maximum landing weight and I had to perform my first actual single-engined approach and landing. As we went downwind in the visual pattern I could see the band of ochre sky heading towards us from the other side of the airfield.

The wind was starting to swing about so I made sure that we wouldn't be too slow, but a bit too enthusiastically, as we crossed the threshold at about 15kts above the normal speed. I touched down as soon as I could and popped the airbrakes out; you never know, they might help, I thought. I started braking at our emergency maximum braking speed, which was relatively low because the air temperature was so high. I told the tower that we may suffer a brake fire and asked for the attendance of a fire vehicle. We came to a stop about 1,000ft from the other end of the runway. Well, so much for our transit of the Empty Quarter and what about all that stuff in the bomb bay panniers?

The diagnosis on the aircraft, XM 269, was that a bolt or bolts had come loose on the flange that held the back of the engine unit to the long exhaust pipe that kept the hot gases from burning the back part of the wing. Thus there was a small leak of hot air and the wires that sensed the temperature back there had got hot enough to illuminate the fire warning light. No remedial action was possible for some time, so we were booked onto the next trooping flight back. That left on the following Friday, five days hence. So we spent the rest of the week at Khormaksar.

It was very hot and humid, but at least we had air conditioning in our accommodation and in most of the public rooms in the Officers' Mess. It was strange to come out of one's room into the hot, humid air and feel one's shirt go instantly damp and limp. Everyone there was waiting for the rainy season to start, which usually was at the beginning of September. One day we were at the outside bar in the Mess gardens, and huge drops of rain started to fall from the sky. Geoff and I naturally ran for cover, but everyone else ran out into the rain, holding their faces up to it with great glee. After a while some of the younger wives' dresses started to become somewhat transparent; that brought previously animated male conversations to a halt, often mid-sentence. That was until the said young ladies realised why it had gone so quiet!

The trooping flight back was crowded, mainly with soldiers going home after their tours of duty. It wasn't until we got to boarding did I become aware, by what was said at the check-in desk, that two unfortunate lads had been bumped off the flight in order to get us back. Apparently our 'nuclear' and NATO status made us valuable cargo. The flight was going to Gatwick, so we were connected with a flight from there to Dusseldorf, where we were met by a driver, who took us back to Laarbruch. We both slept for that journey. The driver dropped us off at our homes, which were on opposite sides of the same road in a village near the base. It was good to be home.

When we went into work on the Monday, I found an official RAF invoice for two wingtip tanks in my mail slot. It took me a while to find out that it was a Flight Commander's practical joke. Well, at least my china was coming by commercial transport – some folks were going to have to wait for XM 269 to be brought home for their goodies to arrive. It did take quite a while for the aircraft to be recovered and, when it did arrive, one side of the jet had lost most of its paint. It had been sandblasted off. So XM 269 soon went off to be repainted – again!

28

When Things Go Wrong

Aeroplanes or, more correctly, bits of them, go wrong from time to time. Sometimes they are just little bits, like an electrical relay, at other times big bits, like an engine or a vital aerodynamic part. There are the really obvious failures whose symptoms you just can't miss, and there are quiet, unseen failures that creep up on you and catch you unawares. Geoff and I had our fair share of bits going wrong in the three and a half years that we committed aviation together and I've already told you about some of them. There were also failures of another kind – of a human sort – that affected others and all of us on the squadron. Sometimes these failures brought death and injury into our midst or they initiated that 'There but for the grace of God go I' response. Then there are the things that go wrong because some natural phenomenon triggered a chain of events, which led to an incident or accident.

The Canberra was, on the whole, a reliable aircraft with reliable engines. The principal handling and safety problem that it had was in controlling the aircraft after an engine failure; the worst case being immediately after lift-off from the runway, when there was a considerable band of airspeed during which the aircraft was off the ground, but below the speed at which one could guarantee to keep control after one engine had stopped. In the case of a fully loaded B(I)8 that gap was about 50kts. If the engine failed during that critical phase of flight, the power of the engine that was still operating normally had to be reduced, full rudder and some aileron had to be rapidly applied and, if at all possible, the aircraft eased away from the ground. The next worse case was an engine failure on the final approach after the one-stage flaps had been lowered. The first response had to be to raise the flaps and increase power on the surviving engine, keeping the aircraft straight with rudder until the normal glide angle and airspeed had been regained. After that a safe landing was usually possible.

Historically the Canberra had, in its very early days, suffered some fatal accidents from the tailplane trim running uncontrollably to full deflection. This had been stopped with a trim cut-out switch, operated simultaneously with the trim switch. In the B(I)8 this safety feature was operated by the flap that had to be raised to give access to the spring-loaded, sliding trim switch itself.

The only other technical problem that recurred at infrequent intervals was not really a safety issue, but it was a real nuisance. That was 'the nosewheel red'. The electric micro-switch that signalled the extinguishing of the red lights on the undercarriage position indicator in the cockpit, was fitted to the wheel-bay doors. The red lights came on as soon as the wheels started to move after the 'up' selection and the action of the doors closing was designed to put it out. However, the nosewheel door micro-switch often went out of adjustment, so that red light would remain on.

This meant that we had to hold the airspeed below 190kts, the speed limit for an unlocked landing gear, then select the undercarriage down, usually burn off fuel and land. However, it became accepted practice to make a low and slow fly-past for someone in the air traffic control tower to inspect the nosewheel bay doors with binoculars. If they appeared to be closed and flush, then we could continue with our sortie. Often, we found that a short while into the flight, the red light would go out. But it was a recurring headache for the electricians.

Another historically significant undercarriage problem was referred to as 'sequence valve malfunction'. This snag affected the main wheels and could cause a major safety incident. The legs of the main landing gear had the largest portion of the undercarriage bay door attached to it and, when it was up and locked, the rest of the undercarriage bay was covered by another door, hinged to the wing root; because of its shape this was known as the D-door. So the retraction sequence was that the main leg and door retracted first and then the D-door followed it to give full coverage and streamlining over the whole undercarriage bay. However, if the valve that controlled this sequence failed the D-door would retract first and then the main leg would retract and trap it; the wheel would then remain half out of the bay. A mainwheel red light would show on the undercarriage indicator. The immediate action would be to drop the speed below 190kts and lower the wheels again. But, in the case of a sequence valve failure, the wheel would not move, because the D-door could not now open first. So the only course of action was to carry out a landing with one main wheel up.

This never happened to me, but one day at Laarbruch a 31 Squadron crew was flying one of the T4s and this sequence valve problem occurred. I was in QRA when it happened and we received a phone call from our ops desk, so we all became 'goofers' and climbed onto one of the QRA building's flat roof to watch. On the final approach we saw the navigator's cabin hatch blow off and flutter to the ground; this was to allow him to get out should the aircraft be too badly damaged on the landing for him to use the normal door. The touchdown was made in the normal place, with flaps down, and the aircraft stayed upright for a remarkably long time. But, eventually and inevitably, the left wing dropped and the jet described a perfect pirouette onto the grass, coming to a stop after turning through 270°. The crew made a rapid exit and the fire vehicles were on the scene very shortly thereafter. There was no fire and everyone seemed to be well. It took a couple of hours for the poor old flying machine to be jacked up and towed away. We were stood down from alert status during that time. It didn't really make much difference, we just went back to our bridge tournament in the knowledge that it would not be interrupted for a while.

The engine fire warning and subsequent engine shutdown in Aden was the most serious thing that went wrong for us, but there was a later event that warranted us jettisoning our tip tanks for a second time. It was on our first flight of 1967, on 3 January. The weather was typically cold with frequent snow showers and a forecast for them to get heavier. We took off on a high-level navigation exercise, which was supposed to last 4 hours. During the climb to high altitude the starboard engine oil pressure started to fall. Normally it was 20–30psi and the in-flight minimum was 15psi.

The higher we climbed the more it fell. I made a turn to see if there was any black smoke from that engine, but I couldn't see any. At about 25,000ft it had fallen to 15psi and by 30,000ft was almost down to zero. I decided to return home and informed the military radar controller of our problem and our intention to return to Laarbruch. I also warned him that we would have to upgrade to an emergency status if I had to shut down the engine. It is well known that jet engines will run for a long time on low oil pressure. However, exactly when the rotating parts get hot enough to seize up is difficult to predict, so it is best to shut the engine down then you know where you stand. We practised single-engine approaches and landings regularly, but not too frequently. More people had died practising them than because of actual engine failures. After pulling back both engines to flight idle for our descent, the starboard oil pressure went completely to zero, so now it was time to shut it down. We carried out all the appropriate drills, put out an emergency call and recovered to Laarbruch. Just as in Aden the jet was still well above the maximum landing weight, so we went into a holding pattern near the airfield to burn off fuel.

After about half an hour I could see a line of big, dark clouds with curtains of snow hanging from them, bearing down on the airfield from the north. I asked the controller if his radar could tell how wide the band of weather was.

'I can see where it starts, about 10 miles north of us, but I can't see the back edge,' he said. Oh great, I thought.

'Please call the Met office and see what their prediction is.'

A couple of minutes later the information that he gave me meant that I would either have to go somewhere else to land or get down at Laarbruch quickly. I decided on the latter, told the tower that I would have to jettison the tip tanks and asked them where I should drop them. The fire section had an old B2 Canberra on the fire practise ground, at the far south-west corner of the airfield, and that's where he wanted us to put them. So we ran in at 1,000ft and 200kts, and I pressed the jettison button just as the old burnt-out jet went out of view at the bottom of the windscreen. The tanks separated cleanly and we landed off the next circuit. As we taxied in it started snowing quite heavily. When we walked into the Ops Room, we were met by a grumpy Flight Commander who said, 'The last invoice you got might have been a joke. This one won't be!' It was satisfying to hear later that our tanks had landed right on the old Canberra: Delta Hotel again! Despite the Squadron Leader's assertion, I didn't have to pay for them.

Our next most serious problem was a multiple birdstrike. After a bombing sortie on Nordhorn range we were transiting back to base at 250ft and 330kts. As we flew over a wooded area a huge flock of starlings, no doubt getting ready to roost, appeared ahead of us. I tried to avoid them but there were just too many. There was a rapid hammering noise and the windscreen in front of me suddenly went pink and opaque. I asked Geoff if he was OK; he told me that he could see out of the nose just fine. By now I had pulled up to a safe height and slowed down. I looked around at the parts of the aircraft I could see and checked all the engine indications. They were both still going and I couldn't see any other damage; but there was a smell of burnt flesh and feathers coming through the air ducts. So at least one of our engines had barbecued a few starlings!

The usual drill after a serious birdstrike is to go to the nearest suitable airfield, carrying out a low speed handling check, with the undercarriage and flaps down, on the way. Well, Laarbruch was by now the nearest suitable airfield and the handling check didn't show any unusual problems. So we flew home sedately and joined the visual circuit to land.

There was only one problem: I couldn't see out straight ahead. The curved Triplex panel in front of the thick, armoured glass directly ahead of me looked like a hammered-glass toilet window. The two side panels were covered with bits of bird, blood and one of them was badly cracked. I decided that I would make a curved approach, straightening up as late as possible and then get Geoff, from his eyrie in the nose, to give me a clue as to how high off the ground we were. As I straightened up he started his talk-down chat.

'About five feet, down, down, down, two feet, ease back a bit, nice hold it there.'

There was a gentle squeak from the wheels; it was one of my better landings.

'Well done, mate,' I said. 'And to think that you were chopped from pilot training because of a lack of height perception! Why don't you re-apply?'

'What and end up having to fly around with someone like me telling me what to do. Not likely, boyo!'

The engineers discovered twenty-seven separate holes in the leading edges of the wings and tail, with lots more impact points. One engine was changed due to minor damage to the compressor blades.

Sometimes it's the navigation kit that lets you down, but our navs were usually soon on to that. One very dark and moonless night, we were climbing out of Malta to go flare dropping and were passing about 15,000ft when there was an exclamation and several Welsh swear words from down below.

'What's up?'

'The Decca has just blown up,' I was informed.

'Well I'm sure we can find our way without it,' I replied encouragingly.

'When I say that it's blown up that's what I mean,' came the disturbing reply. 'I'm applying the fire extinguisher as we speak!'

'Oh. I'll turn back and you let me know when the fire's out.'

I told Malta ATC our problem, started the turn around and then I committed an aviation sin. I looked over my shoulder to find the island to aim at. The sin was that I was not looking at the very helpful, carefully arranged dials that had been placed in an eye-catching manner in front of me to monitor what I was actually doing with the aircraft. I couldn't see the island where I expected it to be. Then what appeared to be a large patch of stars appeared over my left shoulder, but way above my head. That got my attention – it wasn't a hole in the cloud, it was Malta. What is it doing up there? I rapidly got back on the instruments and recovered from what is euphemistically known in the trade as an 'unusual position'. I had it all back under control by about 10,000ft. Geoff had sensed all the rotation, increased G forces and heard the heavy breathing.

He said, 'The fire's out, I've pulled all the relevant circuit breakers, but why are you now trying to make me sick? Haven't I had enough to do? I should get a medal, you know. I can see the headlines in the *Penarth Chronicle* now: "Local RAF lad saves jet from certain destruction. Presentation of medal by HM Queen at Cardiff Castle".' We got back safely but the groundcrew had a lot of work to do down in the confines of Geoff's little den.

One very unusual bit that went wrong on me in early 1965 was the failure of part of the aileron control system. During the recovery into Laarbruch I found that I could only turn the aircraft to the right with great difficulty. I had to hold the left wing up with a lot of right-hand down force on the control yoke, as well as full right aileron trim. I told Laarbruch about it and asked for left-hand turns only and radar positioning for a straight in approach from the east. They duly obliged. However, at about 5 miles from the airfield the controller asked me if I could see an aircraft heading towards me.

'No, I'm still in cloud,' I replied.

'He's closing rapidly – BREAK RIGHT!'

For the third time since the failures I said, 'I can't turn right!'

Silence. We came out of cloud and I couldn't see another aircraft.

The controller said, as reassuringly as he could, 'It's alright. He's gone past you.' Later, the radar plot showed that the other aircraft, a German Air Force F-86 Sabre, had passed very close to us. He had not followed the departure instructions that he had been given.

One of the hazards of flying at high altitudes was the loss of cabin pressurisation. Our cabin wasn't highly pressurised like passenger jets are, which are usually held at about 6,000ft. The Canberra's cabin altitude, indicated on a gauge on the starboard instrument panel, was designed to be half the actual altitude plus 2,000ft; so, at 44,000ft the cabin altitude should be 24,000ft. The worst sort of pressurisation failure was what was known as an explosive decompression, when the loss of pressure was rapid. We were trained to cope with that in a decompression chamber during our aeromedical course; it wasn't a pleasant experience.

En route from Laarbruch to Idris, for another bombing detachment, and while we were at 45,000ft, the cabin pressure suddenly started to rise. Not explosively but quickly enough to make our ears pop. I looked at the cabin altimeter and it was going up steadily. The drill was to get below 25,000ft as rapidly as possible, so I put out an emergency call, closed the throttles, selected full airbrakes out and opened the bomb doors.

Simultaneously I lowered the nose to hold a speed of 0.75 Mach, until the indicated airspeed reached 350kts. This gave us a rapid descent, in excess of 10,000ft per minute. We also selected 100 per cent oxygen and tightened our oxygen masks as the automatic increase in the flow and pressure of oxygen caused them to leak. Now we had to divert to RAF Luqa, on Malta, because we didn't have enough fuel to reach Idris at the lower altitude. Anyway, there were two Canberra squadrons at Luqa, so it was going to be easier to get the problem fixed. It turned out to be a mechanical failure in the pressure-regulating valve.

Later, I did hear about a Canberra crew from one of the other RAF Germany squadrons, who had experienced a rapid decompression over central France. The pilot had carried out all the necessary actions, but just as he called 'bomb doors open' his nav reminded him that their suitcases were in the bomb bay pannier. He shut the doors again, but when they landed they discovered that one case was missing: the pilot's. Amazingly it eventually turned up at his home, a bit bashed and battered, but with all its original contents. Apparently, some Frenchman had found it in a field in the *Massif Centrale* and taken it to the local Gendarmerie, who had discovered the identity and address of the owner from the label on the case and sent it back to him!

Another unusual problem we experienced was caused by clear air turbulence, known as CAT. One day we were heading home from a long, high-altitude tour of Scandinavia, Scotland and England and descending over the North Sea. At about 35,000ft we entered an area of CAT and started getting buffeted about quite badly. I told Geoff to return to his seat and fasten his harness.

Then there was an almighty bang and the aircraft dropped and then rose again in quick succession. I noticed that the accelerometer now read +2.5 G, and I hadn't done anything remotely aggressive during the preceding 3½ hours.

'That was a big one,' I said. 'Are you OK, Geoff?' Then I realised that I wasn't hearing myself on the intercom.

'Can you hear me?' I said, a bit forlornly.

I took my mask off and shouted for Geoff to come up to my cockpit. We were still being buffeted about, but we had been cleared to level off at 25,000ft, so I kept going down and the CAT abated. Then a helmeted head appeared down by my right knee. He took his mask off and I saw his lips move, but I couldn't make out the words. The cabin altitude was now around 14,000ft, a bit too high to risk going without oxygen for any length of time. Nevertheless, I took my helmet and mask off and could now hear Geoff saying that he couldn't hear me at all, but that he could hear ATC. I signalled him to take his helmet off.

'It looks like my part of the comms system has gone completely,' I shouted above the ambient noise, 'You call ATC and get us down to 10,000ft and I'll fly us back with my hat off and you do the radio and pass me their instructions by shouting. OK?'

A thumbs up was the right response. So, we flew successfully back to Laarbruch like that. It was an interesting experience to be flying with no helmet or mask on. It was surprisingly noisy in the cockpit; I could hear the air passing over us, the rushing noise of the air conditioning and the change in engine tone when I moved the throttles. When we got back it was discovered that the vertical movement from the huge lump of CAT that we'd hit had disconnected my ejection seat's radio and intercom lead from the rest of the system. It was in a place that I couldn't reach. In fact, it had been installed with no play in it at all and a very small movement of the seat in the severe turbulence had caused the disconnection.

Other folks' technical problems were both interesting and instructive. The Flight Safety office at Command HQ published a quarterly magazine called *Flight Comment*, so we were kept abreast of things that had gone wrong elsewhere and the lessons we might learn from them. Being a bit of an artist and cartoonist my squadron secondary duty was to write and illustrate the squadron diary, and someone had let on to HQ. In 1965 they asked me to illustrate the cover of the first issue of *Flight Comment*; almost thirty years later, when RAF Germany was wound up, they contacted me again and asked me to illustrate the final cover!

On the squadron, we had a couple of major human error incidents. One of the guys, who shall be nameless to protect his reputation, landed with his wheels still locked up. That and running out of fuel were the two things I most dreaded doing. When it happened he had a gun pack fitted and it transpired that his was the first wheels-up landing in that configuration. The crew got out at the end of their short, very straight slide and were brought back with very long faces to the squadron in the unit's Land Rover. Shortly afterwards, they had to pay a visit to some very senior officer at HQ to present their complements; I expect that it was a very one-sided conversation.

The second event was much more serious. It happened to a new crew on their second sortie in the B(I)8. That trip was flown with full fuel, tip tanks fitted, and involved a heavyweight, practise single-engined transit, approach and overshoot at another airfield. I remember the occasion very well because Geoff and I were scheduled to depart on a bombing sortie at about the same time.

However, when I went to sign for my aircraft I discovered that it had no bombs fitted and it had tip tanks on. It was a simple case of transposition in the communication between the ops desk and the groundcrew office. I popped back and changed the numbers on my flight authorisation and told the duty authoriser. The other guys took the jet I had been originally and wrongly allocated.

We went off to the range and I heard the new pilot call that he was changing frequency for his practise diversion to RAF Gütersloh. When we got back we discovered that the aircraft had crashed on the final approach at Gütersloh, the pilot had ejected and that the navigator was missing, presumed dead. It was a bitter blow to us all, as it was the first fatality on 16 Squadron for several years. The pilot's spine had been injured and he was taken to the RAF Hospital at Wegberg. The investigation by the Board of Inquiry was hampered by his post-stress amnesia, but it was most likely that he had lost control during the asymmetric overshoot. I went to see him in hospital and when I told him that I remembered him changing frequencies he suddenly said, 'Yes – I remember now, hearing you on the radio.' In the end it didn't help much; he never fully recalled the whole, horrible experience.

The navigator's remains were found in the wreckage. He had only just got married and his poor young widow was a very sad and pathetic sight at the military funeral that we all attended. Everyone's hearts went out to her.

Once we were even involved in someone else's accident. It was when we were in Cyprus on an Armament Practise Camp. We had been on Larnaca range doing some shooting and were in transit to Episkopi range for our dive-bombing. As we flew along I heard a very faint 'Mayday, Mayday, Mayday' on the emergency 'Guard' frequency, which we listened to all the time. There was no audible response, so I called the Akrotiri controller to alert him. I then heard him calling on 'Guard', but the aircraft with the emergency didn't seem to be hearing him. As we could hear both, I asked the controller if we could help by being an airborne relay station. He agreed and we called the Mayday aircraft on 'Guard'. It was an RAF Hastings that had lost two out of its four engines. The aircraft captain said they were flying very low and slow, trying to climb and that his crew were presently hurling all sorts of things out of the door into the sea to lighten their load. They were quite some distance from Akrotiri, but a few minutes later the Hastings pilot and the ATC controller were able to successfully communicate. So we signed off and got on with our bombing.

Once we had finished, ATC asked us to fly out on a particular bearing from Akrotiri to see if we could find the Hastings; they still didn't have him on their radar. About 10 minutes later we spotted the lumbering transport, still flying very low. We turned and flew over the top of him and called ATC to give them a chance to get a fix on him; as they did so, he came into radar cover. We returned and landed and as we got out of the aircraft the Hastings was on his final approach. It had been a close call for all on board.

It turned out to be a training flight and the captain/instructor was showing his co-pilot/student how difficult it was to judge height over flat, calm water. He obviously proved his point because the two inboard propellers hit the water and the force was sufficient to shear their drive shafts from the engines. The two outer engines didn't hit the water because the wing's dihedral angle, the slight upsweep from the wing root to the wingtip, meant that the outer's prop discs were just a few inches higher!

On a lighter note, I once had an indication of a fuel pressure failure while carrying out a series of circuits and landings. When the indication came on

I told Geoff that we would have to land. He was, by now, bored out of his skull, so he was very pleased.

'Oh what a shame; and I was having such a good time,' came the heavily sarcastic response.

We landed and taxied in. As we did so the fuel pressure failure indicator changed to normal.

'That's funny,' I said, 'the fuel pressure's back to normal. Oh well, I'd better report it anyway.'

'No, don't do that – it was me. I tripped the circuit breaker with the point of my compasses,' said my wicked navigator.

'Why?'

'Well, the bar's open and it's far too late to be doing circuits.'

'You buy the first round or I'll tell!'

'OK, boyo.'

29

New Buckets

By October 1966, the funny little flat-nosed practise bomb that we had seen in its neat wooden box at Boscombe Down had been replicated in large numbers and crates of them were now occupying a corner of the weapons storage area. This was because we had to train for a new weapon delivery method for our nuclear role. The chubby Mk7 nuclear bomb was being withdrawn and replaced with a new lighter, leaner and meaner bomb: the American B-61. This nuclear weapon was also a variable-yield fission bomb designed for carriage by high-speed aircraft. It had a streamlined casing capable of withstanding supersonic flight speeds. Of course none of these design criteria applied to our strictly subsonic jets. The B-61 was nearly 12ft long, with a diameter of just over a foot and its weight was about 700lb. So it was going to leave us more space around it in the bomb bay and it was less than half the weight of the Mk7.

But the most important change was that this was a ground-burst bomb and under the streamlined glass-fibre nosecone was a steel spike. The delivery mode was going to be what was termed laydown. That is we had to fly over the target at low level and release the bomb, aiming it with our new depressable gunsight, then get the hell out of there as fast and as low as possible. The bomb had a retardation parachute and it would impact at an angle of more than 60°. The spike would stick into the ground and hold the bomb in position while the internal timer ran down; at zero it would go BANG! Like the Mk7, the size of the bang could be preset in flight according to the type of target.

So no more LABS manoeuvres. I think that most people on the squadron were happy with that. There had been several incidents and at least one fatal accident, on another squadron, caused by pilots not flying the recovery correctly. By the time Geoff and I had started our tour LABS manoeuvres had been banned at night. However, we were still expected to do it in cloud. But it wasn't long before one of our guys and one from another squadron had messed up their recoveries in cloud and severely overstressed their poor old aeroplane. The groundcrew reckoned the one on 16 Squadron had pulled over 8G; that was twice the limit! So, the next step was to ban recoveries in cloud. That meant that if we weren't sure what height the cloud tops were, we had to climb up and check before we started a range slot. That wasn't too inconvenient, but it was now practically impossible to do a FRA within timing constraints. So it was all starting to fall into the 'too difficult' box and we were glad that these sorts of restrictions on our freedom of operation would now go away.

The accuracy of a laydown delivery depended on accurate speed and height to give the correct forward throw, which would then give us the gunsight depression for the release point. As we started the work up we were seeing very varied results from all the crews. Some smartarse then correlated the results not to the crews but to the aircraft they were flying. We were flying the release height on the radio altimeter and it turned out that not all of them were quite as accurate as we had thought – so some of us had been flying around 20 or 30ft above or below an actual 250ft above the ground.

The weaponeers worked out a very clever way of calibrating our radio altimeters and it was fun too! We knew the width of the runway and we had a fixed circle in our gunsights. So at a known depressed sight angle, if we flew down the runway with the gunsight circle overlaying the edges of the runway then, by simple trigonometry, we should be at a certain height. So, for a while, we were all getting airborne and flying a low-level circuit to fly straight down the runway at about 300ft to calibrate our radio altimeters. It wasn't long before they had all been re-tuned and we didn't need to calibrate them on every flight. The scores improved markedly and became much more consistent.

In some ways the prospect of not having to do the LABS manoeuvre for real and so expose ourselves to enemy missiles and guns was good. However, we now had to fly right over our targets at 440kts and 200ft and most of us had Warsaw Pact airfields in our target folders. They were likely to be bristling with anti-aircraft facilities. But who said war was going to be easy?

Geoff and I did quite well at this new game. His excellence as a low-level navigator, getting us to the target within seconds of our planned time of arrival and my ability to get the bombs near the target got us assigned to be the junior partners in the weapons empire. We also represented the squadron, along with two other crews, in the annual Salmond Trophy inter-squadron bombing competition. We were starting to become 'establishment' and we were now helping new crews to settle in and learn the job; and most of them were older than us! But we still pulled QRA like everyone else.

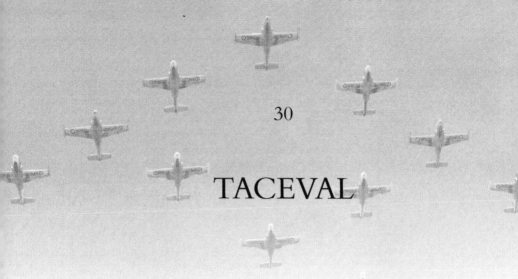

30

TACEVAL

Exercise TACEVAL is NATO-speak for Tactical Evaluation and, on Cold War Canberra squadrons in West Germany, it came around about every eighteenmonths. Exercise TACEVAL was a thorough evaluation and assessment of the whole station's functionality in a war scenario. It could last up to three days and was carried out by a team of folk who came from the host air force and members of the NATO staff. It was supposed to be a no-notice exercise, so there were often rumours flashing around the station or the squadron that the team had been spotted in local parking areas waiting to pounce. Actually, once a TACEVAL had taken place it would be most unusual to have another within the next year, so there was some predictability, certainly within plus or minus six months. Our squadron should, therefore, have had one in 1965, but the operational detachment to Malaysia got in the way. All our other fixed commitments meant that late 1966 was the hot favourite. So those that indulged in the 'Predicting TACEVAL' game started getting twitchier as that autumn turned into winter. That must have included the Station Commander, because the frequency of Exercise MINEVALs went up and there was one just before Christmas 1966.

One of these work-up exercises was called on a Saturday evening. That was a loading and taxiing exercise only, but it did backfire in the early hours of Sunday morning. I was actually at the bowling alley when the station hooter sounded and I hadn't imbibed much, if any, alcohol. However, some of the guys had been at a party and, in the early hours one of them lost his way on the way back from the simulated stream take-off and ran off the taxiway. Being winter the wheel sank up to its axle and the jet had to be pulled out the next day with a tractor. All the while a nuclear weapon was hanging in the bomb bay!

The New Year started with the various members of our management team getting very nervous and the rumour machine going into full gear. The hooter went off again at dawn on 12 January. I think that we all thought that this was it; but no, it was yet another MINEVAL! We flew twice, which was unusual for a MINEVAL, once during the afternoon and again by night. The following day Geoff and I started a two-week QRA stint. On our second shift we received a call from the squadron telling us that the TACEVAL team had been spotted on the road heading for Laarbruch. We treated the rumour like all the others – 'so what?' I took the view that we were always ready so what was the point of getting all worked up about it. My laid-back navigator was, as usual, laid-back; I used to call him the original inertial navigation system.

As evening fell the QRA horn sounded and we all rushed out of the room, with our lifejackets and helmets in hand. Just outside the door I ran straight into a large Wing Commander with a clipboard. Astonishingly it was 'Kit' Carson; I had last seen him at Swinderby in late 1963 where he was our Chief Flying Instructor.

'Hello, sir,' I called out as I bounced off his considerable bulk.

Amazingly he recognised me and said something that sounded friendly, but faded as I kept on running to my jet. Like every other QRA alert, it was all over in minutes, but then we went into a quiz session with the good Wing Commander and a couple of other assessors. By the time it was all over it was time to cook dinner. We all agreed that QRA was, for once, the best place to be.

Normally we would have had the following day off, but this was no longer a normal working day. Having handed over to the next two crews, who were also pleased to be able to escape from the mayhem, we went off duty but straight to the squadron. The crewroom was full of camp beds, where folk had been having a NATO-sponsored sleepover; at least we had slept in proper beds last night. We reported to the Ops Room and found that we were slated to fly a high-low-high trip to the UK and carry out a bombing run on Wainfleet range in the Wash. Our aircraft, WT 340, had had its nuke downloaded and a practise bomb put on the wing pylon. Our target was the ship's hulk on the range and we were given a time on target to achieve. After going through all the simulated political release procedures, we got airborne and set off for East Anglia. The sortie went well; our bomb hit the ship and we were only 6 seconds late. The range officer would pass these numbers to the TACEVAL team, so we were feeling happy.

We got back to find that the scenario had moved on, or perhaps back, to one where we would move from 15 minutes readiness, to cockpit readiness and then to simultaneous release. By the time our hour of sitting waiting in the jet came to an end with the release authentication code word being broadcast, it was dark. Our flight profile and target was the same as our earlier sortie. That went equally well and we got back at about 11 p.m. The stand-down message had come through while we had been away, so we were home by midnight; I slept the sleep of an innocent that night. I had expected that we would be in QRA again the next day, but the roster had been disrupted by the exercise because the 'sickies' had held QRA. We flew an air defence Exercise ROULETTE and we were intercepted by Belgian Air Force Mirage 3s at our usual 40,000ft plus. Service was back to normal.

We learnt later that the squadron and the station had achieved a satisfactory assessment, with some credits thrown in; pleasingly one of these was the response and knowledge of the QRA crews.

31

Testing Times

There was no unit test pilot at Laarbruch, so each squadron carried out post-servicing air tests on its own aircraft. There was no particular training for the task and that gave the management plenty of flexibility when it came to allocating crews to do air tests. I did my first full air test on 12 January 1965, so I had been on the squadron about eight months and I had flown around 150 hours in the B(I)8, 240 hours in the Canberra and 480 hours total flying. Although not written down I would think that those sorts of totals would be a safe minimum for sending a pilot off to carry out his first full air test. As it happened that air test was the one that I wrote about earlier, when part of the aileron control system failed.

Air tests were done following any significant periodic servicing, after an engine change and whenever any component of the flight control system had been changed or otherwise disturbed. Specific parts of the air test schedule were used for tests following particular work. One of the tests that had to be done before all the others, or whenever the tailplane trim or elevators had been changed or fiddled with, was the HSTC – high-speed trim check. The purpose was to make sure that the electrical pitch trimming system could cover the full speed range of the aeroplane; that is from 110kts to 450kts and cope with the very large, nose up trim change when the flaps were dropped at their limiting speed of 140kts. The way the HSTC was done was to accelerate in level flight at 2,000ft to 450kts. There were two possible cases. If you ran out of trim at too low an airspeed then you recorded that speed and returned to base. However, if you reached 450kts and there was still some trim left to go then you had to leave the tailplane trim alone, slow down and return to base. In this case holding the increasing nose down out of trim condition, by pulling back on the control yoke, got more and more difficult. By 150kts you needed two hands and a pull force of over 50lb! The trick was to get the speed down to just under 140kts and drop the flaps. The natural nose up trim change with flap took all the pull force away.

But the biggest challenge during the deceleration was *not* to trim. Flying instructors spent hours and hours in the early days teaching and cajoling their students to trim the aircraft correctly. By the time you got out of training it was absolutely second nature to keep the aircraft in longitudinal trim. The B(I)8 had a flap that covered the pitch trim switch on the right-hand yoke and, whenever I had a Case 2 HSTC result, I would fly home with my thumb pressing down hard on the flap so that I wouldn't waste everyone's time by moving the tailplane from its final position.

The technicians had a graph that they used to calculate by how much they should readjust the system. When they'd done that, off you went again. Each test took about 15 minutes airborne, that was about half the time it took to strap in, start up and taxi out to the runway. In my last month on the squadron, April 1967, I flew no less than seven HSTCs and for all that effort clocked up a total of 1 hour and 40 minutes flying time!

One fine afternoon we were sent over to the other side of the airfield to do a full air test on one of the T4s. When I checked the documentation I saw that the front fuel tank was about half full. Bearing in mind the criticality of the centre of gravity being too far aft I queried why the fuel state was as it was.

'It's from the engine runs,' the Chief Technician in charge told me.

'You should use the aft tank for engine runs,' I replied, 'Then there's no danger of getting the fuel out of balance the wrong way.'

I received one of those looks that meant that he thought that I was not qualified to be giving advice on engine running, or any other carefully preserved groundcrew territory.

'Is there any fuel in the tip tanks, Chief?' I asked, as politely as I could.

'We think that there might be a bit, but we can't tell how much. Why?'

'Well if there is, it will fill the aft tank to the brim as it transfers and could give us an even bigger problem,' I answered.

It was now clear that the Chief and the gathering crowd were beginning to get a little tired of this difficult pilot. You could see them thinking, 'Why doesn't he just get on with it? The sooner he goes, the sooner he gets back and we can all go home.'

'I really would like someone to confirm that we won't run the C of G out of the aft limit,' I said firmly.

The Warrant Officer was extracted from his office and told the problem. He looked over the Form 700, especially at the fuel state, and then looked at me with a steely eye.

'You'll be fine, sir. Just don't use the front tank until its all back in balance.' His unsaid thought was in line with his men's – just get on with it!

So we walked out to the silver and red bird, climbed aboard and started up. Because we had an easterly wind we had a long taxi to the western end of the runway. As we did so, I could feel the aircraft bouncing lightly on its nosewheel as we went over the slightly uneven surface. We held at the stop line to allow another aircraft to land and then, when he had passed, we lined up on the runway for our departure.

I had left the forward tank fuel pumps off until this point (it was mandatory to take-off with all fuel pumps running). I ran the engines up to 7,600rpm, did a final check of the engine temperatures and pressures and released the brakes.

The next move was to apply full power, but as I did so the nose reared frighteningly upwards. I chopped the power, called 'Aborting take-off' to the tower and started braking. The nose had slammed down quite hard when I had reduced the power and, when I stopped braking, it felt extremely light. I held on the runway and asked the tower to organise a tractor. I didn't dare get out because I felt that if I did the nose would go skywards and the jet would sit on its tail. It was a bit like the end of the film *The Italian Job*! Eventually the tractor arrived, fixed the tow bar to the nosewheel and we were towed back in. I had to try very hard not to go into 'I told you so' mode. I just asked politely for them to refuel the aircraft to full and let me know when it was ready.

'Oh, that won't be today now, sir,' was the slightly snotty reply. 'It's too late. Perhaps tomorrow?' I'd forgotten that the guys in the main technical hangar, who looked after the trainers, didn't work squadron hours.

'OK, but it probably won't be me that does it now.' There was an almost audible sigh of relief!

With the exception of the HSTC, most air tests were pretty boring events. The first part was a continuous climb to 45,000ft, at set speeds and with a fixed throttle setting on which we noted, passing every 5,000ft, engine data, such as rpm, oil pressure and jet pipe temperature. After that we had to accelerate to 0.84 indicated Mach number to check that the aircraft's behaviour was as expected. Then we had to check, one at a time, that the engines didn't surge, that is lock into a non-accelerating mode, when we opened the throttle at low speeds. That test was potentially the most exciting; a surge wasn't a big deal, but it was odd to have the throttle fully open and the engine stagnated at a low rpm with the jet pipe temperature rising rapidly. Then it was down to 30,000ft to make sure that the engines relit after shutting them down, again one at a time. This could have also been potentially exciting, but I never had an Avon not relight; one pilot did, but that was because the wire from the relight button to the igniter plugs had broken.

Further descents were carried out until, at 3,000ft, each engine was throttled back and the minimum speed at which the aircraft could be flown with the other engine at full power was noted. This bit of the test required a bit of nerve and strong legs. Throughout the flight all the hydraulic systems were exercised and pressures and times to travel noted down. Anything that was not working properly was also recorded, so that by the time the air test was finished you could hand over a completed test schedule from which the engineers could then generate a fully serviceable jet or call for further tests. However, that noting of other unserviceable items once caught us out.

Again we were sent south side to do a T4 air test. As we drove over I asked Geoff if he'd like to sit up front with me. He readily accepted. We flew the air test and everything appeared to be OK. After landing we handed in the completed schedule and told them that the jet was fit to fly. I even put my signature to it. Then we went for a quick beer on the way home.

The next morning we arrived at the squadron and found that we had been taken off the flying programme and were to report to Wing Commander Edwards, the man in charge of the airfield and operations wing. He was, we were told, very upset. So we set off back to almost where we had just come from, Station Operations, to see the good Wing Commander. As a Squadron Leader he had been our Squadron Commander when we went through Initial Officer Training. He was a tall, distinguished-looking chap with greying hair. Tall and distinguished became rather large and threatening as we stepped into his office.

'You two did the air test on T4 WD 944 yesterday, didn't you?' he said, glowering at us.

'Yes, sir,' I replied, wondering if we'd missed something.

He then turned his attention to Geoff, who had the advantage over me of being level with the Wing Commander's eye line.

'And was there anything wrong?'

'Not that I was aware of,' replied Geoff honestly.

'Where did you sit?' Here it comes, thought Geoff.

'In the front right-hand seat,' he replied, honestly once more.

'Yes, I thought so. When the Station Navigation Officer and I went to fly it last night, the rear ejection seat was loose, the oxygen regulator was faulty and . . .' He went on to list all the things that, in the end, prevented him from doing his almost annual night flight. We were both severely chastised and told never to do it again. I actually did feel sorry about it. The Wing Commander didn't fly often, especially in the dark, so he must have been really angry at not being able to get airborne.

It just showed me that I always needed to take everything I did seriously, without being too solemn about the way I did it. After that experience I tried to follow a saying I first read in the book *Reach for the Sky*: 'Rules were made for the obedience of fools and the guidance of wise men.'

32

Moving On with Reflections

My time on 16 Squadron came to an end as spring took full hold of the German countryside and I had passed my twenty-third birthday. My last flight was a night, low-level navigation exercise with a FRA at Nordhorn, dropping a single bomb on Geoff's call. That was because he was using the Decca Navigation system to steer us towards the target and find the release point. To say that it was done totally blind, the 30-yard score wasn't at all disappointing. It was a fitting and challenging final sortie with good crew cooperation and a nice landing. As I walked away from XM 262 I gave her nose a gentle pat and ambled reluctantly back to the squadron with a lot of sadness in my heart. This tour had been an excellent way to start my time in the RAF and I couldn't imagine that I would find anything better in the years to come. It was time to go, but to what?

Over two years earlier, in January 1965, the Boss had invited us and another crew into his office to tell us that he had recommended the four of us to go forward for training as TSR2 crews. He told us that, if we were selected, our tours in Germany would be extended until the start of pre-OCU training, about another two years. We, of course, were delighted. But that delight was well and truly extinguished by the news, only three months later, that the TSR2 project was cancelled. However, we were then told that all the crews nominated for the TSR2 would be carried over to the General Dynamics F-111K, which was going to be purchased to replace the TSR2. Thanks to the machinations of the Admiralty and Lord Mountbatten, that project was also cancelled, so the whole thing was off. Then we were told that our tour lengths would revert to their original three years. Meanwhile there had been a call for RAF pilots and navigators to be loaned to the Fleet Air Arm to fly the Buccaneer. This was before that aircraft was officially nominated to be the strike/attack Canberra replacement. I asked Geoff if he was interested.

'Look, I have enough trouble finding my way back to the airfield when it hasn't moved while we've been away; how do you think I'll find a carrier in the middle of the oggin?' he said.

Of course I knew that he never had trouble finding anything, but he had just got married and I think that he really didn't want to uproot, go to northern Scotland for training and then disappear for eighteen months on a ship.

'Anyway,' he added, 'you always say that you don't like flying over the sea.'

It was true, I didn't. There was nothing to look at, it was even more tedious than flying over the desert, and the water always looked so cold and uninviting. Also, it seemed that I heard more strange noises from the aircraft and the engines once we had coasted out! So we didn't apply.

At the beginning of 1967 the Boss asked me to go see him. He wanted to know where I would prefer to go next and what sort of job I would like to do. He had received a call from the appointments people to say that I could be offered a tour on Vulcans. Apparently they needed more folk with low flying expertise. To sweeten the pill they were offering acceleration to captaincy within eighteen months, instead of the usual three years. I told the Boss that the whole idea was anathema to me. I had sat in a Vulcan once and that was enough. I could hardly see out of it and to have three guys without bang seats sitting behind me really turned me off; it had been bad enough with just one.

'What I'd really like, Boss, is to do another Canberra tour. Can I just move to another squadron if I can't stay here?'

''Fraid not, old boy,' he said with a fatherly smile. 'How about CFS? Become a flying instructor.'

A light went on in my head. I'd narrowly missed flying the Gnat, maybe this could be a way to make that happen.

'OK, sir. I'll do that.'

I found the appropriate paperwork and filled it in. There was space for my Commanding Officer's remarks. I took it to the Boss and asked him to recommend me for the advanced training role on the Gnat. He did so, giving me a strong recommendation. I sent the form off post haste.

So that was it, by April I had received lots of forms to fill out and my posting notice for No.239 Fixed Wing Instructors' Course at the Central Flying School at RAF Little Rissington in Gloucestershire had come through – I was to report there on 30 May 1967.

Looking back on my tour at Laarbruch, the impression is of busy happiness. But with the benefit of hindsight and forty years of technological development there were many things that we did which were probably operationally futile. The nuclear strike role, with the LABS delivered weapon, was the one that might have had the strongest chance of working satisfactorily. By day and given good weather we could fly lower than anyone else in NATO; but at night or with bad weather our survivability was in question.

When the new laydown delivered nukes came along, we had less chance of being shot down during the pull-up, but we did have to fly right over our targets, which were doubtless going to be very well defended. RAF Tornadoes dropping the JP233 airfield denial weapon in the First Gulf War played out this scenario. It was soon deemed to be too dangerous and was stopped.

In the conventional weapons role we would have had to rely on our fighter pilot friends to give us air supremacy to do most of the attack modes. The use of parachute flares for night attack was a very uncertain way of guaranteeing any success. If there was any decent defence around the target, our arrival at medium altitude would have made us easy targets and the illumination of the target by flares also meant that we were illuminated while flying under them.

Although moderately accurate, the dive-bombing technique put us in a very vulnerable position as we climbed to set up the attack. It was really the end of an era before air weapon delivery moved on to laser-guided, precision weapons and stand-off, cruise missiles. As for low flying successfully at night; that would have to wait for electro-optical devices and head-up or helmet-mounted displays. Little did I realise that just ten years later I would be working on all these things as an experimental test pilot at Farnborough.

Apart from the operational efficacy of a Canberra squadron in the mid-1960s, there were some flight safety issues that were never really addressed. For instance we flew regularly above 45,000ft, but it wasn't until later that the aeromedical folk limited the type of oxygen regulator and mask that we used to NOT ABOVE 40,000ft. We flew long missions over the sea in the middle of winter, as far north as 65°, but we were never equipped with immersion suits. They were just coming into service, but no one thought to procure them for us. Survival time without the suits in the North Atlantic, at night and in winter would have been just a few minutes.

For our war role we had no protection from biological or chemical agents and decontamination procedures were rarely practised. Our aircraft sat in the open, even the QRA jets had only a fairly lightweight, open-ended shelter over them. There was no thought of 'hardening' the base at that time.

Of course, when all these things came in, the whole atmosphere changed. It became more deadly serious; perhaps it should have been all along. But the spirit and *joie de vivre* that we experienced on our tour was probably diminished. We were in that hiatus between the RAF of the Second World War and the modern high-tech air forces we see today. However, one thing is worth noting. In 1967 there were more front-line combat aircraft in RAF Germany than there are in the whole RAF of today.

As a footnote to this story, in 1993, four years after the Cold War was effectively over, I went on an official RAF visit to Poland. At the time I was serving as a member of the Directing Staff at the RAF Staff College and we were building relationships with similar establishments in Eastern Europe. In 1992 we had received our first Polish Air Force student and so we had been invited to send a small party to visit the Polish Air Force Staff College in Warsaw. On the first full day of our visit we were taken by mini-bus to meet the Polish Chief of the Air Staff at an airbase about 30km east of Warsaw. We were also due to meet with squadron members and look over their Mig-29 fighters. When our interpreter told us the name of the airbase I recognised it. Geoff and I had held that airfield as our primary target for over six months! On that day in 1993 I was so glad that the Cold War had thawed out and that we hadn't had to go and throw a 'bucket of sunshine' after all.

Epilogue

At the Central Flying School I was not selected to become an instructor on the Gnat. There were two prospective Qualified Flying Instructors (QFIs) required to fill places on University Air Squadrons (UASs) that had not been filled by pre-course volunteers. QFIs on UASs were required to be officers with Permanent Commissions and I had one. So one day, about two weeks into the course, I was told that I was destined to fly the de Havilland Canada Chipmunk and, on graduation, move to one of the then seventeen UASs in the UK. Despite being sad to miss the diminutive Gnat again I had to accept my fate. I ended up in Scotland as a QFI on the Universities of Strathclyde and Glasgow Air Squadron, where I served for three years. Two further tours as a QFI followed, the first back at CFS, teaching other pilots to instruct on the Chipmunk, and then at the Canberra OCU as a staff instructor and CFS Agent.

I finally broke out of the vicious circle of flying old aeroplanes by being selected for the 1975 Empire Test Pilots' School course. After graduation I flew for five years as an Experimental Test Pilot for the Royal Aircraft Establishments at Farnborough and Bedford. From then on I was destined to spend most of my subsequent flying career in and around the test-flying world, both military and civilian, until 1998. I also entered the world of historic aviation and display flying.

I finally stopped flying in 2004, on my sixtieth birthday, after a tour as the Officer Commanding No.2 Air Experience Flight, giving back to Air Cadets what I had received over forty years earlier. My office was on the south side of the huge Weighbridge Hangar at Boscombe Down, the one I had first seen on my way to Northern Ireland by Pembroke all those years earlier.

Above: The 16 Squadron six-ship formation team, May 1966. (Sqn Ldr S. Foote, OC 16(R) Sqn)

Right: The author in 1982 in the cockpit of an Italian Air Force Aermacchi MB 339 at the Italian Flight Test Centre near Rome. Still with a decent head of hair!

I was once asked to write an article for a Flight Safety magazine. It was the final issue of RAF Germany's *Flight Comment,* for which I had also designed the cover. I gave their young readers an insight into our lives in Germany then; a sort of very condensed version of this book. I was also asked to give 'Ten Commandments' for a life in aviation. I can't remember them all now, but the final one was: 'If you ever stop enjoying your flying – get out of the cockpit and let someone else do it'. I never had to – I just got too old to do the sort of flying I enjoyed most.

By 2004 I had flown, as a pilot, 134 different types of aircraft and amassed over 7,500 hours, mostly one at a time. Whatever and whenever I flew I never, ever lost the fascination for flight, the beauty of the earth and the skies and the thrill of all forms of aviation. For that I am eternally grateful and hope that you have enjoyed sharing a part of my story and my love affair with flying. I hope that, some day, I will be able to tell you many more such tales from the thirty-five years that followed.

Appendix

Pilot's Notes Canberra B(I) Mk8

The following diagrams illustrate:

1) Cockpit foreward view

2) Cockpit Port Console

3) Cockpit starboard side

4) Navigator's Station

Fig. B—Cockpit forward view

KEY TO FIGURE B—COCKPIT
FORWARD VIEW

1. Radio altimeter.
2. Radio altimeter limit lights.
3. ILS indicator.
4. ILS marker light.
5. Machmeter.
6. Emergency lights switch.
7. Anti-dazzle lights switch.
8. Compass light switch.
9. Flare release push-button.
10. Standby inverter MI.
11. SFOM gunsight.
12. Engine fire warning lights and extinguisher push-buttons.
13. Gunsight indicator light.
      Yaw/roll switch.
      T145 cancel light.
      Normal/alternate switch.
      Yaw/roll gyro caging test push-button.
14. Engine fire warning lights test push-button.
15. Engine instruments lights switch.
16. Starboard red and U/V lamps dimmer switches.
17. Windscreen quarter panel demister.
18. Call-light and push-button.
19. Accelerometer.
20. Oxygen remote flow indicator.
21. Turn-and-slip standby supply switch.
22. RPM indicators.
23. JPT indicators.
24. Oil pressure gauges.
25. Fuel pressure warning indicators.
26. Radio compass indicator.
27. Bombs/RP push-button.
28. Camera push-button.
29. Tailplane trim switch (guarded).
30. Generator warning light.
31. Aileron trim indicator.
32. Rudder trim indicator.
33. Tailplane trim indicator.

Fig. A—Cockpit Port Console

APPENDIX

KEY TO FIGURE A—COCKPIT
PORT CONSOLE

1. Canopy jettison lever (under flap).
2. Engine anti-icing switches and magnetic indicators.
3. Bomb doors switch.
4. Bomb doors emergency lever.
5. Switches, left to right:—
   Navigation lights.
   Taxying lamps.
   Landing lamp.
   Identification light, morse.
   Identification light, steady.
   External lights master switch.
6. Anti-collision lights switch.
7. Port console red lamps dimmer switch.
8. Generator switches.
9. Inoperative.
10. HP cocks and relight buttons.
11. Undercarriage master switch.
12. Forward console dimmer switch.
13. Windscreen quarter panel demister.
14. Airbrakes selector switch and guard.
15. Instrument panel port U/V lamps switch.
16. Instrument panel port red lamps switch.
17. Wing tip tank jettison button.
18. Undercarriage emergency lowering handle.
19. Undercarriage up button.
20. Undercarriage position indicator.
21. Parking brake.
22. Undercarriage down button (obscured by tab).
23. Flap position indicator.
24. Flap selector.
25. Throttles.
26. Throttle friction damper.
27. HP cocks friction damper.
28. Press-to-transmit switch.
29. Bomb release safety lock and indicator lights.
30. Rudder trim switches.
31. Aileron trim switches.
32. Gunsight master switch.

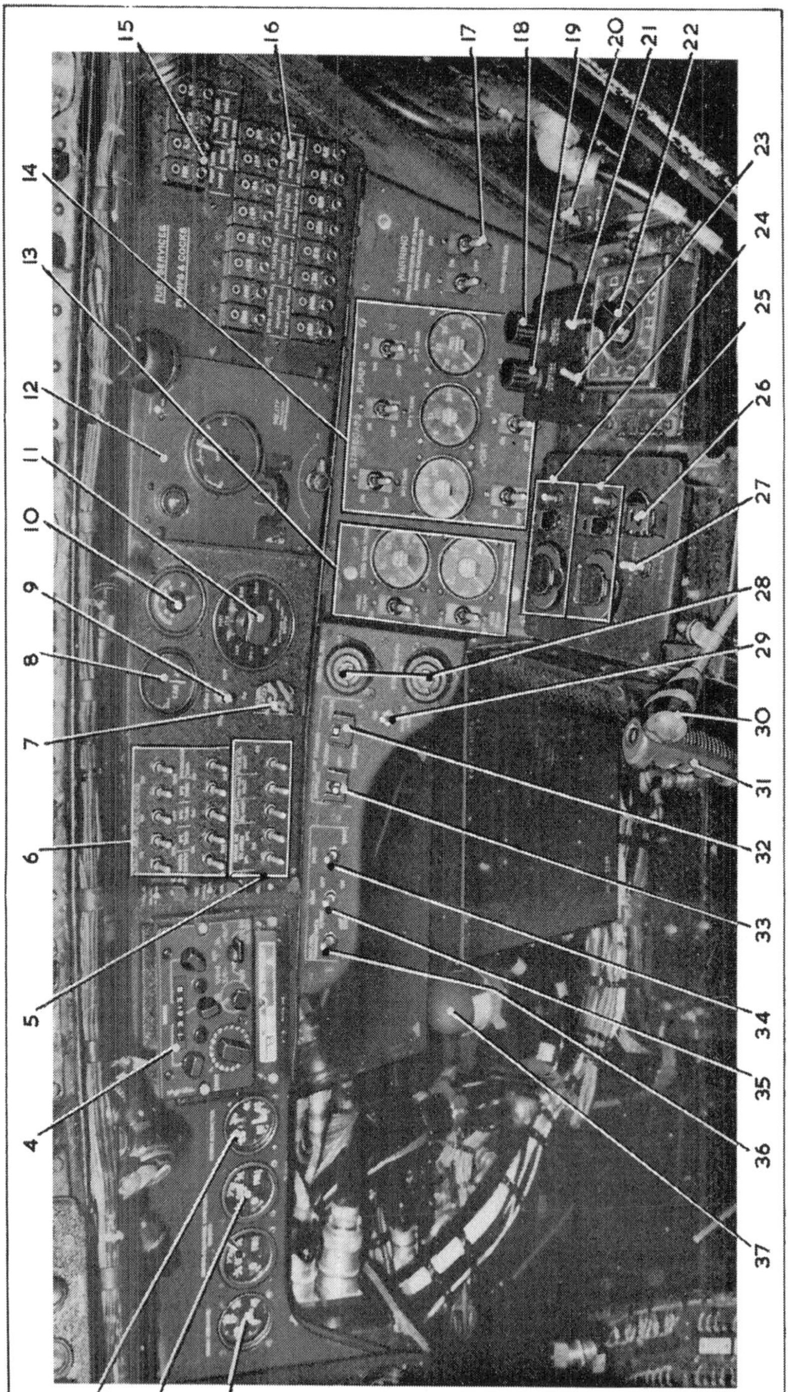

Fig. C—Cockpit starboard side

KEY TO FIGURE C—COCKPIT
STARBOARD SIDE

1. Wheelbrake hydraulic pressure gauge.
2. Oxygen contents gauges.
3. Cabin altimeter
4. v/UHF controller.
5. Switches:—
      Pressurisation warning horn override.
      No. 1 and 2 engine air switches.
      Canopy demist
      Vent valve heater.
      Pressure head heater.
6. Fuel cock switches. Top row starboard, second row port. In pairs from left to right:—
      Integral tank LP cocks.
      No. 1 tank LP cocks.
      No. 2 tank LP cocks.
      No. 3 tank LP cocks.
      Overload tank cocks.
7. Canopy/snatch master switch.
8. Cabin air mixing valve position indicator.
9. Cabin air mixing valve switch.
10. Voltmeter.
11. Radio altimeter height band selector.
12. Oxygen regulator.
13. Top: starboard integral tank fuel gauge and pump switch. Bottom: port integral tank fuel gauge and pump switch.
14. Left to right, Nos. 1, 2 and 3 fuel tank gauges with pump switches above (starboard) and below (port).
15. Overload tank pumps and cocks circuit breakers.
16. Fuel tank pumps and cocks circuit breakers.
17. Overload tank fuel transfer pump switches.
18. ILS volume control.
19. ADF volume control.
20. ILS on/off switch.
21. Intercomm. normal/emergency switch.
22. ILS channel selector.
23. Intercomm. on/off switch.
24. Starboard engine starter push-button, master start and ignition switches.
25. Port engine starter push-button, master start and ignition switches.
26. Battery master switch.
27. Compass/D-Gyro switch.
28. Dimmer switches.
29. Wander lamp switch.
30. Emergency oxygen pull-knob.
31. Hydraulic handpump handle.
32. UHF standby Guard/Channel A switch.
33. UHF standby power switch.
34. v/UHF mute switch.
35. v/UHF tone switch.
36. v/UHF—standby UHF changeover switch.
37. Hand operated fire extinguisher.

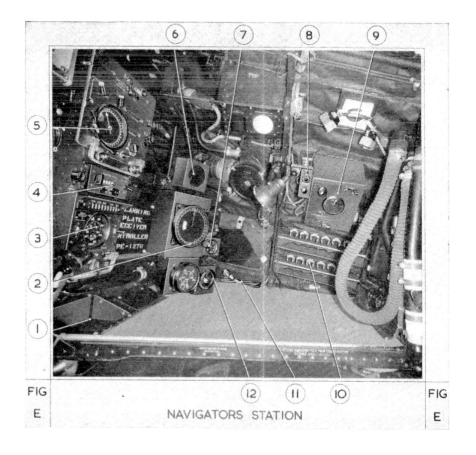

NAVIGATORS STATION

KEY TO FIGURE E—NAVIGATOR'S STATION

1. Rear warning control mounting.
2. G.4B compass master indicator.
3. Blue Silk control panel.
4. Blue Silk impulse counter.
5. GPI Mk. 4A.
6. Rear warning indicator mounting.
7. Outside air temperature gauge.
8. Crew call-light and push button.
9. Navigator's oxygen regulator.
10. Signal pistol cartridge stowages.
11. Position for rear warning suppressor.
12. Ventilation louvre.

Index

INDEX

If you enjoyed this book, you may also be interested in…

The English Electric Lightning Story
MARTIN W. BOWMAN

The unique design of the English Electric Lightning originated in a proposal in 1947, first flying in 1954. It was the standard British fighter for over twenty years and was used by both the Kuwait and Saudi Arabian Air Forces. In 1971 the RAF Lightning squadrons began disbanding, the last one leaving front-line service in 1988. Built for the Cold War, they lasted almost until the fall of the Berlin Wall.

978 0 7524 5080 3

Britain's Cold War
BOB CLARKE

Like no other conflict, the Cold War was more than a struggle between two superpowers, it was a war of ideologies, the Capitalistic West and the Communist East. The conflict infiltrated every facet of British life to the extent it was not really considered a war at all, even if it was. This book uncovers what effects the Cold War had on the British as they recovered from post-war struggles onwards.

978 0 7524 5017 9

The Vulcan Story
PETER R. MARSH

A cornerstone of Britain's nuclear deterrent, the Vulcan was later adapted for conventional bombing and saw its only active service in the Falklands War. Restored with the help of Heritage Lottery funding, the last airworthy Vulcan B2, XH558, in many ways fills the gap left by Concorde.

978 0 7524 4399 4

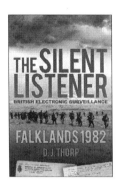

The Silent Listener, Falklands 1982: British Surveillance
MAJOR D.J. THORP

Here, for the first time in print, is the confirmation of the existence and role of the Special Task Detachment during Operation Corporate, with details of the deployment and operational role of a dedicated ground-based electronic warfare (EW) weapons facility. Complimented by previously unpublished photographs and classified documents only just released under the Official Secrets Act, *The Silent Listener* tells the story of the hidden Falklands War.

978 0 7524 6029 1

Visit our website and discover thousands of other History Press books.

www.thehistorypress.co.uk